W9-CFC-234

Prophecy
Watch

THOMAS ICE &
TIMOTHY DEMY

HARVEST HOUSE PUBLISHERS
Eugene, Oregon 97402

This book is a compilation of ten Harvest House Pocket Books from the Pocket Prophecy Series, written by Thomas Ice and Timothy Demy, published by Harvest House Publishers.

All views expressed are solely the individual authors' and do not reflect the position of any governmental agency or department.

Cover by Terry Dugan Design, Minneapolis, Minnesota.

PROPHECY WATCH
Copyright © 1998 by Pre-Trib Research Center
Published by Harvest House Publishers
Eugene, Oregon 97402

Ice, Thomas.
     Prophecy Watch / Thomas Ice and Timothy J. Demy.
       p. cm.
     ISBN 1-56507-685-0
     1. Bible—Prophecies—End of the world.   2. End of the world—Biblical teaching. I. Demy,
     Timothy J. II. Title.
BS649.E63I24   1998
236'.9—dc21   97-30866
                                                                             CIP

To

George Chronis

in recognition of
many faithful years of service
to our Lord
as an "elder indeed" at
Oak Hill Bible Church
Austin, Texas

CONTENTS

PART 1

Signs of the Times

Biblical Prophecy and World Events 7

1. Does the Bible Provide Signs of the
   End Times? 9
2. Biblical Prophecy, Date-Setting, and the
   Year 2000 17
3. Who Are the Date-Setters? 27
4. What Does the Bible Teach About Setting
   Dates? 39
5. What Are the Signs of the End of
   the Church Age? 44
6. What Signs Indicate the Tribulation
   Might Be Near? 56
7. What Are the "Problem" Scriptures
   Regarding Signs? 73

PART 2

The Rapture

Caught Up in the Air! 77

8. Is the Rapture Clearly Taught in
   the Bible? 78
9. What Is the Foundation for a
   Pretrib Rapture? 84
10. What Evidence Supports a
    Pretrib Rapture? 98
11. Why Is the Pretrib Rapture
    Important Today? 114

P A R T 3

The Tribulation and the Antichrist

The Darkness Ahead 119
12. What Is the Tribulation? 121
13. Can the Antichrist Be Identified? 139
14. Does the Tribulation Have a
    Specific Timetable? 158
15. Does Tribulation Prophecy Impact
    Us Today? 174

P A R T 4

Armageddon and the Middle East

A Glimpse of the Future 181
16. What Does the Bible Say
    About Armageddon? 183
17. What Is the Course of the
    Campaign? 187
18. What Else Do We Know About
    Armageddon? 206
19. Why Does Armageddon Matter? 217

P A R T 5

The Millennium

The Mountain of the House of the Lord 221
20. What Is the Millennium? 223
21. What Is the Purpose of the Millennium? 231
22. When Will the Millennium Occur? 237
23. What Are the Characteristics
    of the Millennium? 246
24. Who Will Be in the Millennium? 259
25. Why Does the Millennium Matter? 265

Notes 267
Recommended Reading 273
Index 278

PART 1

Signs of
the Times

Biblical Prophecy and World Events

We have probably all seen cartoons of people wearing or holding placards proclaiming "The end is near!" Some of us have even seen such prophets of doom on the busy street corners of our nation's cities. As we approach and go beyond the year 2000, there is a significant amount of attention and writing about the new millennium by both religious and secular observers and writers. Is there any relationship between the events of which we read, hear, and see in the daily news and biblical prophecy? Yes! Just as when we are traveling and see signs beside the highway telling us what to expect on the road ahead, so also does the Bible provide signs of the times that point to specific events in the future.

God's prophetic plan for humanity is on track and on schedule. History and current events are moving toward a final end in which God's program will be fully realized. With the return of a significant portion of world Jewry to the Promised Land and the subsequent establishment of Israel as a nation in 1948, God's plan is moving closer and closer to fruition. Hardly a day goes by without the media reporting on news from that tiny country in the Middle East—Israel. Such focus is as God's Word said it would be. Israel is God's super-sign of the times, which makes significant many other developments and world events.

The Gulf War that ushered in the '90s caused many Americans to wonder how current events relate to Bible prophecy. Dr. John Walvoord noted that "these events were not precisely the fulfillment of what the Bible predicts for the future. Instead they could be a setting of the stage for the final drama leading to the Second Coming."[1] Even though they are not a specific fulfillment of prophecy, this does not mean that current events are not significant in relation to God's fixed plan for history. "Although the events sparked some premature conclusions that the world is already in the end time, they had a beneficial effect on the study of prophecy," contends Dr. Walvoord. "Many people searched the Scripture, some perhaps for the first time, to learn what the Bible says about the end of the age."[2]

The signs of the times are passing by. Do you see them and recognize them? Are you equipped to interpret them in terms of God's prophetic template for history?

CHAPTER 1

Does the Bible Provide Signs of the End Times?

1. How does the Bible use terms like "end times"?

Sometimes Christians read in the Bible about the "last days," "end times," and so on, and tend to think that these phrases refer to the same thing all the time. In our own lives there are many endings: the end of the work day, the end of the day according to the clock, the end of the week, the end of the month, and the end of the year; the word "end" does not mean that it always refers to the same time. The word *end* is restricted and precisely defined when it is modified by terms such as *day, week, year.* So it is in the Bible that "end times" may refer to the end of the current church age or it may refer to other times.

The Bible teaches that this present age, the church age, will end with the rapture, followed by the tribulation, which will end with the second coming of Messiah to the earth. Thus, we must distinguish between the "last days" of the church age and the "last days" of Israel's tribulation.

Note the following chart, which classifies and distinguishes between passages referring to the end of the church age and the "last days" for Israel:

Biblical Use of Last Days

ISRAEL	CHURCH
"latter days"—Deuteronomy 4:30; 31:29; Jeremiah 30:24; 48:47; Daniel 2:28; 10:14	*"latter days"*—1 Timothy 4:1
"last days"—Isaiah 2:2; Jeremiah 23:20; 49:39; Ezekiel 38:16; Micah 4:1; Acts 2:17	*"last days"*—2 Timothy 3:1; Hebrews 1:2; James 5:3; 2 Peter 3:3

Biblical Use of Last Days (Continued)

ISRAEL	CHURCH
"last day"—John 6:39,40, 44,54; 11:24; 12:48	*"last times"*—1 Peter 1:20; Jude 18
"latter years"—Ezekiel 38:8	*"last time"*—1 Peter 1:5; 1 John 2:18

The Bible clearly speaks of a last days or end time. The contextual referent lets us know whether the Bible is speaking of the last days relating to Israel or the end times in reference to the church.

2. What is "stage-setting"?

The present church age is not a time in which Bible prophecy is being fulfilled. Bible prophecy relates to a time *after the rapture* (the seven-year tribulation period). However, God *is* preparing the world during the present church age for that future time. But this *is not* "fulfillment" of Bible prophecy. So although prophecy is not being fulfilled in our day, we can track "general trends" in preparation for the coming tribulation, especially since it immediately follows the rapture. We call this approach "stage-setting." Just as many people set their clothes out the night before they wear them, so God, in the same sense, is preparing the world for the certain fulfillment of prophecy in a future time.

Dr. John Walvoord explains:

> But if there are no signs for the Rapture itself, what are the legitimate grounds for believing that the Rapture could be especially near of this generation?
>
> The answer is not found in any prophetic events predicted before the Rapture but in understanding the events that will follow the Rapture. Just as history was prepared for Christ's first coming, in a similar way history is preparing for the events leading up to His Second Coming....If this is the case, it leads to the inevitable conclusion that the Rapture may be excitingly near.[3]

The Bible provides detailed prophecy about the seven-year tribulation. (See "The Tribulation and the Antichrist" beginning on page 119.) In fact, Revelation 4 – 19 gives a detailed, sequential outline of the major players and events. Using Revelation as a framework, a Bible student is able to harmonize the hundreds of other biblical passages that speak of the seven-year tribulation into a clear model of the next time period for planet Earth. With such a template to guide us, we can see that already God is preparing or setting the stage of the world in which the great drama of the tribulation will unfold. This future time casts shadows of expectation in our own day because current events provide discernible signs of the times.

3. Are there signs of the end of the church age, the coming rapture, and plans for Israel?

Church Age

It would be too strong to say that there are signs of the end of the church age. Instead, the Bible indicates what the condition of the church will be like, the general course of the age, and then warns about some general trends that will occur toward the latter part of the church age.

Rapture

The rapture is a signless event; thus, there are not and never will be signs of the time indicating that the rapture is near. This is true because the rapture is *imminent,* meaning it could happen at any moment.

If there were signs that related to an event, they would indicate whether it was near or not near. Therefore, the event couldn't happen until *after* the signs were present. Thus, signs would have to precede the event—which means the event couldn't happen until after the signs appeared. Since the rapture could occur at any moment, it can't be related to any signs at all. (See 1 Corinthians 1:7; 16:22; Philippians 3:20; 4:5; 1 Thessalonians 1:10; Titus 2:13; Hebrews 9:28; James 5:7-9; 1 Peter 1:13; Jude 21; Revelation 3:11; 22:7,12,17,20.) However, this does not mean that there aren't signs of the times that relate to other aspects of God's plan.

End-Time Plans for Israel

There are many signs relating to God's end-time program for Israel. However, we must be careful in how we see them relating to us. Since believers today live during the church age, which will end with the rapture of the church, prophetic signs relating to Israel are not being fulfilled in our day. Instead, what God is doing prophetically in our day is preparing the world for the time when He will begin His plan relating to Israel, which will then involve the fulfillment of signs and times. One major indicator that we are likely near the beginning of the tribulation is the clear fact that national Israel has been reconstituted after almost 2,000 years.

4. Are there guidelines for understanding the signs?

Just because there may be legitimate signs in our day pointing to the return of Christ, that doesn't mean that every thought and speculation being brought forth is legitimate. In fact, there is entirely too much unsupported guess work that some current event is related to Bible prophecy. Some people believe that virtually everything that happens is an indication that the Lord's return is near. Wild speculations are all too common today, and too often they are not grounded in a proper biblical approach to the issues. This is why we need to offer some guidelines to discipline our thoughts so that we can guard against extreme and unfounded interpretations of events.

There are at least three key steps that must be processed before developing a proper approach to understanding the signs of the times. Prophecy expert Dr. Ed Hindson calls these three items facts, assumptions, and speculations. He says:[4]

> In our effort to make sense of all this, let me suggest a simple paradigm:
>
> *Facts.* There are the clearly stated facts of prophetic revelation: Christ will return for His own; He will judge the world; there will be a time of great trouble on the earth at the end of the age; the final conflict will be won by Christ; and so on. These basic facts are clearly stated in Scripture.
>
> *Assumptions.* Factual prophecy only tells us so much and no more. Beyond that we must make certain

assumptions. If these are correct, they will lead to valid conclusions, but if not, they may lead to ridiculous speculations. For example, it is an assumption that Russia will invade Israel in the last days. Whether or not that is factual depends on the legitimacy of one's interpretation of Ezekiel's Magog prophecy (Ezekiel 38–39)....

Speculations. These are purely calculated guesses based on assumptions. In many cases they have no basis in prophetic fact at all. For example, the Bible says the number of the Antichrist is "666" (Revelation 13:18). We must try to assume what this means. It is an assumption that it is a literal number that will appear on things in the last days. When one prominent evangelist saw the number 666 prefixed on automobile license plates in Israel a few years ago, he speculated the "mark of the Beast" had already arrived in the Holy Land.

The greatest danger of all in trying to interpret biblical prophecy is to assume that our speculations are true and preach them as facts. This has often caused great embarrassment and confusion. For example, when Benito Mussolini rose to power in Rome in the 1920s, many Christians assumed he might be the Antichrist, who would rule the world from the city of seven hills in the last days. Some even speculated that Adolph Hitler, who rose to power later in Germany, was the False Prophet. Others were sure the False Prophet was the pope, who was also in Rome.

The time has come when serious students of biblical prophecy must be clear about what is fact, what is assumption, and what is speculation.[5]

Thus, when we are approaching the study of biblical prophecy and attempting to relate it to events in our own day, we must first make sure that we start with a proper interpretation of the biblical text before we can draw conclusions upon which to speculate. It stands to reason that if we have an incorrect interpretation of a passage, then the conclusions or assumptions we draw will of necessity

be wrong (unless, by happenstance, we stumble onto a right conclusion).

For example, if we are studying what area of the world the Antichrist will come from, we must start with a correct interpretation of
biblical passages that bear on the subject. Having properly gathered
the biblical data, we then draw conclusions or, as Dr. Hindson called
them, assumptions. Thus, we might conclude that the Antichrist will
arise out of the Revived Roman Empire. Since 2 Thessalonians 2:6-9
indicates that he will not be revealed until after the rapture, we
would not be able to legitimately speculate as to who he might be
within the community of present-day possibilities. We could use
such an interpretation and assumption to exclude a suggested candi-
date from somewhere like Japan, for example.

Legitimate views about the signs of the times must start with
1) sound biblical interpretation, 2) proper assumptions or conclusions drawn from the interpretation, and 3) speculation consistent
with the previous two factors. Only after following such an approach
can we conclude that any contemporary development is a sign of
Christ's return.

5. What is the difference between a valid approach to the signs and "newspaper exegesis"?

It is common for critics of those who believe that there are signs
in our day of Christ's return to dismiss such a notion as "newspaper
exegesis." By this, the critics mean that human ideas—not the
Bible—are the true source of such beliefs because they arise from a
search of newspaper headlines rather than from exegesis (proper
interpretation) of the biblical text. Is this true?

In some cases it would be true, but not necessarily in all. If one
has first gone to Scripture and derived a sound model of end-time
events and there is true correspondence with what is reported in the
newspapers, then it can be valid. However, if one is genuinely
attempting to fit into the Bible today's headlines, then that is wrong
and could rightly be termed "newspaper exegesis."

Some prophecy teachers incorrectly teach that Bible prophecy
is being "fulfilled" in our day. As we previously noted, this is not the
case, except in relation to the reestablishment of the modern state of
Israel. Nevertheless, we do support the notion that there are signs of
the times relating to the fact that God is setting the stage for a time

of future fulfillment. Thus, it is an overstatement to speak of prophecy being fulfilled in our day, but not wrong to speak of signs that God is preparing for fulfillment.

It is common for some prophecy teachers to go to a biblical passage, usually one that will be fulfilled during the tribulation, and find a similarity to that prophecy and something happening in our day. Just because something is similar, does not mean it is the same.

For example, years ago I (Thomas) remember reading in Isaiah 24:5 that the "earth is also polluted by its inhabitants." I had heard a lot in the early '70s about how the earth was being polluted. I then suggested to a couple of friends that this was a prophecy of events taking place in our day. I made the connection based upon the idea of "pollution," without considering the biblical context of Isaiah 24. What is the contextual setting of Isaiah 24? It refers to events that will take place during the future tribulation period. Are we living in the tribulation period today? No! Thus, whatever was happening in current events at that time was not a fulfillment, nor was it related to Isaiah 24 just because I believed there was a point of similarity. If you examine most of the approaches in use today that claim fulfillment of prophecy relating to the tribulation with events of our day, they take a similar approach and thus have made a similar mistake.

Preparation for the Fulfillment of Prophecy

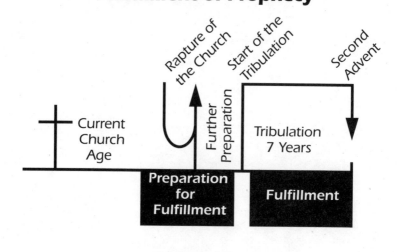

As we have noted before, there does not have to be actual fulfillment for a development to be a sign of the times. This can be so because there can be *preparation* for fulfillment. The preparation is not the fulfillment of a prophecy, but it does indicate that God is preparing to fulfill a prophecy in the near future. Such preparation for fulfillment is a sign of the times.

Dr. Walvoord echoes such a belief about current stage-setting in preparation for fulfillment.

> In our day…there has been a movement of God among Israel which has set the stage as never before for exactly that fulfillment which is predicted for the period immediately after the translation of the church…. More prophecies have either been fulfilled or prepared for fulfillment in our day than in all the previous centuries since the first of our era.[6]

CHAPTER 2

Biblical Prophecy, Date-Setting, and the Year 2000

6. Are there time schemes that relate primarily to the age of the world and to the second coming?

Yes! In fact, date-setting can be traced to pre-Christian Jewish origins. The oldest form of date-setting relates to an ancient view known as the septa-millennial theory. The sexta- or septa-millenary theory in Christianity stated that Christ would return after 6,000 years of history, and He would reign on earth for an additional 1,000 years. This view is based upon the six days of creation with the seventh day of rest (Genesis 2:2) and the belief (developed from Psalm 90:4 and 2 Peter 3:8) that each day was to be reckoned as representative of 1,000 years.

> And by the seventh day God completed His work which He had done; and He rested on the seventh day from all His work which He had done (Genesis 2:2).

> For a thousand years in Thy sight are like yesterday when it passes by, or as a watch in the night (Psalm 90:4).

> But do not let this one fact escape your notice, beloved, that with the Lord one day is as a thousand years, and a thousand years as one day (2 Peter 3:8).

Thus, just as man's work week (Exodus 20:8-11) is 6 days followed by the Sabbath rest, so the scope of history follows the pattern of 6,000 years for man's history, followed by the seventh thousand years of millennial rest (Hebrews 4:9).

> Remember the sabbath day, to keep it holy. Six days you shall labor and do all your work, but the seventh day is a sabbath of the LORD your God; in it you shall not do any work, you or your son or your daughter, your male or your female servant or your cattle or your sojourner who stays with you. For in six days the LORD

made the heavens and the earth, the sea and all that is in them, and rested on the seventh day; therefore the LORD blessed the sabbath day and made it holy (Exodus 20:8-11).

The Septa-Millennial Theory

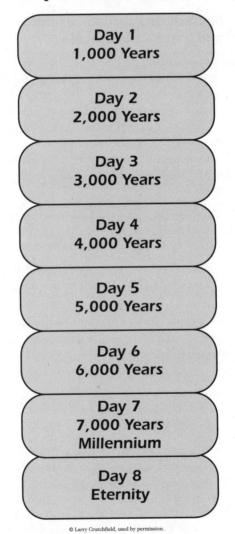

Day 1
1,000 Years

Day 2
2,000 Years

Day 3
3,000 Years

Day 4
4,000 Years

Day 5
5,000 Years

Day 6
6,000 Years

Day 7
7,000 Years
Millennium

Day 8
Eternity

It is significant to note that the book of Revelation (20:2-7) tells us six times that the length of Christ's reign on earth from Jerusalem will be 1,000 years in length. In the minds of those advocating the septa-millennial theory, this gives credibility since we know the seventh day—the day of our Lord's rest—will clearly be 1,000 years long, then it follows that the six days, the time of man, will be 6,000 years.

Nathaniel West tells us:

> The hope of the 1,000 years' kingdom did not originate with John. Plainly enough, it appears as an already given, steadfast, and of itself a well-grounded, matter of expectation, familiar and needing only to be named, something peculiar and of the highest importance, and woven as closely as possible into the whole web of the Christian life.... The Seer...found this term, the 1,000 years, already extant, and assumed that his readers were not unacquainted with it. He retained an expression already in common use....A point undoubtedly common to both Jewish and Christian apocalyptics, is the period of blessedness on earth, called the 1,000 years.[7]

Indeed, we find in Jewish literature (written before John was given the book of Revelation) that some Jews speculated that Messiah's kingdom would be 1,000 years in length.[8] This speculation was based upon the septa-millennial theory, which was developed well before the Christian era. Such speculation was turned to fact with the Holy Spirit's giving of Revelation 20 to the apostle John. Not only is this timeline found within Jewish tradition, but various forms of it are found in many cultures. Bishop Russell of Scotland wrote in the nineteenth century:

> It must be acknowledged that the doctrine concerning it stretches back into antiquity so remote and obscure, that it is impossible to fix its origin. The tradition that the earth, as well as the moral and religious state of its inhabitants, were to undergo a great change at the end of 6,000 years, has been detected in the writings of Pagans, Jews and Christians. It is found in the most ancient of those commentaries of the Old Testament, which we owe to the learning of the Rabbinical

> school;...this will nevertheless leave no room for
> doubt that the notion of the millennium preceded by
> several centuries the introduction of the Christian
> faith.[9]

Daniel Taylor and H.L. Hastings further tell us:

> David Gregory, a learned mathematician and astrono-
> mer of Oxford, Eng., who died in 1710, says: "In the
> first verse of the first chapter of Genesis, the Hebrew
> letter Aleph, which in the Jewish arithmetic stands for
> 1000, is six times found. From hence the ancient Cab-
> alists concluded that the world would last 6000 years.
> Because also God was six days about the creation, and
> a thousand years with him are but as one day; Psalm
> 90:4; 2 Peter 3:8, therefore after six days, that is 6000
> years duration of the world, there shall be a seventh
> day, or millenary sabbath rest. This early tradition of
> the Jews was found in the Sibylline Oracles and in
> Hesiod.[10]

Early church historian, Dr. Larry Crutchfield, has documented
that 21 of 34 writers of the ancient church (covering the first eight
centuries) taught the septa-millennial view.[11] The view was likely
even more widely held than noted previously, since some may have
held the view but not had occasion to mention it.

The earliest, and often considered the classical statement of the
septa-millennial theory, is found in the extra-biblical document
entitled *The Epistle of Barnabas* (ca. 70–100 or 117–138). Barnabas
says,

> Moreover concerning the sabbath likewise it is written
> in the Ten Words, in which he spake to Moses face to
> face on Mount Sinai; *And ye shall hallow the sabbath
> of the Lord with pure hands and with a pure heart.*
> And in another place He saith; *If My sons observe the
> sabbath, then I will bestow My mercy upon them.* Of
> the sabbath He speaketh in the beginning of the cre-
> ation; *And God made the works of His hands in six
> days, and He ended on the seventh day, and rested on
> it, and He hallowed it.* Give heed, children, what this
> meaneth; *He ended in six days.* He meaneth this, that

in six thousand years the Lord shall bring all things to an end; for the day with Him signifieth a thousand years; and this He himself beareth me witness, saying; *Behold, the day of the Lord shall be as a thousand years.* Therefore, children, in six days that is in six thousand years, everything shall come to an end.

And He rested on the seventh day. This He meaneth; when His Son shall come, and shall abolish the time of the Lawless One, and shall judge the ungodly, and shall change the sun and the moon and the stars, then shall He truly rest on the seventh day....Finally He saith to them; *Your new moons and your sabbaths I cannot away with.* Ye see what is His meaning; it is not your present sabbaths that are acceptable unto Me, but the sabbath which I have made, in the which, when I have set all things at rest, I will make the beginning of the eighth day which is the beginning of another world. Wherefore also we keep the eighth day for rejoicing, in the which also Jesus rose from the dead, and having been manifested ascended into the heavens. [Italics represent Barnabas' quotations of Scripture.][12]

Even though adherence to the septa-millennial view has waned somewhat with the passage of time, the theory has always had fervent proponents, down to and including our own day.

Thus, the oldest form of date-setting does not directly relate to the second coming, per se. Instead, the septa-millennial theory predicts the length of earth history, thereby implicating the time of the second advent.

7. Is the year 2000 prophetically significant?

The year A.D. 2000 is important in that many people, Christian and non-Christian alike, believe that the world could come to an end and/or the second coming will occur. However, it is questionable as to whether the Bible places special significance upon this year.

Historically, the reason why some people attach significance to the year 2000 is based on the septa-millenary theory and not just that our calendar date will pass from one millennium to the next. Some believe that the 6,000 years of man will expire on or around the year 2000.

The six-thousandth year since creation, according to the calculations of Irish Bishop James Ussher (1581–1656) is 1996. In 1701, Ussher's chronology was included in the margin of the King James Version of the Bible and is still in many editions today. It has been noted that Ussher was motivated to study past chronology because of his interest in dating the future second coming of Christ.

Even though Ussher's approach to biblical chronology is usually disdained in our day, he calculated the creation week to have commenced in 4004 B.C. on the basis of the numbers found in the Hebrew Masoretic Text of the Genesis 5 and 10 genealogies. (It is clear that the numbers in the Masoretic Text are the correct ones.) Ussher's chronology, when coupled with the septa-millennial theory, leads to the conclusion that Christ would return in the year 1996.

More recently, some people who have followed Ussher's approach and the numbers of the Masoretic Text have argued that his date for creation did not allow for a calendar shift. They conclude that the real date of creation is 4000 B.C. Thus, A.D. 2000 is more likely the six-thousandth year since creation and the time of Christ's second coming. Some add in a "fudge" factor of about 10 years but, by-and-large, if Christ has not returned by the year 2000 then it appears that the septa-millennial theory will have exhausted all possible avenues of adjustment and fulfillment.

> Though few moderns, Christians or otherwise, know the ancient traditions of the world ages and the chronographic countdowns to the millennial Sabbath,... the year 2000 nonetheless serves as a focus of apocalyptic speculation.[13]

As the year A.D. 2000 approaches, there may be an increase in advocates engaging in date-setting. However, one thing seems clear to us: Since America is largely a secular nation, the atmosphere of panic historically associated with the end of the world will probably not occur.

Instead, the only panic that may arise will revolve around those who will stir up fear about those who set calendar dates—what is sometimes called "the millennial glitch." Apparently, many of the world's computers will reset themselves to 1900 when the year 2000 rolls around. This could cause problems with large government agencies that issue monthly payments. It has been estimated that the cost for fixing this problem worldwide may be $600 billion!

8. Wasn't the year 1000 significant?

As the year A.D. 1000 approached, panic swept across Christian Europe. This was likely the most widespread anticipation of the end of the world in history. Richard Erdoes has noted,

> On the last day of the year 999...the old basilica of St. Peter's at Rome was thronged with a mass of weeping and trembling worshipers awaiting the end of the world....Many of those present had given away all their possessions to the poor—lands, homes, and household goods—in order to assure for themselves forgiveness for their trespasses of the Almighty. Many poor sinners...had entered the church in sackcloth and ashes, having already spent weeks and months doing penance and mortifying the flesh.[14]

The year 1000 brought to a climax a whole era that increasingly anticipated Christ's return. In those days:

> Every phenomenon of nature filled them with alarm. A thunderstorm sent them all upon their knees in mid-march. It was the opinion that thunder was the voice of God announcing the Day of Judgment....Fanatic preachers kept up the flame of terror. Every shooting star furnished occasion for a sermon, in which the sublimity of the approaching Judgment was the principle topic.[15]

Ron Rhodes tells us,

> As Christmas (A.D. 999) arrived, there was an outpouring of love. Stores gave away food; merchants refused payment. On December 31 the frenzy reached new heights. Pope Sylvester II held a midnight mass in the Basilica of St. Peter's in Rome. There was a standing-room-only audience—but the people weren't standing; they were on their knees.
>
> After the mass had been said, a deathly silence fell over the congregation. Finally, as the clock uneventfully

> ticked past 12, church bells began ringing. Amid weeping and laughing, husbands and wives embraced. Friends exchanged "the kiss of peace." Enemies were reconciled.
>
> But life soon resumed its normal rhythm. Merchants ceased giving away their goods. Prisoners were captured to be placed back in the slammer. Debts were remembered. And life went on as if nothing happened.[16]

In spite of the obvious fact that the world did not come to an end and Christ did not return, did this serve to discredit the gospel and Christianity? It may have with some, but on the whole such an interest in eternal things actually furthered the cause of Christianity. It is said on the frontiers of Christendom that Christianity was strengthened and the pagan gods diminished through this ordeal. "The years around Anno Domini 1000 saw the kings of Denmark, Norway, Sweden, Poland, and Hungary accept the Christian faith."[17]

The basis for such anticipation was not related to the septa-millennial view. Since the time of Augustine, early in the fifth century, premillennialism fell into disfavor among Catholic interpreters. They tended to equate the present church age with the 1,000 years of Revelation 20, even though they did not believe the number was literal. Nevertheless, a majority of the church placed significance on the year 1000.

9. Has date-setting always occurred in church history?

The early church did not engage in a lot of specific setting of dates since they believed that Christ could return at any moment. However, at the same time, they held to the septa-millennial view, which tended to lead them to believe that there were outer limits to the time in which the world would end.

Date-setting throughout church history has tended to occur around major time periods such as 500, 1000, and now 2000. Yet there have always been those who have produced formulas for setting dates—in spite of the fact that this is clearly prohibited in Scripture. The major aspect that has changed throughout the history of date-setting has been the basis upon which dates are set.

10. Hasn't there been a lot of date-setting in the last few years?

When compared to times in church history when date-setting was popular, there has not been a lot of date-setting in the last few years. For example, there is much less date-setting in our day than 100–150 years ago when historicism was dominant. In spite of the impression given by some, there is not an unusual amount of date-setting today. Those people who do engage in this activity get the attention of the media, perhaps giving an impression that it is commonplace. The media likes to report on these kind of stories, knowing they are of great interest to today's secular and religious societies.

On the other hand, there is a general sense among many evangelicals that we are near the time of the end. It is possible to have a general belief that the Lord's return is near, but not engage in the specific act of date-setting. For example, Dr. John Walvoord stops short of date-setting, but goes on to say that,

> informed Christians are expecting the coming of the Lord as the next important event on the prophetic calendar.
>
> The world today is like a stage being set for a great drama. The major actors are already in the wings waiting for their moment in history. The main stage props are already in place. The prophetic play is about to begin....All the necessary historical developments have already taken place....
>
> Our present world is well prepared for the beginning of the prophetic drama that will lead to Armageddon. Since the stage is set for this dramatic climax of the age, it must mean that Christ's coming for His own is very near. If there ever was an hour when men should consider their personal relationship to Jesus Christ, it is today. God is saying to this generation: "Prepare for the coming of the Lord."[18]

The following poll results were published in a December 1994 article entitled, "Waiting for the Messiah: The new clash over the Bible's millennial prophecies."[19]

• Americans who believe that Jesus Christ will return to Earth:	61%
• Of those who believe Jesus will return, the percentage who think He will come within—	
a few years; few decades:	34%
longer than that:	37%
• Americans who believe the world will come to an end:	59%
• Of those, the percentage who believe the end will occur within—	
a few years:	12%
a few decades:	21%
a few hundred years:	16%
longer than that:	28%
• Americans who believe some world events this century fulfill biblical prophecy:	53%
• Of those, the percentage who believe these specific events fulfill prophecy—	
world wars:	16%
conflict between Israel and its enemies:	10%
establishment of Israel:	6%
AIDS epidemic:	6%

CHAPTER 3

Who Are the Date-Setters?

11. Are some prophetic schemes more susceptible than others to date-setting?

Without a doubt, one's approach to the *timing* of the fulfillment of prophecy in general impacts one's disposition toward date-setting. So when will a prophecy be fulfilled? There are four possibilities, simple in the sense that they reflect the only possibilities in relation to time—past, present, future, and timeless.

The *preterist* (past) believes that most, if not all, prophecy has already been fulfilled, usually in relation to the destruction of Jerusalem in A.D. 70.

The *historicist* (present) sees much of the current church age as equal to the tribulation period. Thus, prophecy has been and will be fulfilled during the current church age.

Futurists believe that virtually all prophetic events will not occur in the current church age, but will take place in the future tribulation, second coming, or millennium.

The *idealist* (timeless) does not believe that the Bible indicates the timing of events or that we can determine their timing in advance. Idealists think prophetic passages mainly teach that great ideas or truths about God are to be applied regardless of timing.

The four prophetic timing possibilities are diagrammed on page 28. The logical implications for date-setting in regard to the four approaches are:

Preterism. In a sense, preterists are the biggest date-setters of all. On one hand, they teach that Christ returned when He provoked the Roman army to destroy Jerusalem in A.D. 70. On the other hand, those preterists who believe in a future second coming rarely date-set, since their focus is on a past—not future—event.

Historicism. It appears that it is impossible to be a historicist and not date-set. Why? Because historicism equates the current church age with the tribulation period through the day/year theory. The day/year theory takes numbers like 2,300 days (Daniel 8:14) and

Basic Approaches to Eschatology

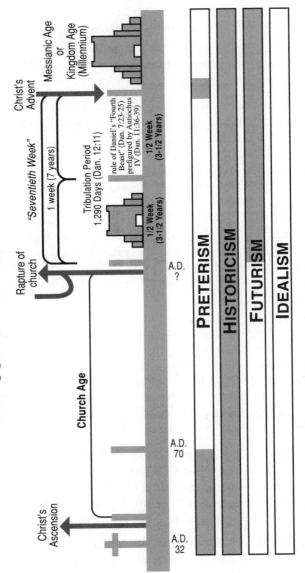

(Shaded areas indicate time of fulfillment)

1,290 days (Daniel 12:11) and declares them to be years. Thus, if one can find the right starting year it is merely a matter of adding the 2,300 or 1,290 years to discover the date of Christ's return. In addition, historicists also relate the seal, trumpet, and bowl judgments to major historical events for the last 2,000 years. For example, the fifth seal in Revelation 6 is identified as the martyrdom under Roman Emperor Diocletian (284–304). Then one might view the French Revolution as the first five bowl judgments of Revelation 16. This approach, coupled with the day/year theory, naturally leads to date-setting. This view was almost unanimously held by Protestants from the Reformation until about 100 years ago. It is also the view of many of the nineteenth-century sects such as Mormonism, Seventh-Day Adventism, and Jehovah's Witnesses.

Futurism. Since futurists believe that end-time events (i.e., the tribulation, second coming, and millennium) are future to this current time period, they should not be inclined to date-setting. However, many futurists do engage in date-setting. It is significant to observe that they have to resort to historicist principles in order to inconsistently presume that current events are fulfilling Bible prophecy in our own day.

Idealism. Idealism logically cannot date-set since the core of this view is the belief that God has not revealed anything relating to the timing of an event. Chronology (if it even exists) for the idealist is an unrevealed mystery.

We may conclude, then, that historicism is far and away the most favorable method for date-setting. In fact, it is impossible to intelligently practice this approach without engaging in date-setting. Futurism should not date-set, but all too often some within its ranks engage in the practice, even though we are not in the tribulation. Preterists rarely date-set, unless one views the A.D. 70 destruction of Jerusalem as date-setting. It is impossible for the idealist to date-set and remain an idealist.

12. Should dispensationalists set dates?

After the Reformation, scholars began to take more literally the Old Testament promises to restore the Jews to their land so that end-time prophecy could be fulfilled. Scholars also began to realize that if these prophecies apply literally to Israel, then this meant the church had a different and distinct program from Israel within God's plan. Thus, the futurist interpretation contributed to the development of a new brand of premillennialism which, today, we know as dispensationalism.

All dispensationalists are futurists, but all futurists are not dispensationalists. Dispensational futurism deserves some special consideration since it is the only viewpoint that in essence sees a two-phase return of Christ—the rapture and the second coming.[20] (This book is written from this perspective.)

An undeveloped futurism was widespread within the early church. It fell into disfavor by the fifth century and was not revived until the early 1800s. It has become the most widely used approach to Bible prophecy among conservatives in our day.

Dispensationalism was developed and championed by Irishman J.N. Darby. Historian Ernest R. Sandeen noted:

> Darby's view of the premillennial advent contrasted with that held by the historicist millenarian school in two ways. First, Darby taught that the second advent would be secret, an event sensible only to those who participated in it....Second, Darby taught that the secret rapture could occur at any moment. In fact, the secret rapture is also often referred to as the doctrine of the any-moment coming.[21]

As this new dispensational futurism gained ground during the last half of the nineteenth century, date-setting, as encouraged by historicism, became less frequent. In fact, a major reason why dispensational futurism became widespread was precisely because it was an anti-date-setting theology. Sandeen observes,

> [Unlike the historicist millenarians,] Darby taught that the prophetic timetable had been interrupted at the founding of the church and that the unfulfilled biblical prophecies must all wait upon the rapture of the church. The church was a great parenthesis which Old Testament prophets had not revealed to them. As was true of all futurists, of course, Darby maintained that none of the events foretold in the Revelation had yet occurred nor could they be expected until after the

secret rapture of the church. Christ might come at any moment.[22]

"Darby avoided the pitfalls," adds Sandeen, "both of attempting to predict a time for Christ's second advent and of trying to make sense of the contemporary alarms of European politics with the Revelation as his guidebook."[23]

Since the focus of dispensational futurism is upon the *signless, any-moment rapture,* and only secondarily on the second coming, it does not follow that dispensationalists should in any way date-set. However, it is possible to believe that we are near the general time of the end as God sets the stage of human history for the coming tribulation.

Many advocates of a dispensational approach to Bible prophecy in our day have attempted date-setting schemes. However, we believe that it is inconsistent with the principles which lead to a dispensational understanding of the Bible and should be avoided. This point becomes clear when examining the basis upon which dispensationalists date-set. Every attempt to date-set by dispensationalists has meant that a nondispensational basis has been employed in their date-setting approach. It is impossible to date-set if one is consistent within the principles of dispensational futurism.

A major approach that has been used recently by some dispensationalists, in addition to the septa-millennial theory, is to employ Israel's feast cycle prophetically. The Bible teaches a cycle of seven feasts that Israel was to celebrate yearly. The seven feasts are: Passover, Unleavened Bread, First Fruits, Feast of Weeks, Trumpets, Day of Atonement, and Tabernacles. The first four feasts are celebrated in the spring, while the remaining three are commemorated in the fall.

A common interpretation by some evangelicals concludes that the feasts also are prophetic of the career of the Messiah. The spring cycle is said to have been fulfilled by Christ at His first coming, while the fall cycle will be fulfilled in the future through events surrounding the second coming.

Usually the date-setting approach goes something like this: The fifth feast (the Feast of Trumpets) is taken as a reference to the rapture. Since Rosh Hashanah (Hebrew for Feast of Trumpets) is yearly celebrated on Tishri 1 according to the Hebrew calendar (this day usually falls in September according to our contemporary calendar), and it is argued that trumpets are related to the rapture (1 Corinthians 15:52), therefore, the rapture will occur on Tishri 1 as the spring cycle of feasts begins to be fulfilled. This scheme argues that if the year of the rapture can be determined, then we would know that it would occur in the fall of that year. Many of the more recent and popular date-setting schemes have implemented Israel's feast cycle in some way.

We do not have a problem with the prophetic aspect of Israel's feast cycle. However, we do believe that Israel's feasts relate to Israel and Israel alone. True, the fulfillment of Israel's feasts relate to salvation for all mankind, but the precise fulfillment relates exclusively to national Israel. In the New Testament, the rapture is a newly revealed event related only to the church and, thus, could not have been predicted through Old Testament revelation like Israel's feasts. Therefore, any attempt to date-set using the feasts is invalid because they are for Israel and not the church.

It should be clear that the church does not fulfill any of Israel's feasts, including the Day of Pentecost. The Feast of Pentecost was given for Israel. It just so happened, that in the plan of God, He scheduled the founding of the church to begin on that day, even though it is not a fulfillment by the church of the Day of Pentecost. This means that any future fulfillment of the feasts will be fulfilled by Israel, not the church.

Whenever one encounters and examines a dispensational date-setting scheme, inevitably the core of the approach will employ passages of Scripture that do not directly relate to God's program for the church. Every approach is wrongly built upon a passage that relates to Israel, events of the tribulation, or events related to the second coming and not to the rapture of the church. Even though some do, no one who is a dispensational futurist *should* attempt to date-set.

13. Have all millennial systems had proponents who set dates?

Yes! As noted in previous questions, the primary factor in date-setting is one's view of the timing of prophecy (i.e., preterism, historicism, futurism, and idealism) not one's millennial view. However, the millennial factor does restrict, to some extent, which approaches to the timing of prophecy are possible for the three millennial positions.

For many, trying to understand the differences between premillennialism, postmillennialism, and amillennialism is a significant challenge. However, it becomes even more complex when the four "timing" approaches to prophecy are added. But, like many complex appearances, it is not too difficult if an effort is put forth to learn the basic characteristics of each aspect. There is then a basis for understanding the commingling of the different aspects. In terms of the logic of the various aspects, what are the possible mixes that can be produced? The chart below summarizes this information.

Prophetic Timing and Millennial Views

TIMING	AMILLENNIALISM	POSTMILLENNIALISM	PREMILLENNIALISM
Preterism	YES	YES	NO
Historicism	YES	YES	YES
Futurism	NO	YES	YES
Idealism	YES	YES	NO

This material has been presented for the purpose of delineating the different viewpoints so that we may gain understanding as to the consistency and implications of various millennial views when combined with prophetic timing elements. The only timing view that can be accommodated by all three millennial views is historicism. We know that historicism is the view most prone to date-setting. Thus, all three millennial views have had proponents within their ranks who have date-set in the past.

14. How have premillennialists set dates?

Premillennialism, and specifically dispensationalism, is the view or system of eschatology (doctrine of the last things) that is presented throughout this book and series. It holds that there will be a future, literal millennium or thousand-year reign of Jesus Christ upon the earth following the events of the rapture, tribulation, and second coming. Premillennialism teaches that the millennium is 1,000 literal years and follows Christ's second advent.

Dispensational premillennialists hold that Israel and the church are two separate and distinct entities throughout all of history, including the millennium. Other premillennialists hold that in the Old and New Testament eras, Israel and the church were the same, but in the millennium they will be separate. Premillennialism can be diagrammed as in the graphic below.

Premillennialism

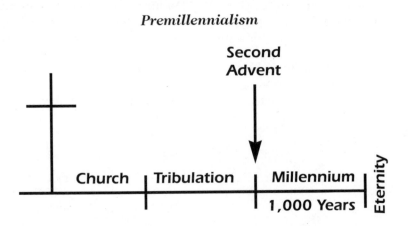

Without a doubt, premillennialists have led the way as those most frequently involved in date-setting. The earliest date-setting combined the septa-millennial approach with a general belief that things such as earthquakes, natural disasters, plagues, moral decline, apostasy, and stellar phenomena in their day were in some way fulfilling biblical prophecy. Based upon some similarity between current events and biblical prophecy, it was often claimed that Christ's return was near.

By the time of the Reformation when historicism was almost unanimously held by all Protestants, many historicist premillennialists were involved in date-setting. Many of the Puritans like Isaac Watts, Joseph Mede, and the Mathers in America were premillennial date-setters.

The most famous date-setter in American history was the Baptist William Miller. Miller was a classic premillennial historicist. He took the 2,300 days from Daniel 8:14 when "the holy place will be properly restored" and turned them into years. Miller's starting year

was 457 B.C., which, he believed, was when Nebuchadnezzar pro-
faned the temple in Jerusalem. When you add up the numbers, you
arrive at the year 1843 as the time of Christ's return. But when that
year came and went like any other year, it was discovered that a year
had been left out for the shift from B.C. to A.D., thus 1844 was the
true year. However, it too came and went and Miller's scheme
became known as the "Great Disappointment" to his thousands of
followers.

In our own day, who can forget the impact made by Edgar
Whisenant and his booklet *88 Reasons Why the Rapture Will Be in
1988*. Whisenant used the Feast of Trumpets approach as the basis
for developing his scheme. Also, a group of Korean Christians set
October 1992 as the time of Christ's return. There are many lesser-
known attempts that appear to be constantly in circulation.

15. How have amillennialists set dates?

Amillennialism is the view or system of eschatology (doctrine of
the last things) teaching that there is no literal earthly millennium.
Although all versions of amillennialism unite around their belief in
no earthly millennium, they sometimes differ as to the exact nature
and time of the millennium. All believe that the millennium is spiritual and not earthly. However, some believe that the spiritual kingdom is present during the current era of the church. Some
amillennialists believe that the present spiritual reign of God's kingdom consists of the influence the church exerts through its many
worldwide ministries. Another form teaches that the millennium is
composed of the reign of all dead Christians in heaven. Still a third
view believes that the millennium is equal to the eternal state that
will commence at the second coming, i.e., the new heavens and new
earth equals the millennium.

Amillennialism teaches that from the ascension of Christ in the
first century until His second coming (no rapture) both good and evil
will increase in the world as God's kingdom parallels Satan's kingdom. When Jesus Christ returns the end of the world will occur with
a general resurrection and general judgment of all people. It is essentially a spiritualization of the kingdom prophecies. Amillennialism
can be diagrammed as shown on page 36.

Amillennialism

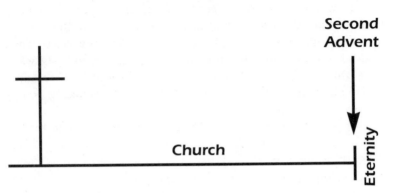

Most of those who have been amillennial date-setters have used the historicist approach as their primary basis for their brand of date-setting. One of the most recent date-setting efforts in our day came from well-known Christian radio teacher and personality Harold Camping. Camping selected September 1994 as the time of Christ's return, which of course failed to materialize. It is hard to classify Camping's approach to date-setting because of his arbitrary use of Scripture, but it apparently is best classified as historicism. Other historicist date-setters include the German Reformers Martin Luther and Philip Melanchthon. They were both date-setters and believed in a form of the septa-millennial theory, as were a number of their colleagues. Luther once taught that Christ's return would occur by 1564.

16. How have postmillennialists set dates?

Postmillennialism is the view or system of eschatology teaching that the current age is the millennium, which is not necessarily 1,000 years in length. Postmillennialists believe the kingdom will gradually be extended through the preaching of the gospel, the eventual conversion of a large majority of people, and the progressive growth of righteousness, prosperity, and development in every sphere of life as this growing majority of Christians struggle to subdue the world for Christ. After Christianity has dominated the world for a long time—the church's glorious reign of victory—then Christ will return. Like amillennialism, there will be a general resurrection, destruction of this present creation, and entry into the eternal state. Postmillennialism differs from premillennialism and amillennialism in that they are optimistic that this victory will be realized without the need for a cataclysmic return of Christ to impose righteousness, but rather will result from the faithful application of the present process. Postmillennialism can be diagrammed as shown below.

Postmillennialism

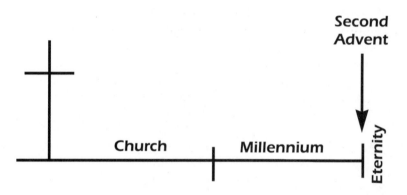

Postmillennial date-setting is a little different than the other two views. In spite of this, some postmillennialists have not been able to resist the lure of date-setting. Postmillennial date-setting has been largely inspired by the historicist timing approach to prophecy. Some have employed the septa-millennial theory to date-setting. However, when a postmillennialist date-sets, he is usually interested in predicting the beginning of the millennial phase of the kingdom.

For example, America's first major postmillennial thinker was Jonathan Edwards. His views paralleled those of Daniel Whitby (1638–1725), the founder of modern postmillennialism. In the mid-1700s, Edwards speculated in his *History of Redemption* that within a century-and-a-half the Mohammedans might be overthrown and the Jews converted. Contemporary signs convinced him that the millennium was at hand.

More recently, a couple of reconstructionist postmillennialists have date-set using the septa-millennial view. Contemporary postmillennialism is not immune to the date-setting temptation. Amazingly,

Francis Nigel Lee and Gary North, who have been quick to poke fun at premillennial date-setters like Whisenant, have also dabbled in the art. Writing in February 1985, North said that the millennium will arrive around the year A.D. 2000. He says, "It will not take long; under 20 years."[24]

17. What about non-Christians who set dates?

God's Word alone is the only legitimate basis for predicting the future. When Israel had lapsed into idolatry in the sixth century B.C., our Lord, speaking through Isaiah declared:

> I declared the former things long ago and they went forth from My mouth, and I proclaimed them. Suddenly I acted, and they came to pass. Because I know that you are obstinate, and your neck is an iron sinew, and your forehead bronze, therefore I declared them to you long ago, before they took place I proclaimed them to you, lest you should say, "My idol has done them, and my graven image and my molten image have commanded them" (Isaiah 48:3-5).

It is part of the sinful and idolatrous nature of man to think that he can know anything—let alone the future—apart from the omniscient God and His revelation. As God's creatures, we are dependent upon Him for everything, especially knowledge. There is no legitimate basis for extrabiblical attempts at knowing the future, even if their predictions appear to support biblical conclusions.

There are a number of non-Christian date-setters in our day who think the world could come to an end around the year A.D. 2000. We have all heard of the famous Nostradamus of the sixteenth century. Many people have interpreted his writings to say that he predicted the end of the world around A.D. 2000. Even if this is true, his occult basis for such a prediction should not even turn the head of a Christian.

A number of New Agers and Native Americans have predicted the end of the world or the arrival of a utopian era around the year A.D. 2000. These predictions are based upon occult and non-Christian practices and are to be categorically rejected by any sincere, Bible-believing Christian.

CHAPTER 4

What Does the Bible Teach About Setting Dates?

18. What did Jesus teach about date-setting?

Our Lord was quite emphatic in teaching about His return. In at least five passages (seven, if parallel passages are included), Jesus specifically warned the disciples and believers against date-setting. Yet, as we have seen, throughout church history there has been an amazing amount of date speculation.

Jesus emphasized prophecy and the understanding of it in His teachings. He did not avoid or dismiss its relevance; He did just the opposite. He emphasized its importance in understanding His life and ministry. Yet, He did explain that there are some aspects of the future that cannot be discerned with precision. His return is certain, but the precise moment is not. Jesus understood the human longing for knowledge of tomorrow, but He did not permit His followers to succumb to soothsayer temptations:

- *Matthew 24:36:* But of that day and hour no one knows, not even the angels of heaven, nor the Son, but the Father alone. (Mark 13:32 is an exact parallel.)

- *Matthew 24:42:* Therefore be on the alert, for you do not know which day your Lord is coming.

- *Matthew 24:44:* For this reason you be ready too; for the Son of Man is coming at an hour when you do not think He will.

- *Matthew 25:13:* Be on the alert then, for you do not know the day nor the hour. (Mark 13:33-37 is a parallel passage.)

- *Acts 1:7:* He said to them, "It is not for you to know times or epochs which the Father has fixed by His own authority."

These passages are absolute prohibitions against date-setting. Some students of prophecy have said these verses teach that it was impossible to know the date in the early church, but in the last days some people will come to know it. Other students have said that the verses teach that no one knows the day or the hour, except those who are able to figure it out through some scheme. Both are absolutely wrong! The date of Christ's coming is a matter of God's revelation. He has chosen not to reveal it even to Christ during His humanity in His first advent (Matthew 24:36). If the Father did not reveal it to the Son in His humanity, why should any person believe the Father would reveal it to him or her? Jesus is very clear: "No!"

19. What else does the Bible teach regarding prophecy?

The teaching of Christ is reinforced elsewhere in the Scriptures as well. In 1 Thessalonians 5:1,2, Paul reasserts the words of Jesus regarding the uncertainty of His return: "Now as to the times and the epochs, brethren, you have no need of anything to be written to you. For you yourselves know full well that the day of the Lord will come just like a thief in the night."

Some people believe there are passages in the Bible which teach that believers will be able to know the date of Christ's return. We will examine some of these passages to show how those who advocate date-setting have misused various verses in their attempts for legitimacy. The Bible does not contain internal contradictions. It is wrong to think that Scripture says "no man can know," but also states that some people will be able to figure it out.

The first passage that is sometimes cited is Luke 21:28: "But when these things begin to take place, straighten up and lift up your heads, because your redemption is drawing near." Some people have taught that this passage implies a license to date-set. However, important contextual indicators are overlooked in such an argument. These indicators include the fact that the passage refers to Jewish believers during the future seven-year tribulation, who, right before the second coming of Christ, are told to *watch,* not date-set, as they endure the final period of severe persecution. This does not relate to date-setting during the current church age, since it relates to events during the seven-year tribulation. Once the tribulation starts, then it will be possible to know the time of Christ's coming. However, this in no way relates to believers today who are living during the church age (not the tribulation). The church age ends with the signless event of the rapture. Thus, there is no way to link, specifically, events of our own day with those of the tribulation for the purpose of setting a date. We are to be watching and waiting for our Lord's return at the rapture precisely because we cannot date-set.

A second passage sometimes cited is Hebrews 10:25: "but encouraging one another; and all the more, as you see the day drawing near." Some teach that this implies that believers are able to see or know that "the day" (the second coming) is drawing near. While some do interpret "the day" as a reference to the second coming, we think that the immediate context and the context of the book of Hebrews is a warning to Jewish believers before the A.D. 70 destruction of Jerusalem and the temple. A warning telling them not to return (i.e., apostatize) to Judaism, since the immediate future contained only wrath for those Jews who reject Jesus as their Messiah. Therefore, "the day" is not a reference to the second coming but instead refers to Jerusalem's destruction by the Romans in A.D. 70. If this passage does refer to the second coming, once again there would be no basis in which to link a specific factor on which to date the second coming. The general statement "as you see the day drawing near" does not mean that we will know specifically when He is coming any more than someone watching the progress of a thunderstorm knows the precise moment when it will rain at his or her location.

A third passage sometimes called upon is 1 Thessalonians 5:4: "But you, brethren, are not in darkness, that the day should overtake you like a thief." It has been taught from this passage that believers would have to know the timing of "the day" [i.e., "the day of the Lord" (see 1 Thessalonians 5:2)] in order to not be overtaken by it. But this date-setting interpretation attaches the wrong sense to Paul's teaching. Paul is saying that they will not be overtaken because they are prepared by virtue of the fact that they are believers. All believers will be taken care of by the Lord (we believe through the pretribulational rapture), so that unlike the unbeliever who will be unprepared and caught off-guard, the believer will be prepared.

20. What's the harm in studying prophecy and setting dates?

There is no harm in studying prophecy. In fact, we can't ignore prophecy and properly study the Bible, but we must not fall into a snare of setting dates. The Bible clearly teaches that God's Word is sufficient for everything needed to live a life pleasing unto Christ (2 Timothy 3:16,17; 2 Peter 1:3,4). This means that if something is not revealed for us in the Bible, it is not needed to accomplish God's plan for our lives. The date of Christ's return is not stated in the Bible, therefore, in spite of what some may say, knowing it is not important for living a godly life. The Lord told Israel, "The secret things belong to the LORD our God, but the things revealed belong to us and to our sons forever, that we may observe all the words of this law" (Deuteronomy 29:29). The date of Christ's coming has not been revealed; it is a secret belonging only to God.

Since the Bible prohibits date-setting, what does it teach? Many of the same passages that prohibit date-setting instruct us in what we should do until the Lord returns. For example, Matthew 24:42 not only warns "for you do not know which day your Lord is coming," but also admonishes believers to "be on the alert." Matthew 24:44 tells believers to "be ready" because "the Son of Man is coming at an hour when you do not think He will." Also, Matthew 25:13 admonishes us to "be on the alert then, for you do not know the day nor the hour."

The alert to which believers are called is not to date-setting, but one of looking for the Savior (since we do not know when Jesus will return). We are to be alert, in contrast to unbelievers who are pictured as sleeping, in regard to the things of God. We are to be alert for the purpose of godly living until the Lord returns because we are in the dark night of this current evil age, which requires an active alertness toward evil.

If the church knew the day or the hour of the rapture then imminence, the posture Christians have in relation to the rapture, would be destroyed. Biblical imminence teaches that Christ can, but does not have to, come at any moment. It also means that *there are no signs which have to be fulfilled in order for the rapture to occur.* Thus, Christ could literally come today or this hour or moment. All attempts at date-setting destroy this imminence. If someone taught that the rapture will happen on a specific date or month or year, then it would mean that Christ could not come before that time. And, thus, the rapture could not be imminent, since Christ could not come until that specific date. Imminence is important because it's often related to commands for holy living. So date-setting also has a negative impact upon ethics. (See our booklet *The Truth About 2000 A.D. and Predicting Christ's Return* for a more thorough examination.)

Although date-setting is clearly prohibited in God's Word, we believe it is valid to understand that God is setting the stage for His great end-time program. What does that mean? As we mentioned earlier, the rapture is a signless event, thus it is impossible to identify specific signs that indicate its nearness. This is why all attempts to date the rapture have had to wrongly resort to the application of passages relating to God's plan for Israel to the church. An example of this misuse would be those who say Israel's feasts (i.e., Rosh Hashanah) relate to dating the rapture as noted previously. However, since the Bible outlines a clear cast and scenario of players, events, and nations involved in the end-time tribulation, we can see God's preparation for the final seven years of Daniel's 70 weeks for Israel.

For example, the fact that Israel has been reestablished as a nation and now controls Jerusalem is a strong indicator that the church age is drawing to an end (Isaiah 11:11–12:6; Ezekiel 20:33-44; 22:17-22; Zephaniah 2:1-3). But this can only be a general indication, since no timetable is specifically given for current preparation. We cannot know for certain that we are the last generation before the rapture since God may choose to "stage set" for another 100 years or more. Dr. Walvoord correctly says,

> There is no scriptural ground for setting dates for the Lord's return or the end of the world....As interpretation principles, they are becoming increasingly aware of a remarkable correspondence between the obvious trend of world events and what the Bible predicted centuries ago.[25]

Jesus Christ will return! It is our responsibility to be prepared for that return and to proclaim the salvation He offers, so others may also be prepared.

CHAPTER 5

What Are the Signs of the End of the Church Age?

21. What is the prophetic nature of the church age?

Apart from a few exceptions, the church age is not a time of prophetic fulfillment. Instead, prophecy will be fulfilled after the rapture, in relation to God's dealing with the nation of Israel in the seven-year tribulation. The current church age in which believers live today does not have a specific prophetic countdown or timetable, as does Israel and its 70 weeks of years prophecy (Daniel 9:14-27). The New Testament does, however, provide general traits that characterize the church age.

Even specific prophecy that is fulfilled during the church age relates to God's prophetic plan for Israel and not directly to the church. For example, the prophesied destruction of Jerusalem and its temple in A.D. 70 relates to Israel (Matthew 23:38; Luke 19:43-44; 21:20-24). Thus, it is not inconsistent that prophetic preparations relating to Israel are already underway with the reestablishment of Israel as a nation in 1948, even though we are still living in the church age.

The church age is not characterized by historically verifiable prophetic events, except its beginning on the Day of Pentecost and its ending with the rapture. But the general course of this age has been prophesied and can provide a general overview of what can be expected during this age.

22. What is the course of the church age?

The course of the current church age is given to Christians in three sets of passages in the New Testament. An understanding of these passages is needed for insight into the signs of the times.

Matthew 13

The parables of Matthew 13 provide insight into the course of the current church age. Actually, since Matthew 13 surveys this present age in its relation to the kingdom, the parables cover the period of time between Christ's two advents—His first and second comings. This includes the tribulation, second coming, and final judgment after the rapture, but nevertheless includes an important overview of our present era. How does Matthew 13 depict this age?

Dr. J. Dwight Pentecost summarizes the description as follows:

> We may summarize the teaching as to the course of the age by saying: (1) there will be a sowing of the Word throughout the age, which (2) will be imitated by a false counter sowing; (3) the kingdom will assume huge outer proportions, but (4) be marked by inner doctrinal corruption; yet, the Lord will gain for Himself (5) a peculiar treasure from among Israel, and (6) from the church; (7) the age will end in judgment with the unrighteous excluded from the kingdom to be inaugurated and the righteous taken in to enjoy the blessing of Messiah's reign.[26]

Revelation 2–3

The next major passage providing an overview of the course of this age is found in the presentation of the seven churches of Revelation 2–3. The perspective of Revelation 2–3 is in reference to the program of the church and not the kingdom. Thus, its overview proceeds from Pentecost to the rapture as indicated by the oft-repeated phrase, "He who has an ear, let him hear what the Spirit says to the churches" (Revelation 2:7,11,17,29; 3:6,13,22). These seven historical churches of the first century provide a pattern of the types of churches that will exist throughout church history.

Revelation 1:19 indicates a threefold division of the book of Revelation: "Write therefore the things which you have seen, and the things which are, and the things which shall take place after these things."

- *Revelation 1:* corresponds with "the things which you have seen," which depicts the resurrected Christ.

- *Revelation 2–3:* corresponds with "the things which are," which covers the church age.

- *Revelation 4–22:* corresponds with "the things which shall take place after these things," which covers the tribulation, second coming, millennium, and eternal state.

It is clear from this division of Revelation that the seven churches of Revelation 2–3 relate to the current church age.

What lessons do these seven epistles to the churches in Revelation teach us about the church age? G.H. Pember, a prophecy scholar of a previous generation, says,

> Hence it seems clear, that the Churches selected must have been chosen because of their representative character. And, taking, also, into consideration the order in which they are placed, we may, probably, see in these Seven Epistles—apart from their literal application—a twofold purpose, affecting all the Churches of God's people upon earth.
>
> For, firstly, if we regard them as a whole, we may, probably, detect in them specimens of every kind of circumstance, temptation, or trial, which God's foreknowledge saw in the future of Christian believers. Hence He is enabled, by means of them, to give advice, comfort, exhortation, or warning, to any of His Own disciples, and at any time during the course of the Church-period.
>
> And, secondly, if considered in the order in which they were given, they will be found to foreshadow the successive predominant phases through which the Nominal Church was to pass, from the time of the vision until the close of the Age.[27]

Bible students like Pember believe that the seven churches "present a prophetic picture of the seven historical periods in which the visible church will develop." This has been called "the historical-prophetical method of interpretation."[28] Such an approach suggests that the church age will pass through these seven stages, thus providing a general prophetic outline beginning with Ephesus and concluding with Laodicea. The prophetic message is conveyed through the subject matter contained in each address and "the bare names of the Churches addressed...and the period of Church-history in which they appear to find their fulfillment."[29] Pember explains the names as follows:

> Ephesus = relaxation. The waning of love at the close of Apostolic times.
>
> Smyrna = bitterness; also myrrh, an unguent especially used for embalming the dead. The epoch of the Ten Great Persecutions.
>
> Pergamum = a tower. Earthly greatness of the Nominal Church, from the accession of Constantine.
>
> Thyatira = she that is unwearied in sacrifices. The Catholic Churches, with their perpetually repeated Sacrifice of the Mass.
>
> Sardis = renovation. The results of the Reformation.
>
> Philadelphia = brotherly love. The gathering in of those who believe the love of Christ to be a stronger bond of union than any ties of sect. This gathering evidently involves preparation for the Lord's return.
>
> Laodicea = the custom, or judgment, of the people. The period in which the people constitute themselves judges of what is right, and so altogether set aside the Word of God. They are, consequently, rejected of the Lord Jesus.[30]

A typical outline of the prophetic aspects of the seven churches is provided by Dr. Arnold Fruchtenbaum:

1. Ephesus [A.D. 30–100] Apostolic Church

2. Smyrna [100–313] Roman Persecution

3. Pergamum [313–600] Age of Constantine

4. Thyatira [600–1517] Dark Ages

5. Sardis [1517–1648] Reformation

6. Philadelphia [1648–1900] Missionary Movement

7. Laodicea [1900–Present] Apostasy[31]

If such an approach is valid, it clearly indicates that history is in the final Laodicean era of the church age. Pember attempts to justify this viewpoint with the following explanation:

> Again, if we turn to the Seventh Epistle, that to the Church of the Laodiceans, we perceive that it describes features which, according to other Scriptures, will characterize the closing days of this Age. For those who are addressed persist, indeed, in retaining a certain form of godliness, but neither regard its significance nor feel its power. They are self-satisfied and complacent on the very eve of judgment. And the Lord, Who is in the act of rejecting them, has withdrawn from their midst, and is only lingering for a moment at the door, to make a last offer to individual believers, and to utter a final warning.[32]

"But, if this be so, the question naturally arises," notes Pember, "Why did the Lord choose so peculiar a form for His revelation?"[33] He provides the following answer:

> Because He did not wish the prophetic import of the Epistles to be distinctly understood, until the Last Days had come. For, while these two chapters have been at all times most useful for reproof, correction, instruction, and exhortation, their predictions were scarcely likely to be discovered, or even suspected, until they were all but fulfilled. And so, they would never, by suggesting events that must first happen, cause believers to say, "My Lord delayeth His coming." And, on the other hand, when, at the time of the End, the Spirit should unveil their meaning, He would, by so doing, bring a deep conviction of the nearness of the Advent to every thoughtful and reverent mind.
>
> And there is also another cause of obscuration in this form of prophecy. For, from the very nature of the case, such predictions cannot be direct and literal, as the prophecies of single events in the fourth and following chapters are, but can only dimly foreshadow things to come, though, if the clue be once obtained, with an outline sufficiently distinct.

> Lastly, we must notice, that in this prophecy, as in that
> of the Seven Parables, a phase that has once com-
> menced may be continued, though often with con-
> tracted area, far beyond the time of its predominance,
> even, indeed, until the Lord's return. There is a plain
> intimation that this will be so in the case of Perga-
> mum—for the Lord has not yet fought against the Bal-
> aamites with the sword of His mouth; in that of
> Thyatira—for the remnant are bidden to hold that fast
> which they have, until He come; in that of Sardis—for
> she is told, that, unless she watches, He will come
> upon her as a thief: and in that of Philadelphia—for He
> promises her that He is coming quickly, and charges
> her to hold fast that which she has, that no one take
> her crown. Indeed, the Nominal Churches will, proba-
> bly, in their last days, as in their first, embrace com-
> munities which, taken together, will exhibit all the
> characteristics mentioned in the two chapters; so that
> each of the Epistles will retain its directly practical
> value until the End. But, at that time, the prevailing
> phase will be the Laodicean.[34]

This understanding of Revelation 2–3 would indicate that the
church has passed through her various stages and is now poised for
the rapture to occur, as always, at any moment. However, only the
general conclusion that we are in the final era is valid, since the Laodicean period could continue for hundreds of years as did the Thyatiran
age.

The Last Days for the Church

Regardless of what Revelation 2–3 may mean, the New Testament clearly speaks about the last days for the church. As explained
previously, a number of New Testament epistles speak of the condition within Christendom near the end of the age. Interestingly, virtually all of these comments come from the Epistles written shortly
before the death of each apostle (i.e., during the last days of the various apostles), writing as if to emphasize the dangers latent during
the church's last days. The following is a list of the seven major passages that deal with the last days for the church: 1 Timothy 4:1-3; 2
Timothy 3:1-5; 4:3,4; James 5:1-8; 2 Peter 2:1-22; 3:3-6; Jude 1-25.

An Overview of the Church Age

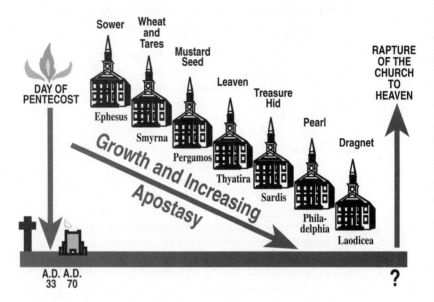

Every one of these passages emphasizes over and over again that the great characteristic of the final time of the church will be that of *apostasy*. Dr. Pentecost concludes:

> This condition at the close of the age is seen to coincide with the state within the Laodicean Church, before which Christ must stand to seek admission. In view of its close it is not surprising that the age is called an "evil age" in Scripture.[35]

The New Testament pictures the condition within the professing church at the end of the age by a system of denials.

- Denial of GOD—Luke 17:26; 2 Timothy 3:4-5
- Denial of CHRIST—1 John 2:18; 4:3; 2 Peter 2:6
- Denial of CHRIST'S RETURN—2 Peter 3:3-4
- Denial of THE FAITH—1 Timothy 4:1-2; Jude 3
- Denial of SOUND DOCTRINE—2 Timothy 4:3-4

- Denial of THE SEPARATED LIFE—2 Timothy 3:1-7
- Denial of CHRISTIAN LIBERTY—1 Timothy 4:3-4
- Denial of MORALS—2 Timothy 3:1-8,13; Jude 18
- Denial of AUTHORITY—2 Timothy 3:4[36]

Dr. Lewis Sperry Chafer, founder and first president of Dallas Theological Seminary, characterized the last days for the church in the following way:

> A very extensive body of Scripture bears on the last days for the Church. Reference is to a restricted time at the very end of, and yet wholly within, the present age. Though this brief period immediately precedes the great tribulation and in some measure is a preparation for it, these two times of apostasy and confusion— though incomparable in history—are wholly separate the one from the other. Those Scriptures which set forth the last days for the Church give no consideration to political or world conditions but are confined to the Church itself. These Scriptures picture men as departing from the faith (1 Tim. 4:1-2). There will be a manifestation of characteristics which belong to unregenerate men, though it is under the profession of "a form of godliness" (cf. 2 Tim. 3:1-5). The indication is that, having denied the power of the blood of Christ (cf. 2 Tim. 3:5 with Rom. 1:16; 1 Cor. 1:23-24; 2 Tim. 4:2-4), the leaders in these forms of righteousness will be unregenerate men from whom nothing more spiritual than this could proceed (cf. 1 Cor. 2:14).[37]

The clear course of the last days for the church consists of constant warnings to the believer to be on guard against doctrinal defection, otherwise known as apostasy. Such a characteristic provides for the Christian today a clear sign of the end times.

Even though specific prophecy is not given concerning the present church age, we have seen that three sets of passages do paint a general picture of the course of this age. All three indicate that apostasy will characterize Christendom during the time when the rapture will take place. This common distinctive provides for believers today a general sign of the times.

23. How does the rapture relate to signs of the times?

Briefly, the rapture does not relate to signs of the times. This is because the rapture of the church will happen at any moment, without the procession of a single sign. Since no signs are in any way attached to this imminent event, then it is impossible ever to discover or connect specific signs to the time of the rapture. This means that believers are always to be watching for the Lord, not signs, when it comes to the rapture. Anyone suggesting that the rapture will occur on a specific date can only make such a prediction based upon speculative elements derived from outside the Bible or upon a misinterpretation of Scripture.

Even though there are no signs specifically relating to the nearness of the rapture, this does not mean that there are not general signs that relate to other aspects of God's plan that are of value for the believer today. Among those who believe the rapture will occur before the tribulation (the perspective of the authors), we observe three basic approaches to interpreting current events and the signs of the time. The three classifications relate to how the interpreter associates prophecy for Israel and the church. We see a spectrum of 1) loose, 2) moderate, and 3) strict.

The Loose View

The loose view is characterized by those who sometimes take prophecy written for Israel and suggest that it is being fulfilled today—during the church age. At times, they relate prophecy about the tribulation as if it is being or has already been fulfilled in the current church age. Such an approach commingles God's plan for Israel with His plan for the church at specific points of prophetic fulfillment. This view is not in keeping with the literal interpretation that leads to a separating of Israel and the church. Current believers cannot be both in the church age and in the tribulation at the same time.

An example of this kind of interpretation would be one who set a date for the rapture or attempts to see a current event from today fulfilling prophecy related to the yet future tribulation or second coming. In the early 1980s a popular prophecy teacher said that Isaiah 19 predicted the assassination of Egypt's President Anwar Sadat. This is impossible since Isaiah 19 refers to events that will take place in the tribulation. Since we are not in the tribulation now, it could not have prophesied such an event. This is an improper mixing of God's prophecy for Israel with the church and is inconsistent with one who believes the rapture occurs before the tribulation.

The Strict View

We will take the third viewpoint next, so that the second view, which we favor, can be compared to the first and third. Some pretribulationists are airtight in maintaining a distinction between God's prophetic plan for Israel and His plan for the church. They tend to say that current events have virtually no significance to today, since the only event a true church age believer is looking for is the rapture.

The strict view holds that the establishment of Israel as a nation in 1948 may not be the beginning of that which was prophesied for the last days. They tend to reason that we really cannot know about the significance of these things until after the rapture. Thus, current events do not indicate "signs of the times" in any significant way. Some even teach that Israel could be kicked out of the land and it would not impact prophecy, since we cannot really confirm whether contemporary events are preparation for biblical fulfillment.

This view is nonspeculative about how current events relate to prophecy, and often speaks strongly against those who try to make a correlation between the Bible and current events. Strict interpreters have a significant following within the academic circles of dispensationalism, likely over a concern about the damage that can result to literal interpretation of prophecy when improper speculation is employed.

The Moderate View

A third approach about how prophecy relates to Israel and the church is the moderate view, the outlook that we favor. Moderates clearly maintain a distinction between God's plan for Israel and the church. The current church age is prophetically pictured only by general trends and characteristics, not by specific fulfillment of events, as will be true of prophecy after the rapture. Therefore, there are no signs or current events which indicate the nearness of the rapture, which is an imminent, any-moment possibility at any time

Interpreting Signs of the Times

RAPTURE = is always an "any moment" possibility
2nd COMING = could be thought to be "near"

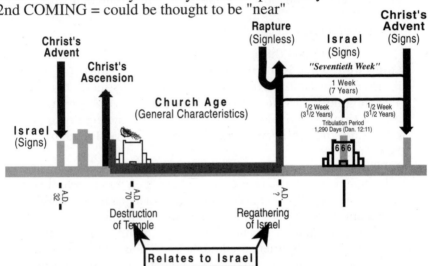

during the church age. But current events may have a prophetic relevance.

Moderates do not date-set or think that a current event fulfills prophecy relating to the tribulation or millennium. However, they tend to think that it is valid to lay out a model or scenario of how things will be after the rapture, since Scripture gives a clear and detailed picture of the tribulation period. Based upon such a model, we can see preparation and stage-setting for those events increasingly fitting together through current events. Since these are not signs for the rapture, but rather stage-setting for events leading up to the second coming, our anticipation of the rapture is heightened. The positioning of players and events related to God's plan for the world during the future tribulation is increasingly casting shadows upon the current church age, thus intensifying anticipation of the any-moment rapture which must take place before any event of the tribulation commences.

Dr. Walvoord explains:

These major situations that are true now, and that were not true fifty years ago, point to the conclusion that the Rapture itself may be very near because the stage has been set for events that will follow the Rapture.

All areas of prophecy combine in the united testimony that history is preparing our generation for the end of the age.

In each area of prophecy a chronological checklist of important prophetic events can be compiled. In each list, in regard to the church, the nations, or Israel, the events of history clearly indicate that the world is poised and ready for the Rapture of the church and the beginning of the countdown to Armageddon.[38]

While no signs of the times specifically relate to the time of the rapture, this does not mean that there are not signs relating to God's overall prophetic plan, specifically to His preparation of the world for the time of the tribulation, which will start after the rapture. This approach has been illustrated as follows: If one sees signs that Christmas is coming (the tribulation) then Thanksgiving must be even closer (the rapture).

CHAPTER 6

What Signs Indicate the Tribulation Might Be Near?

In every generation since Christ's ascension there have been Christians who thought that there was reason for His return in their lifetime. However, almost all of these expectations were derived from the belief that they were experiencing events of the tribulation. Only in the last 200 years have interpreters begun to return to a literal, futurist understanding of the tribulation. Thus, while so many have believed that Christ's return was near, the basis for such an understanding has not always been the same down through the history of the church. That Israel became a nation in 1948 is an undeniable fact of history that indicates that God is up to something in history in our day that could not be said in previous times.

24. What "props" and "actors" is God using to set the prophetic stage?

The "props" and "actors" relating to the next flurry of prophetic activity—the tribulation—revolve around the three major divisions of future prophecy: the church, the nations, and Israel.

While the next event for the true church—the body of Christ—is translation from earth to heaven at the rapture, those unbelievers left in the organized church as an institution will pass into the tribulation and form the base of an apostate super-church that the false prophet will use to aid the worldwide rule of the Antichrist (Revelation 13; 17–18). Dr. Walvoord provides a prophetic checklist relating to the church, listing events that are preparation for fulfillment and actual future fulfillment.

A Prophetic Checklist for the Church

1. The rise of world communism made possible the worldwide spread of atheism.

2. Liberalism undermines the spiritual vitality of the church in Europe and eventually America.

3. The movement toward a super-church begins with the ecumenical movement.

4. Apostasy and open denial of biblical truth is evident in the church.

5. Moral chaos becomes more and more evident because of the complete departure from Christian morality.

6. The sweep of spiritism, the occult, and belief in demons begin to prepare the world for Satan's final hour.

7. Jerusalem becomes a center of religious controversy for Arabs and Christians, while Jews of the world plan to make the city an active center for Judaism.

8. True believers disappear from the earth to join Christ in heaven at the rapture of the church.

9. The restraint of evil by the Holy Spirit is ended.

10. The super-church combines major religions as a tool for the false prophet who aids the Antichrist's rise to world power.

11. The Antichrist destroys the super-church and demands worship as a deified world dictator.

12. Believers of this period suffer intense persecution and are martyred by the thousands.

13. Christ returns to earth with Christians who have been in heaven during the Tribulation and ends the rule of the nations at the Battle of Armageddon.[39]

A similar checklist of prophetic events can be compiled of prophetic stage-setting and actual prophecy yet to be fulfilled in God's plan for the nations. Dr. Walvoord provides the following checklist.

A Prophetic Checklist for the Nations

1. The establishment of the United Nations began a serious first step toward world government.

2. The rebuilding of Europe after World War II made possible its future role in a renewal of the Roman Empire.

3. Israel was reestablished as a nation.

4. Russia rose to world power and becomes the ally of the Arab countries.

5. The Common Market and World Bank show a need for some international regulation of the world economy.

6. Red China rose to world power.

7. The Middle East becomes the most significant trouble spot in the world.

8. The oil blackmail awakens the world to the new concentration of wealth and power in the Mediterranean.

9. The Iron Curtain falls and a new order emerges in Europe.

10. Russia declines as a world power and loses her influence in the Middle East.

11. A world clamor for peace follows the continued disruption caused by the high price of oil, terrorist incidents, and the confused military situation in the Middle East.

12. Ten nations create a united Mediterranean Confederacy— beginnings of the last stage of the prophetic fourth world empire.

13. In a dramatic power play, a new Mediterranean leader upsets three nations of the confederacy and takes control of the powerful ten-nation group.

14. The new Mediterranean leader negotiates a "final" peace settlement in the Middle East (broken three and a half years later).

15. The Russian army attempts an invasion of Israel and is miraculously destroyed.

16. The Mediterranean leader proclaims himself world dictator, breaks his peace settlement with Israel, and declares himself to be God.

17. The new world dictator desecrates the temple in Jerusalem.

18. The terrible judgments of the great tribulation are poured out on the nations of the world.

19. Worldwide rebellion threatens the world dictator's rule as armies from throughout the world converge on the Middle East.

20. Christ returns to earth with His armies from heaven.

21. The armies of the world unite to resist Christ's coming and are destroyed in the Battle of Armageddon.

22. Christ establishes His millennial reign on earth, ending the times of the Gentiles.[40]

As with the church and the nations, God is moving His chosen people—Israel—into place for future fulfillment. Dr. Walvoord lists the following:

A Prophetic Checklist for Israel

1. The intense suffering and persecution of Jews throughout the world lead to pressure for a national home in Palestine.

2. Jews return to Palestine and Israel is reestablished as a nation in 1948.

3. The infant nation survives against overwhelming odds.

4. Russia emerges as an important enemy of Israel, but the United States comes to the aid of Israel.

5. Israel's heroic survival and growing strength make it an established nation, recognized throughout the world.

6. Israel's military accomplishments become overshadowed by the Arabs' ability to wage a diplomatic war by controlling much of the world's oil reserves.

7. The Arab position is strengthened by their growing wealth and by alliances between Europe and key Arab countries.

8. The increasing isolation of the United States and Russia from the Middle East makes it more and more difficult for Israel to negotiate an acceptable peace settlement.

9. After a long struggle, Israel is forced to accept a compromise peace guaranteed by the new leader of the Mediterranean Confederacy of ten nations.

10. The Jewish people celebrate what appears to be a lasting and final peace settlement.

11. During three-and-a-half years of peace, Judaism is revived, and traditional sacrifices and ceremonies are reinstituted in the rebuilt temple in Jerusalem.

12. The Russian army attempts to invade Israel but is mysteriously destroyed.

13. The newly proclaimed world dictator desecrates the temple in Jerusalem and begins a period of intense persecution of Jews.

14. Many Jews recognize the unfolding of prophetic events and declare their faith in Christ as the Messiah of Israel.

15. In the massacre of Jews and Christians who resist the world dictator, some witnesses are divinely preserved to carry the message throughout the world.

16. Christ returns to earth, welcomed by believing Jews as their Messiah and deliverer.

17. Christ's thousand-year reign on earth from the throne of David finally fulfills the prophetic promises to the nations of Israel.[41]

The many items in these checklists constitute specific signs that God's end-time program is on the verge of springing into full gear; additionally, the fact that all three streams of prophecy are converging for the first time in history at the same time constitutes a sign itself. This is why many students of prophecy believe that we are on the edge of history. Dr. Walvoord concludes:

> The world today is like a stage being set for a great drama. The major actors are already in the wings waiting for their moment in history. The main stage props are already in place. The prophetic play is about to begin....
>
> All the necessary historical developments have already taken place.[42]

25. Why is Israel the "super-sign" of the end times?

God's plan for history always moves forward in relation to what He is doing with Israel. Thus, the fact that Israel has been and continues to be reconstituted as a nation is prophetically significant, so significant that it makes Israel God's "super-sign" of the end times. Were Israel not a nation again it would be impossible for events of the end times to occur since so many of them take place in that tiny country or in reference to it. But it has returned and so it is that all other aspects of Bible prophecy are also being prepared for the grand finale of history.

There are dozens of biblical passages that predict an end-time regathering of Israel back to the land. However, it is a common mistake to lump all of these passages into one fulfillment time frame, especially in relation to the modern state of Israel. Modern Israel is prophetically significant and is fulfilling Bible prophecy. But readers of God's Word need to be careful to distinguish which verses are being fulfilled in our day and which references await future fulfillment.

Hebrew Christian scholar Dr. Arnold Fruchtenbaum explains:

> The reestablishment of the Jewish state in 1948 has not only thrown a wrench in amillennial thinking, but it has also thrown a chink in much of premillennial thinking. Amazingly, some premillennialists have concluded that the present state of Israel has nothing to do with the fulfillment of prophecy. For some reason the present state somehow does not fit their scheme of things, and so the present state becomes merely an accident of history. On what grounds is the present state of Israel so dismissed? The issue that bothers so many premillennialists is the fact that not only have the Jews returned in unbelief with regard to the person of Jesus, but the majority of the ones who have returned are not even Orthodox Jews. In fact the majority are atheists or agnostics. Certainly, then, Israel does not fit in with all those biblical passages dealing with the return. For it is a regenerated nation that the Bible speaks of, and the present state of Israel hardly fits that picture. So on these grounds, the

present state is dismissed as not being a fulfillment of prophecy.

However, the real problem is the failure to see that the prophets spoke of two international returns. First, there was to be a regathering in unbelief in preparation for judgment, namely the judgment of the tribulation. This was to be followed by a second world-wide regathering in faith in preparation for blessing, namely the blessings of the messianic age. Once it is recognized that the Bible speaks of two such regatherings, it is easy to see how the present state of Israel fits into prophecy.[43]

First Worldwide Gathering in Unbelief

When the modern state of Israel was born in 1948, it not only became an important stage-setting development but began an actual fulfillment of specific Bible prophecies about an international regathering of the Jews in unbelief before the judgment of the tribulation. Such a prediction is found in the following Old Testament passages: Isaiah 11:11,12; Ezekiel 20:33-38; 22:17-22; 36:22-24; Zephaniah 2:1,2; and Ezekiel 38–39 presupposes such a setting.

The following passages speak of Israel's regathering in preparation for a coming judgment that will remove unbelief from their midst.

- *Ezekiel 20:33-38:* "As I live," declares the Lord GOD, "surely with a mighty hand and with an outstretched arm and with wrath poured out, I shall be king over you. And I shall bring you out from the peoples and gather you from the lands where you are scattered, with a mighty hand and with an outstretched arm and with wrath poured out; and I shall bring you into the wilderness of the peoples, and there I shall enter into judgment with you face to face. As I entered into judgment with your fathers in the wilderness of the land of Egypt, so I will enter into judgment with you," declares the Lord GOD. "And I shall make you pass under the rod, and I shall bring you into the bond of the covenant; and I shall purge from you the rebels and those who transgress against Me; I shall bring them out of the land where they sojourn, but they will not enter the land of Israel. Thus you will know that I am the LORD."

- *Ezekiel 22:17-22:* And the word of the LORD came to me saying, "Son of man, the house of Israel has become dross to Me; all of them are bronze and tin and iron and lead in the furnace; they are the dross of silver. Therefore, thus says the Lord GOD, 'Because all of you have become dross, therefore, behold, I am going to gather you into the midst of Jerusalem. As they gather silver and bronze and iron and lead and tin into the furnace to blow fire on it in order to melt it, so I shall gather you in My anger and in My wrath, and I shall lay you there and melt you. And I shall gather you and blow on you with the fire of My wrath, and you will be melted in the midst of it. As silver is melted in the furnace, so you will be melted in the midst of it; and you will know that I, the LORD, have poured out My wrath on you.'"

Zephaniah 1:14-18 is one of the most colorful descriptions of "the day of the LORD," which we commonly call the tribulation period. Zephaniah 2:1,2 says that there will be a worldwide regathering of Israel before the day of the Lord.

- *Zephaniah 2:1,2:* Gather yourselves together, yes, gather, O nation without shame, before the decree takes effect—the day passes like the chaff—before the burning anger of the LORD comes upon you, before the day of the LORD's anger comes upon you.

Second Worldwide Gathering in Belief

Many passages in the Bible speak of Israel's regathering, in belief, at the end of the tribulation, in conjunction with Christ's second coming, in preparation for commencement of the millennium. These references are not being fulfilled by the modern state of Israel. Some of the citations include: Deuteronomy 4:29-31; 30:1-10; Isaiah 27:12,13; 43:5-7; Jeremiah 16:14,15; 31:7-10; Ezekiel 11:14-18; Amos 9:14,15; Zechariah 10:8-12; Matthew 24:31; and many more.

- *Ezekiel 11:14-18:* Then the word of the LORD came to me, saying, "Son of man, your brothers, your relatives, your fellow exiles, and the whole house of Israel, all of them, are those to whom the inhabitants of Jerusalem have said, 'Go far from the LORD; this land has been given us as a possession.' Therefore say, 'Thus says the Lord GOD, "Though I had removed them far away among the nations, and though I had scattered them among the countries, yet I was a sanctuary for them a little while in the countries where they had gone."' Therefore say, 'Thus says the Lord GOD, "I shall gather you from the peoples and assemble you out of the countries among which you have been scattered, and I shall give you the land of Israel."' When they come there, they will remove all its detestable things and all its abominations from it."

- *Amos 9:14,15:* "Also I will restore the captivity of My people Israel, and they will rebuild the ruined cities and live in them, they will also plant vineyards and drink their wine, and make

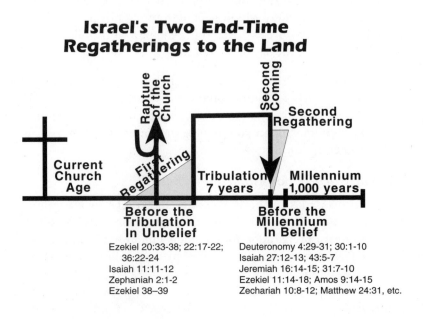

Israel's Two End-Time Regatherings to the Land

Before the Tribulation In Unbelief	Before the Millennium In Belief
Ezekiel 20:33-38; 22:17-22; 36:22-24	Deuteronomy 4:29-31; 30:1-10
Isaiah 11:11-12	Isaiah 27:12-13; 43:5-7
Zephaniah 2:1-2	Jeremiah 16:14-15; 31:7-10
Ezekiel 38–39	Ezekiel 11:14-18; Amos 9:14-15
	Zechariah 10:8-12; Matthew 24:31, etc.

gardens and eat their fruit. I will also plant them on their land, and they will not again be rooted out from their land which I have given them," says the LORD your God.

- *Matthew 24:31:* "And He will send forth His angels with A GREAT TRUMPET and THEY WILL GATHER TOGETHER His elect from the four winds, from one end of the sky to the other."

The fact that the last 50 years has seen a worldwide regathering and reestablishment of the nation of Israel, which is now poised in just the setting required for the revealing of the Antichrist and the start of the tribulation, is God's grand indicator that all of the other areas of world development are prophetically significant. Dr. Walvoord writes,

> Of the many peculiar phenomena which characterize the present generation, few events can claim equal significance as far as Biblical prophecy is concerned with that of the return of Israel to their land. It constitutes a preparation for the end of the age, the setting for the coming of the Lord for His church, and the fulfillment of Israel's prophetic destiny.[44]

Israel, God's "super-sign" of the end times, is a clear indicator that time is growing shorter with each passing hour. Are you ready for the meeting in the sky?

26. How is Jerusalem a sign of the times?

Scripture not only teaches that Israel will be reconstituted for the end times, but even more specifically, Jerusalem will be restored and play a major role during the tribulation. Thus, the current occupation of Jerusalem by Israeli Jews, which happened in 1967, is another stage-setting sign of the times.[45]

The fact that God is restoring Israel to the land and, in conjunction, has reunited the entire city of Jerusalem under Jewish control, sets the stage for fulfillment during the tribulation period for dozens of prophecies that will take place in relation to Jerusalem. If the Jews were not in control of Jerusalem, then those prophecies could not be fulfilled. But, indeed, they are in control of the ancient city, which indicates that God is preparing the world for the fulfillment of predicted events.

The book of Zechariah focuses on Jerusalem. Chapters 8–14 provide us with much prophecy about Jerusalem. Zechariah 8:7,8 says, "Behold, I am going to save My people from the land of the east and from the land of the west; and I will bring them back, and they will live in the midst of Jerusalem...." This will be fulfilled during the millennium. However, before Jerusalem arrives at such a blessed destiny she has many rocky days ahead.

The Bible predicts that during the tribulation Jerusalem will be viewed by all the nations as the source of the world's problems:

> Behold, I am going to make Jerusalem a cup that causes reeling to all the peoples around; and when the siege is against Jerusalem, it will also be against Judah. And it will come about in that day that I will make Jerusalem a heavy stone for all the peoples; all who lift it will be severely injured. And all the nations of the earth will be gathered against it (Zechariah 12:2,3).

"A cup that causes reeling" and "a heavy stone" are not positive pictures describing Jerusalem. Yet already we see in our own day that, all too often when something happens in Jerusalem, worldwide criticism inevitably comes streaming forth against the Jews of Jerusalem. The stage is being set!

The well-known battle of Armageddon will take place at the end of the tribulation in relation to an international response to Jerusalem.

> For I will gather all the nations against Jerusalem to battle, and the city will be captured, the houses plundered, the women ravished, and half of the city exiled, but the rest of the people will not be cut off from the city. Then the LORD will go forth and fight against those nations, as when He fights on a day of battle. And in that day His feet will stand on the Mount of Olives, which is in front of Jerusalem on the east; and the Mount of Olives will be split in its middle from east to west by a very large valley, so that half of the mountain will move toward the north and the other half toward the south. And you will flee by the valley of My mountains, for the valley of the mountains will reach to Azel; yes, you will flee just as you fled before the earthquake

in the days of Uzziah king of Judah. Then the LORD, my God, will come, and all the holy ones with Him! (Zechariah 14:2-5).

Dr. John Walvoord declares the fact that Jerusalem is a stage-setting sign of the end times when he says,

> The prophecies about Jerusalem make it clear that the Holy City will be in the center of world events in the end time....
>
> ...the conflict between Israel and the Palestinian Arabs will focus more and more attention on Jerusalem....
>
> In all of these situations Jerusalem is the city to watch, as the city of prophetic destiny prepares to act out her final role.
>
> The total world situation may be expected more and more to be cast into the mold that prophecy indicates. From many indications it seems that the stage and the actors are ready for the final drama, in which Jerusalem will be the key.[46]

27. How are efforts to rebuild the Jewish temple a sign of the times?

The Bible indicates that by the midpoint of the seven-year tribulation (most likely some time before that) there will be a rebuilt temple in Jerusalem (Daniel 9:27; Matthew 24:15,16; 2 Thessalonians 2:3,4; Revelation 11:1-29). In order for that to happen, the Jews first needed to reoccupy the land of Israel and the city of Jerusalem. Israel became a nation in 1948, the old city of Jerusalem was captured by the Israelis in 1967, and increasing efforts are underway to rebuild a Jewish temple on the Temple Mount in Jerusalem.[47]

The tribulation temple only has to be there by the midpoint of the seven-year tribulation so that the Antichrist can defile it. Nevertheless, with each year that passes, Jews in Israel increasingly desire a rebuilt temple and prepare for its eventuality. Such stage-setting is a sign for our time of the increasing nearness of the Lord's return.

28. How is the revived Roman Empire and the European union a sign of the times?

Scripture teaches that the Antichrist will rise to power out of a federation of nations that correlate in some way with the Roman Empire of 2,000 years ago. Dr. J. Dwight Pentecost explains:

> Now, when we turn to the prophecies of Daniel 2 and 7 and to Revelation 13 and 17 and other parallel passages, we find that at the end time, during the Tribulation period, the final form of Gentile world power is a federation of ten separate nations, the ten toes or ten horns. It seems as though Europe's leaders are advocating that which Daniel prophesied hundreds of years before Christ, when he said that the final form of Roman world power would be a federation of independent states who elect one man to take authority over them while maintaining their own sovereign authority. The more movement we see in Europe for a common market and a federation of nations, the closer the coming of our Lord must be.[48]

One would have to be totally ignorant of developments within the world of our day not to admit that, through the efforts of the European union, "Humpty Dumpty" is finally being put back together again. This is occurring, like all of the other needed developments of prophecy, at just the right time to be in place for the coming tribulation period. Prophecy popularizer Hal Lindsey tells us:

> A generation ago, no one could have dreamed that an empire formed of the nations that were part of old Rome could possibly be revived. But today, as Europe is on the advent of real unity, we see the potential fulfillment of another vital prophecy leading to the return of our Lord Jesus Christ.[49]

29. How is Russia a sign of the times?

In conjunction with tribulation events, Ezekiel 38–39 teaches that there will be an invasion into Israel by a coalition lead by "Gog of the land of Magog, the prince of Rosh, Meshech, and Tubal" (Ezekiel 38:2). Gog appears to be modern Russia. Coalition partners in the invasion are Persia (modern Iran), Cush (Ethiopia), Put (Libya), and

Gomer and Beth-togarmah (likely modern Turkey) (Ezekiel 38:5,6). Chuck Missler concludes, "All the allies of Magog (Russia) are reasonably well identified and all of them are Muslim."[50]

The twentieth-century rise of Russia as a military power and her alignment with those nations who will invade Israel under Gog's leadership, once again, in concert with all of the other prophetically significant factors, are a sign that the stage is set indicating the nearness of our Lord's return. The modern Russian bear is a player in end-time prophecy and thus should be watched as a sign of the times. Mark Hitchcock, a specialist on the Gog invasion, agrees:

> Russia is a wounded, starving bear and is more dangerous than ever before. Vladimir Zhirinovsky is gaining power in Russia, and the entire focus of his political plan is a massive military campaign into the Middle East.
>
> The stage is being set. The events of Ezekiel 38–39 are more imminent than ever before. The consummation of history could begin at any time. All that remains is for the curtain to be raised.[51]

30. How is political, economic, and religious globalism and the rise of Antichrist a sign of the times?

As never before current events are working in concert with one another, preparing the way for the rise of globalism and the infamous character historically known as the Antichrist. The Bible indicates (Revelation 13:12-17) that the beast (another name for the Antichrist) will expand his rule from his European base to the world during the last three-and-a-half years of the tribulation. Today preparation is well under way for the coming globalism and the rule of Antichrist.

Globalism

Only in the last 50 years has globalism become a realistic option at the practical level. Revelation 17–18 indicates that Antichrist's global empire will revolve around political, economic, and religious issues. Many who reject the Bible and God's plan for history believe that the ultimate solution to this world's political, economic, and religious problems have only global answers. They are right...if the Bible is not true. But of course Scripture is true, so ultimately they

are wrong. Dr. Ed Hindson comments on the motives behind the rise
of the modern global thrust:

> All previous attempts at structuring a world order
> have, without fail, fallen on the harsh realities of man's
> pride, arrogance, greed, avarice, and self-destruction.
> Woodrow Wilson's League of Nations failed to stop
> World War II, and the present United Nations has
> struggled since its very inception. Yet there seems to
> be something within the international community pro-
> pelling us toward a unified world system. Many fear
> that driving force is Satan himself.[52]

The thrust toward global religious unity has never been stronger
than in our day. The flames have been fanned the last few decades by
the rising popularity of New Age thought, which has invaded every
aspect of North American society, including the evangelical church.
Dr. Charles Ryrie speaks:

> The Superchurch of World Religions is on its way:
> powerful, worldwide, and invincible—for three-and-
> one-half years.
>
> The progress toward organizational unity waxes and
> wanes, but the movement is steadily going forward.
> Whatever happens to ecumenical organizations, how-
> ever, do not overlook what is happening on the theo-
> logical scene. Universalism and revolution in the name
> of the church are sweeping the theological world.
> Organizational unity and theological heresy may be
> compared to two runners. One may pass the other
> temporarily, causing the lead to seesaw back and forth
> between them. But as they approach the finish line
> they will join hands, and from their combined forces
> will emerge Superchurch.
>
> The stage is set. The script has been written. The props
> are in place. The actors are in the wings. Soon we shall
> hear, "Curtain!"[53]

Antichrist

The world is clearly being prepared for the rise of the Antichrist
out of Europe, as the Bible demands. While many items could be

cited as evidence of such preparation, none is more striking than the rise of an electronic, cashless society, which will facilitate fulfillment of the "mark of the beast" during the tribulation.

> And he causes all, the small and the great, and the rich and the poor, and the free men and the slaves, to be given a mark on their right hand, or on their forehead, and he provides that no one should be able to buy or to sell, except the one who has the mark, either the name of the beast or the number of his name. Here is wisdom. Let him who has understanding calculate the number of the beast, for the number is that of a man; and his number is six hundred and sixty-six (Revelation 13:16-18).

At what other time in history, other than our own, could such a prophecy be successfully implemented?

> It is becoming increasingly apparent that today's developing cashless system will become the instrument through which the Antichrist will seek to control all who buy or sell, based upon whether they are a follower of Jesus Christ or a follower of the European ruler, and thus, Satan. It is obvious that any leader wanting to control the world's economy would avail themselves of the power that an electronic cashless system holds as a tool for implementing total control....
>
> ...But surely the coming cashless society is one of the signs that prophecy is being fulfilled.[54]

31. Is Babylon a sign of the times?

Babylon is depicted throughout the Bible as the focus of the kingdom of man that is set in opposition to God, Israel, and His plan for history. It is not surprising to realize that many biblical passages speak of an end-time role for Babylon as God's enemy (Revelation 14:8; 17–18). "What are the specific signposts that can serve as indicators of God's end-time program for the world?" asks Dr. Charles Dyer. "The third sure signpost is the rebuilding of Babylon."[55] Is Babylon being rebuilt in our day? Yes it is!

Dr. Joseph Chambers traveled to Iraq, shortly before the Gulf War, and witnessed firsthand Saddam Hussein's rebuilding of Babylon. "I have walked through those ruins and have seen repeatedly the ancient bricks of Nebuchadnezzar with the bricks of Saddam Hussein laid on top and workers proceeding to erect wall after wall and building after building," declares Dr. Chambers. "Every nuance of God's infallible Word is being fulfilled."[56]

God's prophetic plan includes His restoration of many of Israel's ancient enemies who will once again, but for the last time, plague God's people. Dr. Chambers says,

> The only biblical fulfillment in our generation that sur-
> passed the rebuilding of ancient Babylon is the regath-
> ering of Israel to their God-given homeland. Babylon
> represents to the world system what Israel represents
> to biblical ideas and Christianity. The climax of all the
> ages is at hand.[57]

The rise of ancient Babylon in our day constitutes another sign of the times that sets the stage. Once again, this development, after thousands of years, just happens to be occurring in conjunction with all the other developments necessary for the fulfillment of the prophecies of the coming tribulation.

CHAPTER 7

What Are the "Problem" Scriptures Regarding Signs?

32. What does "this generation shall not pass away" mean?

Hal Lindsey, in his landmark book, *The Late Great Planet Earth,* taught that Christ would return within a 40-year generation of the reestablishment of Israel. This conclusion was based upon his interpretation of Matthew 24:34.

> Now learn the parable from the fig tree: when its branch has already become tender, and puts forth its leaves, you know that summer is near; even so you too, when you see all these things, recognize that He is near, right at the door. Truly I say to you, this generation will not pass away until all these things take place (Matthew 24:32-34).

Lindsey speculates as follows:

> What generation? Obviously, in context, the generation that would see the signs—chief among them the rebirth of Israel. A generation in the Bible is something like forty years. If this is a correct deduction, then within forty years or so of 1948, all these things could take place. Many scholars who have studied Bible prophecy all their lives believe that this is so.[58]

Forty years from 1948 is 1988, yet we are a full decade after this time and the rapture has not occurred. We believe that a better interpretation is to understand "this generation" as a reference to those who see the events of the seven-year tribulation, especially the "abomination of desolation" (Matthew 24:15), as a sign of the second coming, not the rapture. If this interpretation is true, then it would not matter how long a generation is, since the signs would not last more than seven years. Further, we can draw from other passages (cited earlier) the same general conclusion about the reestablishment of Israel as constituting a sign of the nearness of the Lord's return.

33. Are wars, earthquakes, famines, and false Christs signs of the times?

Many prophecy teachers and scholars differ in their understanding of Matthew 24:3-14. One group believes that these verses describe the course of the current church age leading up to the start of the tribulation in Matthew 24:15 and on. If this interpretation is true, then it would mean that wars, earthquakes, famines, and the appearance of false Christs would be constantly on the increase as we approach the tribulation period. Thus, these items would constitute further signs of the times.

We believe that the wars, earthquakes, famines, and false Christs are better understood as corresponding to the first four seal judgments of Revelation 6, which will take place in the first half of the seven-year tribulation. (See Part 3.) This would mean that Matthew 25:15 and on would refer to the second half of the tribulation known as the great tribulation. Therefore, wars, earthquakes, famines, and false Christs during any part of the church age would not constitute signs of the times indicating a near return of Christ.

34. Is the moral decline of modern society a sign of the times?

We do not believe that the general moral decline of society (which we do not deny) is a specific sign of the end of the age. As noted in questions 13 and 14 in this section, such a decline was predicted to occur within the church as part of the apostasy. However, we do not know of a passage that predicts such a decline for society as a whole.

It can also be noted that it is hard to quantify such decline. No matter how bad things get, they can always get a little worse. So it is impossible to know specifically how bad things must be in order for something to be a prophetic sign.

35. Is the recent and rapid rise in knowledge a sign of the times?

Many prophecy teachers believe that, based on Daniel 12:4, shortly before Christ's return the world will experience an increase in the speed of travel coupled with an explosion of information:

> But as for you, Daniel, conceal these words and seal up
> the book until the end of time; many will go back and
> forth, and knowledge will increase (Daniel 12:4).

No one would quarrel with the fact that the twentieth century has indeed witnessed an exponential increase in both the speed of travel and the accumulation of knowledge and thus would be a sign in our time that the end is near. But is this really what Daniel is saying in the passage?

Another possible interpretation of the passage is given by Dr. Charles Ryrie in the Ryrie Study Bible when he says, "As the end approaches, people will travel about seeking to discover what the future holds."[59] If this is the correct understanding of the passage, then it would not be a sign of the times. It would mean that many Jews during the tribulation will study the book of Daniel in an attempt to find out what is going on. Thus, the scope would be limited to the future time of the tribulation and could not justly be applied to our own day.

There does not appear to be any real textual basis for the first interpretation. The meaning of the Hebrew words and grammar do not support such a view.

The second interpretation makes the best sense of the passage, especially when the first half of the verse is taken to relate to the second half, which it does. Thus, Daniel is told to preserve the book until later times when great effort to study the text will produce an increase in the understanding of the writing.

A Framework for Tomorrow

God's plan for the future is definite, well-defined, and exciting. We do not live in a world of chance. Prophecy means that certain things will definitely happen, while other possibilities are eliminated. We live in God's world, under His control, heading down a path preordained by Him. We have a framework teaching us what to expect from the future. This is why, in light of Bible prophecy, Dr. Walvoord declares:

> Never before in history have all the factors been
> present for the fulfillment of prophecy relating to end-
> time religious trends and events. Only in our genera-

tion have the combined revival of Israel, the formation of a world church, the increasing power of Muslim religion, the rise of the occult, and the worldwide spread of atheistic philosophy been present as a dramatic setting for the final fulfillment of prophecy. As far as world religion is concerned, the road to Armageddon is already well prepared, and those who will travel to their doom may well be members of our present generation.[60]

The Bible clearly teaches that Christians are to be alert and anticipating the fulfillment of biblical prophecy. Prophecy matters! It helps us put into proper perspective present circumstances and gives us hope for the future, because it is history written in advance. For the believer, looking for Christ's coming for His church at the rapture, every day is a day of hope. The Lord Jesus Christ will return; the Bible tells us so, and the signs point to it!

PART 2

The Rapture

Caught Up in the Air!

A recent survey by *U.S. News & World Report* found that 61 percent of Americans believe that Jesus Christ will return to earth, and 44 percent believe in the rapture of the church.[1] With so much popular certainty, why is there so much interpretative confusion over these events? Perhaps it's because people need to be more aware of the specific details.

The doctrine of the pretribulational rapture is an important biblical teaching not only because it provides insights into the future, but also because it provides Christians with motivation for contemporary living.

The pretribulational rapture doctrine teaches that, prior to the seven-year tribulation, all members of the body of Christ (both living and dead) will be caught up in the air to meet Christ and then be taken to heaven.

CHAPTER 8

Is the Rapture Clearly Taught in the Bible?

1. What is the rapture?

The teaching of the rapture is most clearly presented in 1 Thessalonians 4:13-18. In this passage Paul informs his readers that living Christians at the time of the rapture will be reunited with those who have died in Christ before them. In verse 17 the English phrase "caught up" translates the Greek word *harpazó*, which means "to seize upon with force" or "to snatch up." This word is used 14 times in the Greek New Testament in a variety of ways.

Sometimes the New Testament uses *harpazó* with the sense of "stealing," "carrying off," or "dragging away" (Matthew 12:29; John 10:12). It also can have the meaning of "to lead away forcibly" (John 6:15; 10:28,29; Acts 23:10; Jude 23). However, for our purposes, a third usage is significant: God's Spirit carrying someone away. We see this image four times (Acts 8:39; 2 Corinthians 12:2,4; 1 Thessalonians 4:17; Revelation 12:5).[2]

This latter definition is illustrated in Acts 8:39 where Philip, upon completion of the baptism of the Ethiopian eunuch, is "caught up" and divinely transported from the desert to the coastal town of Azotus. Similarly, the church will, in a moment of time, be taken from earth to heaven. It is not surprising that one contemporary author has called this unique event "The Great Snatch."

Some critics have noted that the word *rapture* is never used in the Bible. While this is true of English versions, Latin translators of the Greek New Testament *did* use the word *rapere*, which is the root of the English term *rapture*. Throughout much of the history of the Western church, Latin was the accepted language of theological discussion. As a result, many theological terms developed out of this language (i.e., Trinity). Our current term *rapture* is also such a term. As will be seen in the answer to the next question, there are many terms used in the New Testament to refer to the rapture event.

2. What New Testament terms refer to the rapture?

The New Testament uses a variety of terms to describe the multi-faceted aspects of the rapture.

- *harpazó*—"caught up," "to seize upon with force," "to snatch up."

  "Then we who are alive and remain shall be *caught up* together with them in the clouds to meet the Lord in the air, and thus we shall always be with the Lord" (1 Thessalonians 4:17).

- *episunagógé*—"gathering together," "assembly."

  "Now we request you, brethren, with regard to the coming of our Lord Jesus Christ and our *gathering together* to Him" (2 Thessalonians 2:1).

- *allassó*—"to change," "to transform," "to exchange."

  "Behold, I tell you a mystery; we shall not all sleep, but we shall all be *changed*, in a moment, in the twinkling of an eye, at the last trumpet; for the trumpet will sound, and the dead will be raised imperishable, and we shall be *changed*" (1 Corinthians 15:51,52).

- *paralambanó*—"to take to," "to receive to oneself."

  "If I go and prepare a place for you, I will come again, and *receive* you to Myself, that where I am, there you may be also" (John 14:3).

- *epiphaneia*—"a manifestation," "an appearance."

  "...looking for the blessed hope and *the appearing* of the glory of our great God and Savior, Christ Jesus" (Titus 2:13).

- *rhuomai*—"to draw to oneself," "to rescue," "to deliver."

  "...and to wait for His Son from heaven, whom He raised from the dead, that is Jesus, who *delivers* us from the wrath to come" (1 Thessalonians 1:10).

- *apokalupsis*—"an uncovering," "laying bare," "a revealing, revelation."

  "Therefore, gird your minds for action, keep sober in spirit, fix your hope completely on the grace to be brought to you at *the revelation* of Jesus Christ" (1 Peter 1:13).

- *parousia*—"a being present, presence," "a coming," "an arrival."

PROPHECY WATCH

> "Be patient, therefore, brethren, until *the coming* of
> the Lord. Behold, the farmer waits for the precious
> produce of the soil, being patient about it, until it gets
> the early and late rains. You too be patient; strengthen
> your hearts, for *the coming* of the Lord is at hand"
> (James 5:7,8).

Not every use of these words in the New Testament is a rapture
reference. The context determines the meaning.

3. What do these terms teach concerning the nature of the rapture?

A review of these terms teaches that the rapture will be an event
initiated by Christ when He comes in the clouds and appears to
believers. His revelation will result in drawing, gathering, catching
up, and receiving to Himself those same believers. During this event,
Christians of all time will be transformed: the living will be translated apart from death, while those asleep in Christ will be resurrected. All these will then accompany the Son to the Father's
heavenly house, which has been prepared for them.

4. When does the rapture take place in relation to the tribulation?

There are five major views within premillennialism concerning
the timing of the rapture in relation to the seven-year tribulation.

Pretribulationism

This view teaches that all Christians will be taken in the rapture,
which will occur before the tribulation.

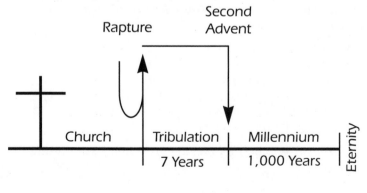

Partial Rapture

This view teaches that the rapture occurs before the tribulation, but only "spiritual" Christians will be taken; other Christians will remain through the tribulation.

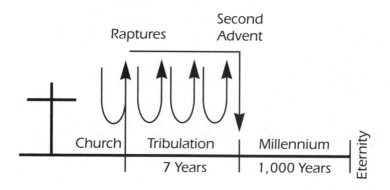

Midtribulationism

This view teaches that all Christian will be taken in the rapture in the middle (after the first 3½ years) of the tribulation.

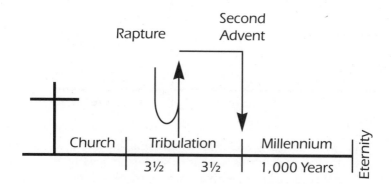

Prewrath Rapture

This view teaches that all Christians will be taken in the rapture approximately three-fourths of the way through the tribulation.

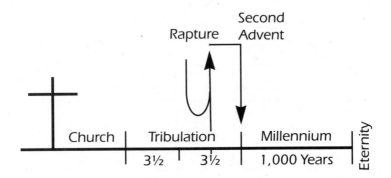

Posttribulationism

This view teaches that all Christians will be raptured at the end of the tribulation.

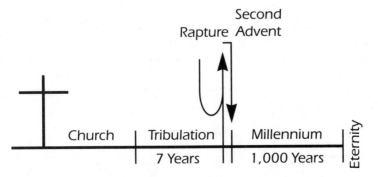

There are many arguments for and against each of these views. However, the purpose of this work is to set forth a positive overview of the pretribulational perspective. Our approach will be to follow a biblically logical order. Just as a builder constructs a house by first laying a proper foundation upon which to build the house, so also sound doctrine rests upon a sure foundation. The following chart summarizes pretribulationism using three elements: the foundation, the body of the house, and the roof.

Practical Motivation for Godly Living

Pretrib Rapture

- Contrasts Between Comings
- Interval Needed Between Comings
- Doctrine of Imminency
- Nature of Tribulation
- Nature of the Church
- Nature of the Holy Spirit

Premillennialism	Futurism	Israel/Church Distinction

Consistent Literal Interpretation

The four elements of the biblical *foundation* supporting pretribulationism are consistent literal interpretation, premillennialism, futurism, and a distinction between God's program for Israel and the church. In the illustration, the *body of the house* represents six major arguments found in the Bible for pretribulationism. These are not the only reasons to believe in a pretrib rapture, but they encompass much of the evidence. The *roof* of the house represents the practical implications springing forth from a consistently applied pretribulationism.

CHAPTER 9

What Is the Foundation for a Pretrib Rapture?

5. How should prophecy be interpreted?

Consistent literal interpretation is essential to properly under-standing what God is saying in the Bible. Yet some people believe that consistent literal interpretation is either impossible or imprac-tical. One critic believes it to be a "presumption" that "is unreason-able" and "an impossible ideal."[3] In spite of false characterization, what do we mean by consistent literal interpretation?

The dictionary defines *literal* as "belonging to letters." Further, it says literal interpretation involves an approach "based on the actual words in their ordinary meaning...not going beyond the facts."[4] "Literal interpretation of the Bible simply means to explain the original sense of the Bible according to the normal and custom-ary usages of its language."[5] How is this done? It can only be accom-plished through an interpretation of the written text, which includes consideration of the grammatical (according to the rules of grammar), historical (consistent with the historical setting of the passage), and contextual (in accord with its context) method of interpretation.

Grammatical Interpretation

The grammatical aspect of literal interpretation considers the impact that grammar plays on a passage. This means that a student of the text should correctly analyze the grammatical relationships of words, phrases, and sentences to one another. Dr. Roy Zuck writes:

> When we speak of interpreting the Bible grammati-cally, we are referring to the process of seeking to determine its meaning by ascertaining four things: (a) the meaning of words (lexicology), (b) the form of words (morphology), (c) the function of words (parts of speech), and (d) the relationships of words (syn-tax).[6]

Dr. Zuck gives further amplification of the four areas noted previously:

> In the meaning of words (lexicology), we are con-
> cerned with (a) etymology—how words are derived
> and developed, (b) usage—how words are used by the
> same and other authors, (c) synonyms and ant-
> onyms—how similar and opposite words are used, and
> (d) context—how words are used in various contexts.
>
> In discussing the form of words (morphology) we are
> looking at how words are structured and how that
> affects their meaning. For example the word *eat* means
> something different from *ate*, though the same letters
> are used. The word *part* changes meaning when the
> letter *s* is added to it to make the word *parts*. The func-
> tion of words (parts of speech) considers what the vari-
> ous forms do. These include attention to subjects,
> verbs, objects, nouns, and others....The relationships
> of words (syntax) are the way words are related or put
> together to form phrases, clauses, and sentences.[7]

The grammatical aspect of literal interpretation lets us know
that any interpretation conflicting with grammar is invalid.

Historical Interpretation

Proper interpretation of the Bible means that the historical context must be taken into account. This aspect means that one must
consider the historical setting and circumstances in which the
books of the Bible were written. Dr. Paul Tan explains:

> The proper concept of the historical in Bible interpre-
> tation is to view the Scriptures as written during given
> ages and cultures. Applications may then be drawn
> which are relevant to our times. For instance, the sub-
> ject of meat offered to idols can only be interpreted
> from the historical and cultural setting of New Testa-
> ment times. Principles to be drawn are relevant to us
> today.[8]

Contextual Interpretation

"A passage taken out of context is a pretext." This slogan is certainly true! Yet one of the most common mistakes made by those who are found to have misinterpreted a passage in the Bible is that of taking a verse out of its divinely ordered context. Even though a sentence may be taken from the Bible, it is not the Word of God if it is placed into a context that changes the meaning from that which God intended in its original context. Dr. Zuck writes:

> The context in which a given Scripture passage is written influences how that passage is to be understood. Context includes several things:
>
> - the verse(s) immediately before and after a passage
> - the paragraph and book in which the verses occur
> - the dispensation in which it was written
> - the message of the entire Bible
> - the historical-cultural environment of that time when it was written.[9]

A widely used example of a verse taken out of context is 2 Chronicles 7:14: "My people who are called by My name humble themselves and pray...." Usually this is quoted as an explanation for why America is in decline. Because "My people" are addressed, it is said that the success of a nation is dependent upon the obedience of Christians to the Lord. Thus, God blesses or curses a nation in accordance with Christian obedience. Then 2 Chronicles 7:14 is cited as a formula for national restoration because the passage says to "humble themselves and pray, and seek My face and turn from their wicked ways, then I will hear from heaven, will forgive their sin, and will heal their land."

We believe that this is an illustration of a passage taken out of context because of the following contextual factors:

- "My people" is said in 2 Chronicles 6:24 to be "Israel," as is also indicated by the flow of the historical context.

- Solomon is preparing to dedicate the recently completed temple, and 7:14 is God's renewal of the Mosaic covenant under which Israel and only Israel operates.

Since this passage involves Israel and not the church, it is improper to speculatively relate it to present-day American Christianity. Proper contextual interpretation allows for the general observation that God delights in a humble and obedient people, but obedience and prayer should be offered according to His plan for the church.

Figures of Speech

Literal interpretation recognizes that a word or phrase can be used either plainly (denotative) or figuratively (connotative). As in our own conversations today, the Bible may use plain speech, such as "He died yesterday" (denotative use of language). Or the same thing may be said in a more colorful way: "He kicked the bucket yesterday" (connotative use of language). An important point to be noted is that even though we may use a figure of speech to refer to someone's death, we are using that figure to refer to an event that literally happened. Some interpreters mistakenly think that because a figure of speech may be used to describe an event (i.e., Jonah's experience in the belly of the great fish in Jonah 2), the event was not literal. Such is not the case. A "golden rule of interpretation" has been developed to help us discern whether or not a figure of speech was intended by an author:

> When the plain sense of Scripture makes common
> sense, seek no other sense; therefore, take every word
> at its primary, ordinary, usual, literal meaning unless
> the facts of the immediate context, studied in the light
> of related passages and axiomatic and fundamental
> truths, indicate clearly otherwise.[10]

Literalists understand that a figure of speech is employed by Isaiah teaching that the Adamic curse upon nature will be reversed in the millennium when he says, "And all the trees of the field will clap their hands" (Isaiah 55:12). This figure is discerned by specific factors in the context in which it was written, all dealing with the removal of the curse upon nature at this future time. Even though figurative language is employed, it will literally happen in history.

Literal Versus Literal

Dr. Elliott Johnson has noted that much of the confusion over literal interpretation can be removed when one properly understands the two primary ways the term has been used down through church history: "(1) the clear, plain sense of a word or phrase as over against a figurative use, and (2) a system that views the text as providing the basis of the true interpretation."[11] Thus, literalists by and large have used the term *literal* to refer to their system of interpretation (the consistent use of the grammatical-historical system, Johnson's second definition). And once inside that system, *literal* refers to whether or not a specific word or phrase is used in its context in a figurative or literal sense (Johnson's first definition).

Johnson's second use of literal (i.e., systematic literalism) is simply the grammatical-historical system consistently used. The grammatical-historical system was revived by the Reformers. It was set against the spiritual (spiritualized) or deeper meaning of the text that was a common approach during the Middle Ages. The literal meaning was used simply as a springboard to a deeper ("spiritual") meaning, which was viewed as more desirable. A classic spiritualized interpretation would, for example, see the four rivers of Genesis 2—the Pishon, Havilah, Tigris, and Euphrates—as representing the human body, soul, spirit, and mind. Coming from such a system, the Reformers saw the need to get back to the literal or textual meaning of the Bible.

The system of literal interpretation is the grammatical-historical or textual approach to interpretation. Use of literalism in this sense could be called "macroliteralism." Within macroliteralism, the consistent use of the grammatical-historical system yields the interpretative conclusion, for example, that *Israel* always and only refers to national Israel. The church will not be substituted for Israel if the grammatical-historical system of interpretation is consistently used because there are no indicators in the text of Scripture that such is the case. Therefore, one must bring an idea from outside the text by saying that the passage really means something that it does not actually say. This kind of replacement approach is a mild form of spiritualized or allegorical interpretation. So it is true to speak of those who replace *Israel* with *the church* as not taking the Bible literally and spiritualizing the text, since such a belief is contrary to a macroliteral interpretation.

Consistent literal interpreters, within the framework of the grammatical-historical system, do discuss whether or not a word, phrase, or the literary genre of a biblical book is a figure of speech (connotative) or is to be taken literally/plainly (denotative), based on the context of a given passage. Some passages are quite naturally clearer than others, and a consensus among interpreters develops, whereas other passages may find literal interpreters divided as to whether or not these passages should be taken as figures of speech. However, this is more a problem of application than of method.

God's Word is to be understood through literal interpretation. It is an important foundation stone supporting the pretribulational rapture. When the Bible is consistently interpreted literally, from Genesis to Revelation, the pretribulational position is hard to avoid.

6. What is premillennialism?

The second foundation stone supporting the pretribulational rapture of the church is the biblical doctrine known as premillennialism. Premillennialism teaches that the second advent will occur before Christ's thousand-year reign from Jerusalem upon earth. In the early church, premillennialism was called *chiliasm,* from the Greek term meaning "1,000" used six times in Revelation 20:2-7. Dr. Charles Ryrie cites essential features of premillennialism as follows: "Its duration will be 1,000 years; its location will be on this earth; its government will be theocratic with the personal presence of Christ reigning as King; and it will fulfill all the yet-unfulfilled promises about the earthly kingdom."[12]

Premillennialism is contrasted with the postmillennial teaching that Christ will return after He has reigned spiritually from His throne in heaven for a long period of time during the current age, through the church, and the similar amillennial view that also advocates a present, but pessimistic, spiritual reign of Christ. Biblical premillennialism is a necessary foundation for pretribulationism since it is impossible for either postmillennialism or amillennialism to support pretribulationism.

Premillennialism is merely the result of interpreting the whole Bible, Genesis to Revelation, in the most natural way—literally. Many of the critics admit that if the literal approach is applied consistently to the whole of Scripture, then premillennialism is the natural result. If the Old Testament promises are ever going to be

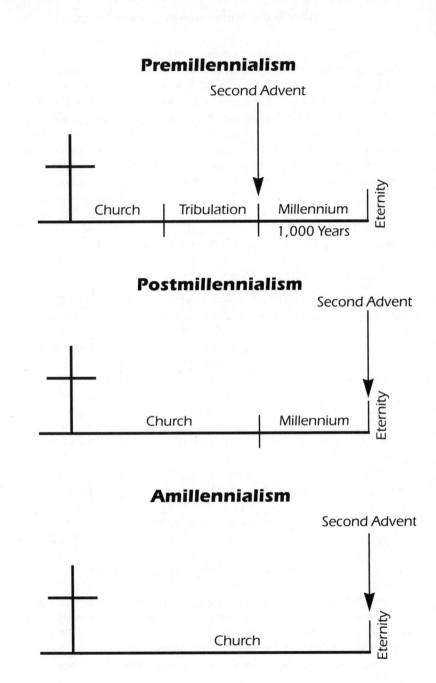

fulfilled literally for Israel as a nation, then they are yet in the future. This is also supportive of premillennialism. Premillennialism also provides a satisfactory and victorious end to history in time as man, through Christ, satisfactorily fulfills his creation mandate to rule over the world. Premillennialism is a necessary biblical prerequisite to build the later biblical doctrine of the rapture of the church before the seven-year tribulation.

7. Is the fulfillment of biblical prophecy past, present, or future?

We believe the answer to this question is "future." The third biblical foundation for a systematic understanding of the pretribulation rapture is futurism. An important, but seemingly little-recognized aspect of proper interpretation of Bible prophecy is the role of timing. When will a prophecy be fulfilled in history? There are four possibilities. The four views are simple in the sense that they reflect the only four possibilities in relation to time: past, present, future, and timeless.

The *preterist* (past) believes that most, if not all, prophecy has already been fulfilled, usually in relation to the destruction of Jerusalem in A.D. 70. The *historicist* (present) sees much of the current church age as equal to the tribulation period. Thus, prophecy has been and will be fulfilled during the current church age. *Futurists* (future) believe that virtually all prophetic events will not occur in the current church age, but will take place in the future tribulation, second coming, or millennium. The *idealist* (timeless) does not believe either that the Bible indicates the timing of events or that we can determine their timing in advance. Therefore, idealists think that prophetic passages mainly teach great ideas or truths about God to be applied regardless of timing. The following is a summary of the four views in contrast to each other

The Significance of Futurism

Of the four views noted previously, the only one that logically and historically has supported the pretribulational position is futurism. Why? Because the timing of the rapture relates to when the tribulation will occur in history. Preterism declares that the tribulation has already taken place. Historicism says that the tribulation started in the fourth century with events surrounding Constantine's Christianization of the Roman Empire and continues until the second coming. Idealism denies that there is a timing of events. Thus, only futurism, which sees the tribulation as a yet future event, could even allow for a rapture before the beginning of that seven-year period. This does not mean, however, that all futurists are pretribulationists; they are not. *But to be a pretribulationist, one must be a futurist.*

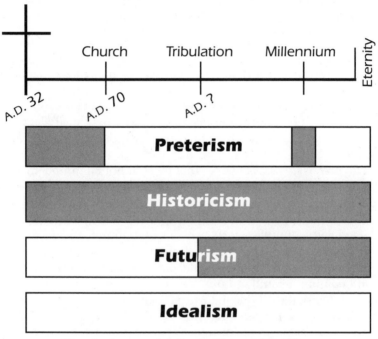

Shaded areas indicate time of fulfillment

Support for Futurism

A defense of futurism can be developed from the Bible by comparing and contrasting futurism with the other three approaches. For example, *futurism instead of preterism* can be shown by demonstrating from specific texts of Scripture that "coming" in the debated passages refers to a bodily return of Christ to planet Earth, not a mystical coming mediated through the Roman army. One area that supports *futurism over historicism* is demonstrated by the fact that numbers relating to days and years are to be taken literally. There is no biblical basis for days really meaning years. A major argument for *futurism over idealism* is the fact that numbers do count. In other words, why would God give hundreds of chronological and temporal statements in the Bible if He did not intend to indicate such?

Let's look at some general support for the futurist approach. First and foremost, only the futurist can interpret the whole Bible literally and, having done so, harmonize those conclusions into a consistent theological system. Just as the people, places, and times were meant to be understood literally in Genesis 1–11, so the texts that relate to the end times are to be taken literally. Days mean days; years mean years; months mean months. The only way that the book of Revelation and other prophetic portions of the Bible make any sense is if they are taken literally, which means that they have not yet happened. Thus, they are future.

The Bible is one-third prophecy, and the majority of that is yet unfulfilled prophecy. Since a consistently literal approach to the whole Bible (including prophecy) is the proper way of understanding God's revelation to man, the futurist approach is the correct way of looking at the timing of biblical prophecy. Only the futurist understanding of biblical prophecy can support the pretribulational rapture.

8. What is the relationship between Israel and the church in prophecy?

"The New Testament consistently differentiates between Israel and the church," claims Dr. Arnold Fruchtenbaum.[13] Fruchtenbaum supports this conclusion through a powerful twofold argument in which he first demonstrates the biblical view of Israel and then shows that the church is viewed in the New Testament as a separate entity.

The fourth biblical foundation upon which the pretrib rapture is built is the fact that God has two peoples: Israel and the church. What do we mean by this distinction, and how does it impact pretribulationism?

Belief that God's single plan for history includes the two peoples, Israel and the church, does not imply that there are different ways of salvation. When it comes to the issue of salvation, there is only one way since all people down through history descend from a single source: Adam. Christ's saving work is the only way of salvation for anyone, whether the person is a member of Israel or the church.

Israel

Fruchtenbaum notes that "the term *Israel* is viewed theologically as referring to all descendants of Abraham, Isaac, and Jacob, also known as Jews, the Jewish people, Israelites, Hebrews, etc."[14] He notes that national election distinguishes Israel from those peoples who were not chosen (that we know as Gentiles), and he outlines four reasons for Israel's election: 1) They were "chosen on the basis of God's love...to be 'a kingdom of priests and a holy nation' (Exodus 19:6)...to represent the Gentile nations before God." 2) "God chose Israel to be the recipient of His revelation and to record it (Deuteronomy 4:5-8; 6:6-9; Romans 3:1,2)." 3) Israel "was to propagate the doctrine of the One God (Deuteronomy 6:4)." 4) Israel "was to produce the Messiah (Romans 9:5; Hebrews 2:16,17; 7:13,14)."[15]

No biblically oriented Christian would deny these purposes relating to Israel. The differences begin to emerge when we consider Israel in relation to the church. "Some theologians insist," notes Fruchtenbaum "that at some point the church receives the promises given to Israel and thus becomes the 'New Israel' (known as replacement theology). Some believe the terms *church* and *Israel* are used virtually 'interchangeably,' most citing Galatians 6:16 and some Romans 9:6."[16]

However, people commonly known as dispensationalists interpret the Bible literally and, thus, do not confuse the terms *Israel* and *the church,* since there is no basis in the text of any biblical passage for supporting such an approach.

Having noted important aspects of the biblical use of *Israel,* we will now examine the nature of the church.

The Church

Six reasons are given by Fruchtenbaum from the Bible supporting the notion that the church is a distinct work in God's household from His people Israel.

1. "The first evidence is the fact that *the church was born at Pentecost,* whereas Israel had existed for many centuries."[17] This, supported by "the use of the future tense in Matthew 16:18, shows that it did not exist in gospel history."[18] The church, born at Pentecost, is called the body of Christ (Colossians 1:18). Entrance into the body is through Spirit baptism (1 Corinthians 12:13), in which Jew and Gentile are united. It is evident that the church began on the Day of Pentecost since Acts 1:5 views Spirit baptism as future, while Acts 10 links it to the past, specifically to Pentecost.

2. "The second evidence is that *certain events in the ministry of the Messiah were essential to the establishment of the church*—the church does not come into being until certain events have taken place."[19] These events include the resurrection and ascension of Jesus to become head of the church (Ephesians 1:20-23). "The church, with believers as the body and Christ as the head, did not exist until after Christ ascended to become its head. And it could not become a functioning entity until after the Holy Spirit provided the necessary spiritual gifts (Ephesians 4:7-11)."[20]

3. "The third evidence is *the mystery character of the church.*"[21] A mystery in the Bible is a hidden truth not revealed until the New Testament (Ephesians 3:3-5,9; Colossians 1:26,27). Fruchtenbaum lists "four defining characteristics of the church [that] are described as a mystery. (1) The body concept of Jewish and Gentile believers united into one body is designated as a mystery in Ephesians 3:1-12. (2) The doctrine of Christ indwelling every believer, the Christ-in-you concept, is called a mystery in Colossians 1:24-27 (cf. Colossians 2:10-19; 3:4). (3) The church as the Bride of Christ is called a mystery in Ephesians 5:22-32. (4) The Rapture is called a mystery in 1 Corinthians 15:50-58. These four mysteries describe qualities that distinguish the church from Israel."[22]

4. "The fourth evidence that the church is distinct from Israel is the *unique relationship between Jews and the Gentiles,* called one new man in Ephesians 2:15."[23] During the current church age God is saving a remnant from the two previous entities (Israel and Gentiles) and combining them into a third new object—the church. This unity of Jews and Gentiles into one new man covers only the church age, from Pentecost until the rapture, after which time God will restore Israel and complete her destiny (Acts 15:14-18). First Corinthians

10:32 reflects just such a division when it says, "Give no offense either to Jews or to Greeks or to the church of God."

5. "The fifth evidence for the distinction between Israel and the church is found in Galatians 6:16."[24] "It appears logical to view 'the Israel of God' (Galatians 6:16) as believing Jews in contrast to unbelieving Jews called 'Israel after the flesh' (1 Corinthians 10:18)."[25] This passage does not support the false claim of replacement theologians who claim that Israel is supplanted by the church. Instead, the Bible teaches that a remnant of Israel is combined with elect Gentiles during this age to make up a whole new entity the New Testament calls the church (Ephesians 2).

Replacement theology tries to teach that because Gentile believers are described as "Abraham's offspring" (Galatians 3:29), this is equivalent to saying that they are Israel. This is clearly not the case. Paul's description of Gentile believers in Galatians 3:29 simply means that they participate in the spiritual (i.e., salvation) blessings that come through Israel (Romans 15:27; 1 Corinthians 9:11,14). "Those who are the spiritual seed are partakers of Jewish spiritual blessings but are never said to become partakers of the physical, material, or national promises."[26] Therefore, Israel's national promises are left intact, awaiting a yet future fulfillment.

6. "In the book of Acts, both Israel and the church exist simultaneously. *The term Israel is used twenty times and* ekklesia *(church) nineteen times, yet the two groups are always kept distinct.*"[27] Thus, the replacement theologian has no actual biblical basis upon which he bases his theological claim that Israel and the church have become one.

The Significance of the Distinction

If Israel and the church are not distinguished, then there is no basis for seeing a future for Israel or for the church as a new and unique people of God. If Israel and the church are merged into a single program, then the Old Testament promises for Israel will never be fulfilled and are usually seen by replacement theologians as spiritually fulfilled by the church. The merging of Israel's destiny into the church not only makes into one what the Scriptures understand as two, but it also removes a need for future restoration of God's original elect people in order to literally fulfill His promise that they will one day be the head and not the tail (Deuteronomy 28:13).

The more that believers see a distinct plan for Israel and a distinct plan for the church, the more they realize that when the New Testament speaks to the church it is describing a separate destiny and hope for it. The church becomes more distinct in the plan of God. Israel's future includes the seven-year tribulation, and then, shortly before Christ's return to Jerusalem, its acceptance of Jesus as Messiah when the veil is removed and it looks upon the one who was pierced. On the other hand, the distinct hope (the rapture before the seventieth week of Daniel) for the church is Christ's any-moment return.

Thus, a distinction between Israel and the church, as taught in the Bible, provides a basis of support for the pretribulational rapture. Those who merge the two programs cannot logically support the biblical arguments for pretribulationism.

CHAPTER 10

What Evidence Supports a Pretrib Rapture?

9. Why are the rapture and the second coming separate events?

In the previous section we gave a basis or foundation for pretribulationism. In this section we will begin laying out specific biblical evidence for the pretribulational rapture. The first place to start is with the biblical notion that the rapture of the church is distinct from Christ's second coming to the earth.

John Feinberg notes that distinguishing between the rapture and second coming is important in establishing pretribulationism against the nonpretribulational claim that the Bible does not teach such a view:

> The pretribulationist must show that there is enough dissimilarity between clear rapture and clear second advent passages as to warrant the claim that the two kinds of passages *could* be speaking about two events which *could* occur at different times. The pretribulationist does not have to prove at this point...that the two events must occur at different times, but only that the exegetical data from rapture and second advent passages do not make it impossible for the events to occur at different times. If he can do that, the pretribulationist has shown that his view is not impossible. And, he has answered the posttribulationist's strongest line of evidence.[28]

A key factor in understanding the New Testament's teaching of the pretribulational rapture revolves around the fact that *two* future comings of Christ are presented. The first coming is the catching up into the clouds of the church before the seven-year tribulation, and the second coming occurs at the end of the tribulation when Christ returns to the earth to begin His 1,000-year kingdom. Anyone desirous of insight into the biblical teaching of the rapture and second advent must study and decide whether Scripture speaks of one or two future events.

Framing the Issue

Posttribulationists usually contend that if the rapture and the second coming are two distinct events, separated by about seven years, then there ought to be at least one passage in Scripture that clearly teaches this. However, the Bible does not always teach God's truth in accordance with our preconceived notions or in such a way that directly answers all of our questions. For example, a Unitarian could design a similar kind of question regarding the Trinity. "Where is at least one passage in Scripture that clearly says that the persons of the Godhead are distinct?" We who believe the Trinity reply that the Bible teaches the Trinity but in a different way.

Many important biblical doctrines are not given to us directly from a single verse; we often need to harmonize passages into systematic conclusions. Some truths are directly stated in the Bible, such as the deity of Christ (John 1:1; Titus 2:13). But doctrines like the Trinity and the incarnate nature of Christ are the product of biblical harmonization. Taking into account all biblical texts, orthodox theologians over time recognized that God is a Trinity and that Christ is the God-Man. Similarly, a systematic consideration of all biblical passages reveals that Scripture teaches two future comings.

Posttribulationists often contend that the pretribulational position is built merely upon an assumption that certain verses "make sense" if and only if the pretribulational model of the rapture is assumed to be correct. However, they often fail to make it clear to their readers that posttribulationism is just as dependent upon assumptions. The error of posttribulationists stems from failure to observe actual biblical distinctions.

For example, Christ's ministry has two phases that revolve around His two comings. Phase one took place at Christ's first coming when He came in humiliation to suffer. Phase two will begin at Christ's second coming when He will reign on earth in power and glory. Failure to distinguish these two phases was a key factor in Israel's rejection of Jesus as Messiah at His first coming. In the same way, failure to see clear distinctions between the rapture and second advent leads many people to a misinterpretation of God's future plan.

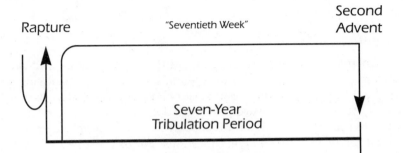

Rapture

"Seventieth Week"

Second
Advent

Seven-Year
Tribulation Period

Rapture and Second Coming Passages

RAPTURE PASSAGES	SECOND COMING PASSAGES
John 14:1-3	Daniel 2:44,45
Romans 8:19	Daniel 7:9-14
1 Corinthians 1:7,8	Daniel 12:1-3
1 Corinthians 15:51-53	Zechariah 12:10
1 Corinthians 16:22	Zechariah 14:1-15
Philippians 3:20,21	Matthew 13:41
Philippians 4:5	Matthew 24:15-31
Colossians 3:4	Matthew 26:64
1 Thessalonians 1:10	Mark 13:14-27
1 Thessalonians 2:19	Mark 14:62
1 Thessalonians 4:13-18	Luke 21:25-28
1 Thessalonians 5:9	Acts 1:9-11
1 Thessalonians 5:23	Acts 3:19-21
2 Thessalonians 2:1	1 Thessalonians 3:13
2 Thessalonians 2:3 (?)	2 Thessalonians 1:6-10
1 Timothy 6:14	2 Thessalonians 2:8
2 Timothy 4:1	1 Peter 4:12,13
2 Timothy 4:8	2 Peter 3:1-14
Titus 2:13	Jude 14,15
Hebrews 9:28	Revelation 1:7
James 5:7-9	Revelation 19:11–20:6
1 Peter 1:7,13	Revelation 22:7,12,20
1 Peter 5:4	
1 John 2:28–3:2	
Jude 21	
Revelation 2:25	
Revelation 3:10	

The Nature of the Rapture

The rapture is most clearly presented in 1 Thessalonians 4:13-18. It is characterized in the Bible as a "translation coming" (1 Corinthians 15:51,52; 1 Thessalonians 4:15-17) in which Christ comes *for* His church. The second advent is Christ returning with His saints, descending from heaven to establish His earthly kingdom (Zechariah 14:4,5; Matthew 24:27-31). Dr. Ed Hindson observes:

> The rapture (or "translation") of the church is often paralleled to the "raptures" of Enoch (Genesis 5:24) and Elijah (2 Kings 2:12). In each case, the individual disappeared or was caught up into heaven. At His ascension, our Lord Himself was "taken up" into heaven (Acts 1:9). The biblical description of the rapture involves both the resurrection of deceased believers and the translation of living believers into the air to meet the Lord (1 Thessalonians 4:16-17; 1 Corinthians 15:51,52).[29]

Differences between the two events are harmonized naturally by the pretribulational position, while other views are not able to account comfortably for such distinctions. Notice the chart on the previous page that gives passages for the rapture and the second coming.

The following chart delineates the differences between the rapture and the second coming.

Rapture and Second Coming Contrasts

RAPTURE/TRANSLATION	SECOND COMING ESTABLISHED KINGDOM
1. Translation of all believers	1. No translation at all
2. Translated saints go to heaven	2. Translated saints return to earth
3. Earth not judged	3. Earth judged and righteousness established
4. Imminent, any-moment, signless	4. Follows definite predicted signs, including tribulation
5. Not in the Old Testament	5. Predicted often in Old Testament
6. Believers only	6. Affects all men
7. Before the day of wrath	7. Concluding the day of wrath
8. No reference to Satan	8. Satan bound

Rapture and Second Coming Contrasts (Continued)

RAPTURE/TRANSLATION	SECOND COMING ESTABLISHED KINGDOM
9. Christ comes *for* His own	9. Christ comes *with* His own
10. He comes in the *air*	10. He comes to the *earth*
11. He claims His bride	11. He comes with His bride
12. Only His own see Him	12. Every eye shall see Him
13. Tribulation begins	13. Millennial kingdom begins

Dr. John Walvoord concludes that these "contrasts should make it evident that the translation of the church is an event quite different in character and time from the return of the Lord to establish His kingdom, and confirms the conclusion that the translation takes place before the tribulation."[30]

Additional Differences

Paul speaks of the rapture as a "mystery" (1 Corinthians 15:51-54)—that is, a truth not revealed until its disclosure by the apostles (Colossians 1:26), making it a separate event, while the second coming was predicted in the Old Testament (Daniel 12:1-3; Zechariah 12:10; 14:4).

The movement for the believer at the rapture is from earth to heaven, while it is from heaven to earth at the second advent. At the rapture the Lord comes *for* his saints (1 Thessalonians 4:16), while at the second coming the Lord comes *with* His saints (1 Thessalonians 3:13). At the rapture the Lord comes only for believers, but His return to the earth will impact all people. The rapture is a translation/resurrection event where the Lord takes believers to the Father's house in heaven (John 14:3), while at the second coming, believers return from heaven to the earth (Matthew 24:30). Hindson says, "The different aspects of our Lord's return are clearly delineated in the scriptures themselves. The only real issue in the eschatological debate is the time *interval* between them."[31]

The Scriptures concerning Christ's coming in the air to rapture His church are too distinct to be reduced into a single coming at the end of the tribulation. These biblical distinctions provide a strong basis for the pretribulational rapture.

---

10. Why is an interval necessary between the two comings?

An interval or gap of time is needed between the rapture and the second coming in order to facilitate many events predicted in the Bible in a timely manner. Numerous items in the New Testament can be harmonized by a pretrib time gap of at least seven years, while proponents of other views, especially posttribulationists, are forced to postulate scenarios that would not realistically allow for normal passage of time. The following events are best temporally harmonized with an interval of time as put forth by pretribulationism.[32]

• Second Corinthians 5:10 teaches that all believers of this age must appear before the judgment seat of Christ in heaven. This event, often known as the "bema judgment" from the Greek word *bema,* is an event never mentioned in the detailed accounts connected with the second coming of Christ to the earth. Since such an evaluation would require some passage of time, the pretrib gap of seven years nicely accounts for such a requirement.

• Revelation 19:7-10 pictures the church as a bride who has been made ready for marriage (with "fine linen," which represents "the righteous acts of the saints") to her groom (Christ). The bride has already been clothed in preparation for her return at the second coming with Christ to the earth (Revelation 19:11-18). It follows that the church would already have to be complete and in heaven (because of the pretrib rapture) in order to have been prepared in the way that Revelation 19 describes. This requires an interval of time which pretribulationism handles well.

• The 24 elders of Revelation 4:1–5:14 are best understood as representatives of the church. Dr. Charles Ryrie explains:

> In the New Testament, elders as the highest officials in the church do represent the whole church (cf. Acts 15:6; 20:28), and in the Old Testament, twenty-four elders were appointed by King David to represent the entire Levitical priesthood (1 Chronicles 24). When those twenty-four elders met together in the temple precincts in Jerusalem, the entire priestly house was represented. Thus it seems more likely that the elders represent redeemed human beings....The church is

included and is thus in heaven before the tribulation begins.[33]

If they refer to the church, then this would necessitate the rapture and reward of the church before the tribulation and would require a chronological gap for them to perform their heavenly duties during the seven-year tribulation.

• Believers who come to faith in Christ during the tribulation are not translated at Christ's second advent but carry on ordinary occupations such as farming and building houses, and they will bear children (Isaiah 65:20-25). This would be impossible if all saints were translated at the second coming to the earth, as post-tribulationists teach. Because pretribulationists have at least a seven-year interval between the removal of the church at the rapture and the return of Christ to the earth, this is not a problem because many people will be saved during the interval and thus be available to populate the millennium in their natural bodies in order to fulfill Scripture.

• It would be impossible for the judgment of the Gentiles to take place after the second coming if the rapture and second coming are not separated by a gap of time. How would both saved and unsaved, still in their natural bodies, be separated in judgment if all living believers are translated at the second coming? This would be impossible if the translation takes place at the second coming, but it is solved through a pretribulational time gap.

• Dr. John F. Walvoord points out that if "the translation took place in connection with the second coming to the earth, there would be no need of separating the sheep from the goats at a subsequent judgment, but the separation would have taken place in the very act of the translation of the believers before Christ actually sets up His throne on earth (Matthew 25:31)."[34] Once again, such a "problem" is solved by taking a pretrib position with its gap of at least seven years.

• A time interval is needed so that God's program for the church, a time when Jew and Gentile are united in one body (cf. Ephesians 2–3), will not become commingled in any way with His unfinished and future plan for Israel during the tribulation. Dr. Renald Showers notes:

All other views of the Rapture have the church going through at least part of the 70th week, meaning that all other views mix God's 70-weeks program for Israel and Jerusalem together with His program for the church.[35]

A gap is needed in order for these two aspects of God's program to be harmonized in a nonconflicting manner.

The pretribulational rapture of the church not only allows for the biblical distinction between the translation of church-age saints at the rapture and the second coming, but it also handles without difficulty the necessity of a time gap which harmonizes a number of future biblical events. This requirement of a seven-year gap of time adds support to the likelihood that pretribulationism best reflects the biblical viewpoint.

11. Why is imminency significant for the rapture?

The New Testament teaching that Christ could return and rapture His church at any moment, without prior signs or warning (imminency), is such a powerful argument for pretribulationism that it is one of the most fiercely attacked doctrines by pretrib opponents. Nonpretribulationists sense that if the New Testament teaches imminency, then a pretrib rapture is virtually assured.

What is a definition of *imminency?* Dr. Showers defines and describes *imminency* as follows:

> 1) An imminent event is one which is always "hanging overhead, is constantly ready to befall or overtake one; close at hand in its incidence" ("imminent," *The Oxford English Dictionary,* 1901, V, 66.). Thus, imminence carries the sense that it could happen at any moment. Other things *may* happen before the imminent event, but nothing else *must* take place before it happens. If something else must take place before an event can happen, then that event is not imminent. In other words, the necessity of something else taking place first destroys the concept of imminency.

> 2) Since a person never knows exactly when an imminent event will take place, then he cannot count on a certain amount of time transpiring before the immi-

nent event happens. In light of this, he should always be prepared for it to happen at any moment.

3) A person cannot legitimately set or imply a date for its happening. As soon as a person sets a date for an imminent event he destroys the concept of imminency, because he thereby is saying that a certain amount of time must transpire before that event can happen. A specific date for an event is contrary to the concept that the event could happen at any moment.

4) A person cannot legitimately say that an imminent event will happen soon. The term "soon" implies that an event *must* take place "within a short time (after a particular point of time specified or implied)." By contrast, an imminent event *may* take place within a short time, but it does not *have* to do so in order to be imminent. As I hope you can see by now, "imminent" is not equal to "soon."[36]

The fact that Christ could return soon, at any moment (but may not), is a support for pretribulationism. What New Testament passages teach this truth? Those verses stating that Christ could return at any moment, without warning, and those instructing believers to wait and look for the Lord's coming, including:

- *1 Corinthians 1:7*—"awaiting eagerly the revelation of our Lord Jesus Christ."

- *1 Corinthians 16:22*—"Maranatha."

- *Philippians 3:20*—"For our citizenship is in heaven, from which also we eagerly wait for a Savior, the Lord Jesus Christ."

- *Philippians 4:5*—"The Lord is near."

- *1 Thessalonians 1:10*—"to wait for His Son from heaven."

- *Titus 2:13*—"looking for the blessed hope and the appearing of the glory of our great God and Savior, Christ Jesus."

- *Hebrews 9:28*—"so Christ...shall appear a second time for salvation without reference to sin, to those who eagerly await Him."

- *James 5:7-9*—"Be patient, therefore, brethren, until the coming of the Lord...for the coming of the Lord is at hand....Behold, the Judge is standing right at the door."

- *1 Peter 1:13*—"fix your hope completely on the grace to be brought to you at the revelation of Jesus Christ."

- *Jude 21*—"waiting anxiously for the mercy of our Lord Jesus Christ to eternal life."

- *Revelation 3:11; 22:7,12,20*—"I am coming quickly!"

- *Revelation 22:17,20*—"And the Spirit and the bride say, 'Come.' And let the one who hears say, 'Come.'... He who testifies to these things says, 'Yes, I am coming quickly.' Amen. Come, Lord Jesus."

As we consider these passages, we note that Christ may come at any moment—that the rapture is actually imminent. Only pretribulationism can give a full, literal meaning to such an any-moment event. Other rapture views must redefine *imminence* more loosely than the New Testament would allow. Dr. Walvoord declares, "The exhortation to look for 'the glorious appearing' of Christ to His own (Titus 2:13) loses its significance if the Tribulation must intervene first. Believers in that case should look for signs."[37] If the pretrib view of imminence is not accepted, then it would make sense to look for signs related to events of the tribulation (i.e., the Antichrist, the two witnesses) and not for Christ Himself. But the New Testament, as demonstrated above, uniformly instructs the church to look for the coming of Christ, while tribulation saints are told to look for signs.

The New Testament exhortation to be comforted by the Lord's coming (John 14:1-3; 1 Thessalonians 4:18) would no longer have meaning if believers first had to pass through any part of the tribulation. Instead, comfort would have to await passage through the events of the tribulation. No, the church has been given a "blessed hope" in part because our Lord's return is truly imminent.

The early church had a special greeting for one another, as recorded in 1 Corinthians 16:22, which was "Maranatha!" Maranatha consists of three Aramaic words: *Mar* ("Lord"), *ana* ("our"), and *tha* ("come"), meaning "our Lord, come." Such a unique greeting reflects an eager expectation of the blessed hope as a very real presence in the everyday lives of these ancient Christians. The life of the church today could only be improved if "maranatha" were to return as a sincere greeting on the lips of an expectant people. Maranatha!

12. Why is the nature of the tribulation significant?

The Bible teaches that the tribulation (the seven-year, seventieth week of Daniel) is a time of preparation for Israel's restoration and conversion (Deuteronomy 4:29,30; Jeremiah 30:3-11; Zechariah 12:10).[38] While the church will experience tribulation in general during this present age (John 16:33), she is never mentioned as participating in Israel's time of trouble, which includes the great tribulation, the day of the Lord, and the wrath of God.

Not one Old Testament passage on the tribulation refers to the church (Deuteronomy 4:29,30; Jeremiah 30:4-11; Daniel 8:24-27; 12:1,2), nor does the New Testament ever speak of the church in relation to the tribulation (Matthew 13:30,39-42,48-50; 24:15-31; 1 Thessalonians 1:9,10; 5:4-9; 2 Thessalonians 2:1-11; Revelation 4–18). Such silence speaks loudly and supports the pretrib position.

If pretribulationism is indeed the teaching of Scripture, then we would expect that passages dealing with the tribulation would consistently make no mention of the church. This is exactly what we find. However, Israel is mentioned often throughout these texts. Dr. Robert Gromacki has studied Revelation 4–19, which gives the most detailed overview of the seven-year tribulation in the Bible, and has shown the following:

> However, there is a strange silence of the term in chapters 4–19. That fact is especially noteworthy when you contrast that absence with its frequent presence in the first three chapters. One good reason for this phenomenon is the absence of the true church and true evangelical churches in the seven years preceding the Second Coming. The true believers of the church have gone into the presence of Christ in heaven before the onset of the events of the seven year period. The church is not mentioned during the seal, trumpet, and bowl judgments because the church is not here during the outpouring of these judgments.[39]

Only pretribulationism is able to give full import to tribulation terms like "the time of Jacob's distress" (Jeremiah 30:7), as a passage specifically stating that the tribulation is for Jacob (i.e., Israel). Since God's purpose for the tribulation is to restore Israel (Jeremiah 30:3,10) and judge the Gentiles (Jeremiah 30:11), it is clear that this purpose does not include the church. This explains why the church will be taken to heaven before this time.

13. Why is the nature of the church significant?

God's plan and purpose for the church would naturally relate to whether He will remove His bride before the tribulation or have her go through it. Only pretribulationism is able to give full biblical import to the New Testament teaching that the church differs significantly from Israel. The church is said to be a mystery (Ephesians 3:1-13) by which Jews and Gentiles are now united into one body in Christ (Ephesians 2:11-22). This explains why the church's translation to heaven is never mentioned in any Old Testament passage that deals with the second coming after the tribulation, and why the church is promised deliverance from the time of God's wrath during the tribulation (1 Thessalonians 1:9,10; 5:9; Revelation 3:10).

It is helpful in determining the timing of the rapture to note that the translation of the church is never mentioned at all in passages that speak of the second coming of Christ after the tribulation.[40] The apostle Paul notes in the following passages that the church is not appointed to God's wrath that will be dispensed during the seven years of the tribulation:

- *Romans 5:9*—"Much more then, having now been justified by His blood, we shall be saved from the wrath of God through Him."

- *1 Thessalonians 1:9,10*—"You turned to God from idols to serve a living and true God, and to wait for His Son from heaven, whom He raised from the dead, that is Jesus, who delivers us from the wrath to come."

- *1 Thessalonians 5:9*—"For God has not destined us for wrath, but for obtaining salvation through our Lord Jesus Christ."

Because God has promised that the church cannot enter the time of "the wrath of the Lamb" or "the great day of their wrath" (Revelation 6:16,17), the church will be taken to heaven before this time.

Forgiveness of sins through Christ prepares the church so that it will not be overtaken by the day of the Lord (1 Thessalonians 5:1-9), which includes the tribulation. This will be accomplished through the rapture, mentioned in the preceding chapter (1 Thessalonians 4:13-18).

Through the church of Philadelphia (Revelation 3:10), the church is explicitly promised deliverance from "the hour of testing," which is the tribulation. Here is a clear passage teaching that the church will escape the tribulation, since God has purposed that it will be "to test those who dwell upon the earth."

- **Revelation 3:10**—"Because you have kept the word of My perseverance, I also will keep you from the hour of testing, that hour which is about to come upon the whole world, to test those who dwell upon the earth."

Believers are promised deliverance from the *hour* of testing. This means that the church is totally absent from the time period of this hour of testing. It is said to be a worldwide time of testing. Further, it will test "those who dwell upon the earth." The single Greek word for "earth dwellers" is used ten other times in Revelation (6:10; 8:13; 11:10 [twice]; 13:8,12,14 [twice]; 17:2,8) as "a company of people constantly in view through the Apocalypse as objects of God's wrath because of their rebellion against Him.... These are men given up to evil and hatred of God's saints."[41] Thus, a contrast between what God has in store for His church and unbelievers could not be greater. Every aspect of this passage supports pretribulationism.

The godly remnant of the tribulation is pictured as Israelites, not members of the church. Thus, pretribulationists do not confuse general terms like *elect* and *saints,* which are used in the Bible of all the saved of the ages, with specific terms like *church* and *those in Christ,* which refer to believers of this age only.

The nature and purpose of the church is said to be unique and separate from Israel. This provides a biblical basis for removal of the church before God completes the final seven years leading up to Israel's redemption. We have seen that there are specific passages promising the church's removal before the time of the tribulation gets underway. This can only make sense with a pretrib understanding.

14. How is the work of the Holy Spirit related to the rapture?

Second Thessalonians 2:1-12 discusses a man of lawlessness being held back until a later time. Interpreting the restrainer of evil (2:6) as the indwelling ministry of the Holy Spirit at work through the body of Christ during the current age supports the pretribulational interpretation. Since "the lawless one" (the beast or Antichrist) cannot be revealed until the restrainer (the Holy Spirit) is taken away (2:7,8), the tribulation cannot occur until the church is removed.

Key to this scenario is whether the Holy Spirit is the restrainer. After surveying various interpretations of the passage, Dr. Robert Thomas concludes:

> To one familiar with the Lord Jesus' Upper Room Discourse, as Paul undoubtedly was, fluctuation between neuter and masculine recalls how the Holy Spirit is spoken of. Either gender is appropriate, depending on whether the speaker (or writer) thinks of natural agreement (masc. because of the Spirit's personality) or grammatical (neuter because of the noun *pneuma*; see John 14:26; 15:26; 16:13,14)....This identification of the restrainer with deep roots in church history...is most appealing. The special presence of the Spirit as the indweller of saints will terminate abruptly at the *parousia* as it began abruptly at Pentecost. Once the body of Christ has been caught away to heaven, the Spirit's ministry will revert back to what he did for believers during the OT period.... His function of restraining evil through the body of Christ (John 16:7-11; 1 John 4:4) will cease similarly to the way he terminated his striving in the days of Noah (Genesis 6:3). At that point the reins will be removed from lawlessness and the Satanically inspired rebellion will begin. It appears that *to katechon* ("what is holding back") was well known at Thessalonica as a title for the Holy Spirit on whom the readers had come to depend in their

personal attempts to combat lawlessness (1 Thessalonians 1:6; 4:8; 5:19; 2 Thessalonians 2:13).[42]

A natural interpretation of this passage leads to identifying the Holy Spirit as the restrainer. This view supports pretribulationism.

15. Are there other arguments for pretribulationism?

In addition to arguments already presented in this work, there are additional reasons to believe in pretribulationism. These arguments vary in their degree of support of pretribulationism, but should not be overlooked or ignored.

• Our Lord told His disciples of the possibility of believers escaping the tribulation in Luke 21:36: "But keep on the alert at all times, praying in order that you may have strength to escape all these things that are about to take place, and to stand before the Son of Man." It was later revealed through the apostles that such a possibility would indeed become a reality for the church.

• Divine deliverance is a pattern often exercised by God preceding His judgment. This is clearly illustrated in the cases of Enoch, Noah, Lot, Rahab, and others (2 Peter 2:5-9). For example, when we look at the story of Enoch, we find an illustration of both deliverance and rapture before judgment. Notice the strong emphasis on physical deliverance from judgment as the New Testament in Hebrews 11:5 comments on this Old Testament event:

> By faith Enoch was taken up so that he should not see death; and he was not found because God took him up; for he obtained the witness that before his being taken up he was pleasing to God.

• God will call His ambassadors home before declaring war on the world, just as in contemporary international relations a nation calls home its ambassador prior to a declaration or act of war. Dr. Ed Hindson notes, "In 2 Corinthians 5:20, believers are called 'Christ's Ambassadors' who appeal to the world to be reconciled to God before it is too late. In biblical times, one's ambassadors were recalled when it was time to make war with the enemy."[43] Such a notion supports only pretribulationism.

• Revelation 4–19 is widely recognized as descriptive of the tribulation. On the other hand, Revelation 2–3 provides instruction relating to the church. The pretrib rapture is reflected in the fact that the apostle John is invited to come up to heaven (Revelation 4:1) at the very point in the biblical text (between Revelation 3 and 4) where pretribulationists say the rapture will occur.

CHAPTER 11

Why Is the Pretrib Rapture Important Today?

16. How does the rapture promote holy living?

Like all aspects of biblical doctrine, teaching on the rapture has a practical dimension. Earlier we noted that the rapture scenario is modeled after the engagement and marriage cycle in ancient Israel. After the engagement, known as a betrothal, which was more binding than modern engagements, the bridegroom was to busy himself with building a room at his father's house so that when the marriage did occur they would have a place to live (John 14:1-3). This interim period, usually at least a year, was viewed as a time of testing the bride's loyalty to see if she would remain chaste and true to the groom. All the while, during the absence, the bride busied herself by preparing her wardrobe and looking forward to the day when she would be united to her beloved. So it is with the church while Christ is absent.

The church is looking for Christ's return at the rapture, as an engaged young woman would anticipate marriage with her beloved: "And though you have not seen Him, you love Him" (1 Peter 1:8). The life each believer lives until Christ's return is a test of loyalty and faithfulness, which is motivated out of a desire to be found pure when He does come for His church.

The rapture is not just wishful "pie-in-the-sky in the by-and-by" thinking. Rather, it is vitally connected to Christian living in the "nasty here-and-now." Any believer with love in his or her heart for the coming Savior will want to live a pure and holy life until His return:

> Beloved, now we are children of God, and it has not
> appeared as yet what we shall be. We know that, when
> He appears, we shall be like Him, because we shall see
> Him just as He is. And everyone who has this hope
> fixed on Him purifies himself, just as He is pure
> (1 John 3:2,3).

Note that this passage directly links our present Christian conduct to a future event—the rapture. Why? Because our destiny as God's children is not complete in this life, and it is toward that future goal that we are moving. At the rapture, when we will receive our resurrection bodies, our character will also be perfected. But in the meantime, we are to be purified in present conduct by fixing our hope on the return of Christ. According to this passage, this should be a motivation to holy living.

Many people do not realize how often the New Testament mentions our future blessed hope as a motive for godly living in the present. Note also the following verses:

> Since all these things are to be destroyed in this way, what sort of people ought you to be in holy conduct and godliness, looking for and hastening the coming of the day of God, on account of which the heavens will be destroyed by burning, and the elements will melt with intense heat!...Therefore, beloved, since you look for these things, be diligent to be found by Him in peace, spotless and blameless, and regard the patience of our Lord to be salvation; just as also our beloved brother Paul, according to the wisdom given him, wrote to you (2 Peter 3:11,12,14,15).

In this passage, Peter's admonition refers to the second coming and not to the rapture, but he takes the same approach used by John in that he shows how a future event should impact the present life of a believer. Peter reasons that "holy conduct and godliness" should spring forth from a right contemplation of God's future judgment. Further, Christians are to "be diligent to be found by Him in peace, spotless and blameless" in this present life. Since Peter calls for "diligence," it is required that a believer put forth a specific effort toward holy living. It does not just happen. We also see an opportunity for salvation during the interim between the Lord's comings.

There are over 20 specific references in the New Testament that link the present conduct of believers to our future destiny. Our rapture hope is said to urge a watchfulness for Christ Himself (1 Corinthians 15:58); to encourage faithfulness in church leaders (2 Timothy 4:1-5); to encourage patient waiting (1 Thessalonians 1:10); to result in expectation and looking (Philippians 3:20; Titus 2:13; Hebrews 9:28); to promote godly moderation (Philippians 4:5);

to excite "heavenly mindedness" (Colossians 3:1-4); to bring forth successful labor (1 Thessalonians 2:19,20); to experience comfort (1 Thessalonians 4:18); to urge steadfastness (2 Thessalonians 2:1,2; 1 Timothy 6:14; 1 Peter 5:4); to infuse diligence and activity (2 Timothy 4:1-8); to promote mortification of the flesh (Colossians 3:4,5; Titus 2:12,13); to require soberness (1 Thessalonians 5:6; 1 Peter 1:13); to contribute to an abiding with Christ (1 John 2:28; 3:2); to support patience under trial (James 5:7,8); and to enforce obedience (2 Timothy 4:1).

Dr. Renald Showers summarized some practical implications of the pretrib rapture when he noted:

> The imminent coming of Christ should have an incredible practical effect on the lives of individual Christians and the church as a whole. The fact that the glorified, holy Son of God could step through the door of heaven at any moment is intended by God to be the most pressing, incessant motivation for holy living and aggressive ministry (including missions, evangelism, and Bible teaching), and the greatest cure for lethargy and apathy. It should make a major difference in every Christian's values, actions, priorities and goals.[44]

17. How does the rapture promote evangelism?

We noted in Question 16 that 2 Peter 3 teaches that our Lord's return is to be seen by Christians not as a delay, but as an opportunity for those who have not yet trusted Christ to come to faith. Thus, the imminent coming of Christ at the rapture has often spurred many into an urgent state of evangelistic zeal.

Dr. Tim LaHaye has pointed out that those impacted by a biblical belief in the pretrib rapture often produce "an evangelistic church of soul-winning Christians, for when we believe Christ could appear at any moment, we seek to share Him with our friends lest they be left behind at His coming."[45]

In our own lifetime, we know of many contemporaries who have come to faith in Christ as a result of evangelistic efforts through the vehicle of prophetic preaching. Specifically, hundreds of thousands of Christians have been motivated to give an evangelistic witness as a result of books such as Hal Lindsey's *Late Great Planet Earth*. And thousands of people have come to faith in Christ as a result of the influence of Lindsey's books that focus on the pretrib rapture.

Belief in pretribulationism promotes evangelism when believers are impacted by the fact that Christ could return at any moment, without any prior warning. Thus, a premium is placed upon any and every opportunity to evangelize the lost. Wherever those who believe in an any-moment return of Christ have realized the implications of such a view, it has always provided a powerful motive for evangelism.

18. How does the rapture promote world missions?

If pretribulationism has provoked many to evangelism, then it would also serve as a great stimulus for world missions. Such has been the case.

Dr. LaHaye has noted:

> Belief in the imminent return of Christ impels Christians and churches to develop a worldwide missionary vision of reaching the lost for Christ in this generation. We have more reason to believe that Christ will come in our lifetime than any generation since He ascended into heaven and promised to return. Naturally, we should eagerly desire to reach friends with His good news.[46]

Dr. Timothy Weber, a church historian, has noted that belief in the rapture has been a great incentive for missions in the last 150 years:

> By the 1920s premillennialists were claiming that they made up "an overwhelming majority" of the [missions] movement. Others estimated that believers in the imminent second coming made up from 75 to 85 percent of the missionary force worldwide....American premillennialists were better represented on the mission fields than in the home churches....Instead of cutting missionary involvement, premillennialism increased it.[47]

In spite of the fact that some critics say belief in an any-moment return of Christ is a hindrance to missions, reality demonstrates just the opposite to be the case. Belief in pretribulationism has had and will continue to have a positive impact upon the worldwide missionary effort.

Hope for the Future

The doctrine of the pretribulational rapture offers Christians great hope for the future. The Bible never intends that doctrine and the spiritual life be separated. The study of prophecy and an understanding of the rapture provide us with both a knowledge of the Word of God and a daily hope for the return of Christ as we wait for Him and proclaim His gospel.

PART 3

The Tribulation and the Antichrist

The Darkness Ahead

Almost everyone has experienced turbulent and traumatic times during which there was great uncertainty or perhaps even enormous pain and sorrow. Such times are often periods of individual, familial, and perhaps even national crises in which every personal, physical, and emotional resource is called into action in order to successfully endure the problem. Sorrow, grief, persecution, tragedy, catastrophe, famine, war, and uncertainty are all very real dynamics in daily life and newspaper headlines. However, according to the Bible, there will be a future time of even greater agony known as "the tribulation." This era will come after the rapture of the church and will be the greatest period of suffering the world has known. It will be the ultimate "future shock."

The Bible also clearly prophesies and warns of a future political leader whose actions and power will cause international chaos. Under his rule, democracy will fall to dictatorship, and prosperity will give way to persecution.

Wall Street's economic forecasters and speculators are often divided into optimists and pessimists (or "bulls" and "bears") based upon their "reading" of economic indicators and trends. In this same sense, interpreters of the Bible can read its prophetic passages and understand much of God's plan for the future. The difference with prophecy is that through careful and prayerful study, much of the speculation can be removed. Unlike tomorrow's markets, God's plan is clear and certain. Does belief in the rapture necessitate that Christians be pessimistic and apathetic? Certainly not! We are to be realistic and expectant. We are realistic about the future, and we are expectant about the coming of the Lord Jesus Christ for His church. However, we also acknowledge that once the rapture occurs there will be a time of intense worldwide torment.

The Bible has more to say about the tribulation than any other prophetic time period. During these seven years, the Antichrist will emerge, persecution of new Christians and the Jewish people will ensue, and the great battle of Armageddon and the second coming of Christ will transpire.

The New Testament teaches that the current church age will also include trials and tribulation. Jesus said, "In the world you have tribulation, but take courage; I have overcome the world" (John 16:33). The apostle Paul warned, "And indeed, all who desire to live godly in Christ Jesus will be persecuted" (2 Timothy 3:12). However, the world's persecution of the church in this age is not the wrath of God. The future tribulation will be a time of God's wrath upon a Christ-rejecting world—a time from which the church has been promised by our Lord to be exempted (Revelation 3:10; 1 Thessalonians 1:10; 5:9).

Christians can daily live in confidence that human history will end with Jesus Christ as the victor. The future is certain. Yet Jesus told His disciples that before the final victory "there will be a great tribulation, such as has not occurred since the beginning of the world until now, nor ever will" (Matthew 24:21). In its intensity and agony, it will be unfortunate and undesirable. But its certainty and course is not unforeseen or unpredicted. The Bible says that it will be tragic but true.

CHAPTER 12

What Is the Tribulation?

1. Where does the Bible teach about the tribulation?

Old Testament Passages

Throughout the Bible there are many direct and indirect references to the tribulation.[1] One of the first and earliest Old Testament passages to prophesy of this period is found in Deuteronomy 4:27-31. These verses foretell both the scattering of the Jews and their restoration with the Lord if they seek Him:

> And the LORD will scatter you among the peoples, and you shall be left few in number among the nations, where the LORD shall drive you. And there you will serve gods, the work of man's hands, wood and stone, which neither see nor hear nor eat nor smell. But from there you will seek the LORD your God, and you will find Him if you search for Him with all your heart and all your soul. When you are in distress and all these things have come upon you, in the latter days, you will return to the LORD your God and listen to His voice. For the LORD your God is a compassionate God; He will not fail you nor destroy you nor forget the covenant with your fathers which He swore to them.

Before Israel had set foot in their promised land, the Lord foretold an outline of their entire history (included in the book of Deuteronomy). Their destiny is said to be a time of "distress" or "tribulation" (KJV) "in the latter days" right before Israel "will return to the LORD your God and listen to His voice." Later in Deuteronomy, Moses expands upon this time of tribulation and notes that its purpose will include a time of retribution to the Gentiles for their ill-treatment of the Jews. Note Deuteronomy 30:7:

> And the LORD your God will inflict all these curses [Deuteronomy 28] on your enemies and on those who hate you, who persecuted you.

Continuing along the same line, Isaiah 26:20,21 notes that the tribulation includes the purpose of punishing the inhabitants of the earth for their sins. This passage also labels the tribulation an "indignation" from which Israel was to hide herself:

> Come, my people, enter into your rooms, and close your doors behind you; hide for a little while, until indignation runs its course. For behold, the LORD is about to come out from His place to punish the inhabitants of the earth for their iniquity; and the earth will reveal her bloodshed, and will no longer cover her slain.

Isaiah continues to describe the Lord's wrath and judgment of the tribulation on behalf of Israel in Isaiah 34:2,3,8:

> For the LORD's indignation is against all the nations, and His wrath against all their armies; He has utterly destroyed them, He has given them over to slaughter. So their slain will be thrown out, and their corpses will give off their stench, and the mountains will be drenched with their blood....For the LORD has a day of vengeance, a year of recompense for the cause of Zion.

In the preaching of Jeremiah there is also reference to the tribulation. Not only did Jeremiah predict the Babylonian captivity of the Jews, but he also foretold of a time of yet future trials for Israel. We read of this time in Jeremiah 30:5-9, which is often known as "the time of Jacob's trouble":

> For thus says the LORD, "I have heard a sound of terror, of dread, and there is no peace. Ask now, and see, if a male can give birth. Why do I see every man with his hands on his loins, as a woman in childbirth? And why have all faces turned pale? Alas! for that day is great, there is none like it; and it is the time of Jacob's distress, but he will be saved from it. And it shall come about on that day," declares the LORD of hosts, "that I will break his yoke from off their neck, and will tear off their bonds; and strangers shall no longer make them their slaves. But they shall serve the LORD their God, and David their king, whom I will raise up for them."

One of the most important passages for the study of the future is Daniel 9:24-27:

> Seventy weeks have been decreed for your people and your holy city, to finish the transgression, to make an end of sin, to make atonement for iniquity, to bring in everlasting righteousness, to seal up vision and prophecy, and to anoint the most holy place. So you are to know and discern that from the issuing of a decree to restore and rebuild Jerusalem until Messiah the Prince there will be seven weeks and sixty-two weeks; it will be built again, with plaza and moat, even in times of distress. Then after the sixty-two weeks the Messiah will be cut off and have nothing, and the people of the prince who is to come will destroy the city and the sanctuary. And its end will come with a flood; even to the end there will be war; desolations are determined. And he will make a firm covenant with the many for one week, but in the middle of the week he will put a stop to sacrifice and grain offering; and on the wing of abominations will come one who makes desolate, even until a complete destruction, one that is decreed, is poured out on the one who makes desolate.

In these four verses Daniel provides a clear and concise framework for prophetic study. This is a critical passage. A proper understanding of these verses provides students of prophecy with scriptural signposts. From this passage we learn that the tribulation is a seven-year period, divided by the "abomination of desolation" into two three-and-a-half-year periods. Since Daniel's 70 weeks are 70 weeks of years, the final week of years (i.e., the tribulation) would thus be a seven-year period. Note the diagram "Daniel's Seventy Weeks" on page 132 for further details and explanations.

Like Jeremiah, Daniel calls this future period "a time of distress." In Daniel 12:1, this time is described not just as "a time of distress," but also as a time when Israel "will be rescued":

> Now at that time Michael, the great prince who stands guard over the sons of your people, will arise. And there will be a time of distress such as never occurred since there was a nation until that time; and at that

> time your people, everyone who is found written in the book, will be rescued.

The whole book of Joel is about "the day of the Lord," which is a synonym for "the tribulation." Notice a couple of citations from Joel which refer to the tribulation:

> Alas for the day! For the day of the LORD is near, and it will come as destruction from the Almighty (1:15).

> Blow a trumpet in Zion, and sound an alarm on My holy mountain! Let all the inhabitants of the land tremble, for the day of the LORD is coming; surely it is near, a day of darkness and gloom, a day of clouds and thick darkness. As the dawn is spread over the mountains, so there is a great and mighty people; there has never been anything like it, nor will there be again after it to the years of many generations (2:1,2).

The prophet Amos, a shepherd from the Judean town of Tekoa, also prophesied about the tribulation in Amos 5:18-20:

> Alas, you who are longing for the day of the LORD, for what purpose will the day of the LORD be to you? It will be darkness and not light; as when a man flees from a lion, and a bear meets him, or goes home, leans his hand against the wall, and a snake bites him. Will not the day of the LORD be darkness instead of light, even gloom with no brightness in it?

Even though Zephaniah is one of the shortest books in the Bible, one of the most important passages relating to the tribulation is found there. The Lord, through Zephaniah, just about exhausts the thesaurus as He pours out a vivid description of the tribulation in chapter 1:14-18:

> Near is the great day of the LORD, near and coming very quickly; listen, the day of the LORD! In it the warrior cries out bitterly. A day of wrath is that day, a day of trouble and distress, a day of destruction and desolation, a day of darkness and gloom, a day of clouds and thick darkness, a day of trumpet and battle cry, against the fortified cities and the high corner towers. And I will bring distress on men, so that they will walk

like the blind, because they have sinned against the
LORD; and their blood will be poured out like dust, and
their flesh like dung. Neither their silver nor their gold
will be able to deliver them on the day of the LORD's
wrath; and all the earth will be devoured in the fire of
His jealousy, for He will make a complete end, indeed a
terrifying one, of all the inhabitants of the earth.

Some other Old Testament prophecies of this era include Joel
2:28-32 and Isaiah 2:12-22; 24.

New Testament Passages

The New Testament, building upon an Old Testament foundation, expands our picture of the tribulation. The first extended passage to deal with the tribulation in the New Testament is Matthew
24:4-28 (see also Mark 13; Luke 17:22-37; and Luke 21:5-36 for parallel passages). In this discourse, Jesus describes for the disciples the
tribulation period. In verses 4-14, He speaks about the first half of
the tribulation, and, in verses 15-28, He describes the second half
leading up to the second coming. According to Jesus, the tribulation
will be intense and extensive and will include both human and natural disasters. Of the first three-and-a-half years He says:

See to it that no one misleads you. For many will come
in My name, saying, "I am the Christ," and will mislead
many. And you will be hearing of wars and rumors of
wars; see that you are not frightened, for those things
must take place, but that is not yet the end. For nation
will rise against nation, and kingdom against kingdom,
and in various places there will be famines and earthquakes. But all these things are merely the beginning
of birth pangs. Then they will deliver you to tribulation, and will kill you, and you will be hated by all
nations on account of My name. And at that time many
will fall away and will deliver up one another and hate
one another. And many false prophets will arise, and
will mislead many. And because lawlessness is
increased, most people's love will grow cold. But the
one who endures to the end, he shall be saved. And
this gospel of the kingdom shall be preached in the

whole world for a witness to all the nations, and then
the end shall come (Matthew 24:4-14).

Jesus then told the disciples that the second half of the tribulation would be no better than the first half. In fact, the trauma and
suffering would escalate to such a point that it would end only after
the battle of Armageddon and the second coming of Christ:

> Therefore when you see the ABOMINATION OF DESOLA-
> TION which was spoken of through Daniel the prophet,
> standing in the holy place (let the reader understand),
> then let those who are in Judea flee to the mountains;
> let him who is on the housetop not go down to get the
> things out that are in his house; and let him who is in
> the field not turn back to get his cloak. But woe to
> those who are with child and to those who nurse babes
> in those days! But pray that your flight may not be in
> the winter, or on a Sabbath; for then there will be a
> great tribulation, such as has not occurred since the
> beginning of the world until now, nor ever shall. And
> unless those days had been cut short, no life would
> have been saved; but for the sake of the elect those
> days shall be cut short. Then if anyone says to you,
> "Behold, here is the Christ," or "There He is," do not
> believe him. For false Christs and false prophets will
> arise and will show great signs and wonders, so as to
> mislead, if possible, even the elect. Behold, I have told
> you in advance. If therefore they say to you, "Behold,
> He is in the wilderness," do not go forth, or, "Behold,
> He is in the inner rooms," do not believe them. For just
> as the lightning comes from the east, and flashes even
> to the west, so shall the coming of the Son of Man be.
> Wherever the corpse is, there the vultures will gather.

Paul's Thessalonian epistles have been characterized as the
Pauline Apocalypse, since they deal extensively with the prophetic.
Twice—in 1 Thessalonians 1:10 and 5:9—Paul refers to the tribula-
tion when speaking of a future time of wrath (see also Romans 5:9):

> ...and to wait for His Son from heaven, whom He
> raised from the dead, that is Jesus, who delivers us
> from the wrath to come.

> For God has not destined us for wrath, but for obtaining salvation through our Lord Jesus Christ.

In 2 Thessalonians 2:1,2, Paul tells his readers that they should not be deceived into thinking that the tribulation (i.e., the day of the Lord) had already started:

> Now we request you, brethren, with regard to the coming of our Lord Jesus Christ, and our gathering together to Him, that you may not be quickly shaken from your composure or be disturbed either by a spirit or a message or a letter as if from us, to the effect that the day of the Lord has come.

He then continues in verses 3-13 to further describe some of the events of the tribulation era:

> Let no one in any way deceive you, for it will not come unless the apostasy comes first, and the man of lawlessness is revealed, the son of destruction, who opposes and exalts himself above every so-called god or object of worship, so that he takes his seat in the temple of God, displaying himself as being God. Do you not remember that while I was still with you, I was telling you these things? And you know what restrains him now, so that in his time he may be revealed. For the mystery of lawlessness is already at work; only he who now restrains will do so until he is taken out of the way. And then that lawless one will be revealed whom the Lord will slay with the breath of His mouth and bring to an end by the appearance of His coming; that is, the one whose coming is in accord with the activity of Satan, with all power and signs and false wonders, and with all the deception of wickedness for those who perish, because they did not receive the love of the truth so as to be saved. And for this reason God will send upon them a deluding influence so that they might believe what is false, in order that they all may be judged who did not believe the truth, but took pleasure in wickedness. But we should always give thanks to God for you, brethren beloved by the Lord, because God has chosen you from the beginning for salvation

through sanctification by the Spirit and faith in the
truth.

The most extensive biblical comments on the tribulation are
found in the writings of John, specifically in Revelation 6–19. In
these chapters, John provides a detailed exposition of the tribulation
days. An example of John's specific mention of the tribulation can be
seen in Revelation 7:14:

> And I said to him, "My lord, you know." And he said to
> me, "These are the ones who come out of the great
> tribulation, and they have washed their robes and
> made them white in the blood of the Lamb."

These chapters in Revelation are rich in both imagery and content and leave little doubt in the reader's mind regarding the crisis
that is yet to come.

2. Is the great tribulation the same as the tribulation?

We believe the Bible distinguishes between the tribulation
period (7 years) and the great tribulation (the final 3½ years). In
Matthew 24:9 the term *tribulation* most likely refers to the full
seven-year period of the tribulation. On the other hand, Matthew
24:21 speaks of the "great tribulation," which begins with the abomination of desolation, that takes place at the midpoint of the seven-
year period (Matthew 24:15).

In Matthew 24:15-20, Jesus told His disciples that after the midpoint of the tribulation, Antichrist will break his covenant with
Israel. Following this there will be an increase in persecution, "For
then there will be a great tribulation, such as has not occurred since
the beginning of the world until now, nor ever shall" (Matthew
24:21).

Is the phrase "great tribulation" a technical phrase referring to
the last three-and-a-half years of the tribulation, or is it simply a
descriptive term for those years? The Bible clearly teaches two segments, but does it label them differently? In other words, does the
Bible itself label the first three-and-a-half years as "the tribulation"
and the second three-and-a-half years as "the great tribulation," or
are the terms "tribulation" and "great tribulation" synonyms for the
entire seven-year era?

Premillennial pretribulational interpreters are divided on how this term is used in the Bible. However, *there is no doctrinal orthodoxy or major interpretive issue at stake for whichever view is taken.* For either view, the basic seven-year, two-segment tribulation remains. What changes is how those two segments of three-and-a-half years are labeled. In a formula format, some understand

> seven-year tribulation (3½ years + 3½ years) = great tribulation (3½ years + 3½ years)

and others understand

> seven-year tribulation (3½ years + 3½ years) = tribulation (3½ years) + great tribulation (3½ years).

Regardless of the view taken, *both have a seven-year tribulation with two parts, and both recognize an increase in intensity during the last three-and-a-half years.*

3. How does "the time of God's wrath" relate to the tribulation?

It appears that "the time of God's wrath" and "the tribulation" encompass the same seven-year time period. How is that so?

Since the Bible uses many terms to describe a wide range of activities associated with God's judgment during the tribulation, and since "tribulation" and "God's wrath" are sometimes used to refer to the same time period (i.e., the seven-year tribulation), then it follows that the time of God's wrath takes place during the tribulation.

Scriptural support can be provided for the above conclusion by the following: We have seen that Deuteronomy 4:30 describes this latter-day time period as a time of tribulation. Zephaniah 1:15 calls this same day "of trouble and distress" (i.e., tribulation) "a day of wrath." New Testament writers pick up this Old Testament term and use it as an overall characteristic of what we know as the seven-year tribulation period, since it is a time when God's stored-up wrath breaks loose within human history and moves to repay a Christ-rejecting world, which will be motivated by Satan to act in persecuting Christians and Jews (Romans 2:5; 5:9; Colossians 3:6; Revelation 14:10,19; 15:1,7; 16:1,19; 19:15). For example, Romans 2:5 says,

> But because of your stubbornness and unrepentant
> heart you are storing up wrath for yourself in the day
> of wrath and revelation of the righteous judgment of
> God.

Thus we see that what is experienced as tribulation by mankind is said in the Bible to be motivated by the wrath of God, which is shown to be building up during this current age of grace.

4. How do Daniel's 70 weeks relate to the tribulation?

Daniel's 70 weeks, prophesied in Daniel 9:24-27, are the framework within which the tribulation (the seventieth week) occurs.[2] The seven-year period of Daniel's seventieth week provides the time span to which a whole host of descriptives are associated. Some of those descriptive terms include: tribulation, great tribulation, day of the Lord, day of wrath, day of distress, day of trouble, time of Jacob's trouble, day of darkness and gloom, wrath of the Lamb. The graphic presentation of the 70 weeks on page 132 assists greatly in understanding this intricate prophecy.

The chart of Daniel's 70 weeks presents a premillennial pretribulational perspective. That is, it shows the rapture occurring before the tribulation and the second coming of Christ before the millennium. Although not all evangelicals hold to a pretribulational rapture (favoring instead a midtribulational or posttribulation view), there is agreement that the Antichrist will arise during the tribulation. He may be known, recognized, or even in power before the rapture, but he will only be revealed or manifested as Antichrist during the tribulation (2 Thessalonians 2:6,8).

Explanation of Daniel's 70 Weeks of Years

$$69 \times 7 \times 360 = 173,880 \text{ days}$$
March 5, 444 B.C. + 173,880 = March 30, A.D. 33

Verification

444 B.C. to A.D. 33 = 476 years
476 years × 365.2421989 days = 173,855 days
+ days between March 5 and March 30 = 25 days
Total = 173,880 days

Rationale for 360-Day Years

Half week—Daniel 9:27
Time, times, and half a time—Daniel 7:25; 12:7; Revelation 12:14
1260 days—Revelation 12:6; 11:3
42 months—Revelation 11:2; 13:5
Thus: 42 months = 1260 days = time, times, and half a time + half week
Therefore: month = 30 days; year = 360 days[3]

After Christ returns and removes the church from the earth, the Antichrist will ascend to power and, as the "little horn" spoken of in Daniel 7:24,25, will lead a 10-nation confederation of western powers during the tribulation years. The Antichrist's future reign is certain, but it will not commence until after the rapture occurs and the tribulation begins.

5. How does the "day of the Lord" relate to the tribulation?

The Bible uses the term "day of the Lord" to refer to the same general time period as the tribulation. This was seen earlier in Zephaniah 1:14,15 in which both terms were used to describe different aspects of the same time span.

From God's perspective, this time will be the day of the Lord. It will be a time dominated by and directly under the control of God. No longer will the Lord control history indirectly through invisible means; during this time He will visibly intervene in human history. Divine intervention then produces, from the human perspective, a time of tribulation to be endured, if possible. Thus, the relationship is that of different perspectives of the same time period.

6. How does "the time of Jacob's trouble" relate to the tribulation?

The phrase "the time of Jacob's trouble" (KJV), or "the time of Jacob's distress" (NASB), comes from the prophecy found in Jeremiah 30:5-7:

> For thus says the LORD, "I have heard a sound of terror, of dread, and there is no peace. Ask now, and see, if a male can give birth. Why do I see every man with his

Daniel's Seventy Weeks
(Daniel 9:21-27)

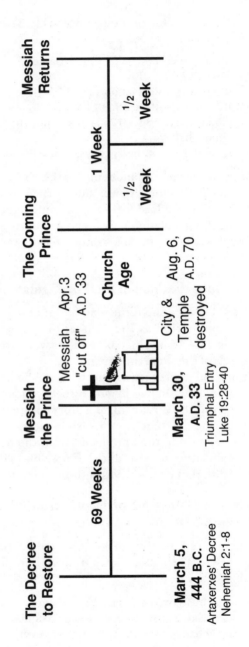

hands on his loins, as a woman in childbirth? And why have all faces turned pale? Alas! for that day is great, there is none like it; and it is the time of Jacob's distress, but he will be saved from it."

In this passage the prophet Jeremiah speaks of a future time when great distress or tribulation will come upon all Israel (symbolically referred to as "Jacob"). Is this time the same as the coming tribulation, or is it an event already past? It is best to understand this time of distress as something that is yet future for Israel—a time which we know as the seventieth week of Daniel or the tribulation. Biblical expositor and prophecy scholar Dr. Charles H. Dyer writes of this passage and its meaning:

> To what "time of trouble" was Jeremiah referring? Some have felt that he was pointing to the coming fall of Judah to Babylon or to the later fall of Babylon to Medo-Persia. However, in both of these periods the Northern Kingdom of Israel was not affected. It had already gone into captivity (in 722 B.C.). A better solution is to see Jeremiah referring to the still-future Tribulation period when the remnant of Israel and Judah will experience a time of unparalleled persecution (Daniel 9:27; 12:1; Matthew 24:15-22). The period will end when Christ appears to rescue His elect (Romans 11:26) and establish His kingdom (Matthew 24:30-31; 25:31-46; Revelation 19:11-21; 20:4-6).[4]

Thus, the time of Jacob's trouble emphasizes that aspect of the future tribulation which focuses upon the difficulty that Jews or the descendants of Jacob will experience during this time.

7. How does the kingdom of God relate to the tribulation?

While all Bible students generally agree that God always has and will rule spiritually over His creation, this "spiritual" rule is to be distinguished in Scripture from the kingdom of God. Dr. Stanley Toussaint notes that the kingdom of God is "a kingdom that is earthly and literal, and is the fulfillment of the Old Testament promises, covenants, and prophetic predictions for Israel."[5] In other words, the kingdom of God is the future Davidic kingdom, also known as the 1,000-year millennium (Revelation 20:2-8).

Having already noted that the tribulation is the seven-year period of our Lord's judgment, how does it relate to the kingdom of God? The tribulation is the judgment phase which prepares the way for the righteous rule of Christ from Jerusalem. Christ must clean up this sinful world before He commences His 1,000-year righteous kingdom.

8. How do "birth pangs" relate to the tribulation?

In Matthew 24:4-7, Jesus describes for the disciples some of the beginning signs of the tribulation. He then states in verse 8, "But all these things are merely the beginning of birth pangs." In the following verses (24:9-28), Jesus continues with a description of the tribulation years. In Jeremiah 30:5-7, the same imagery of childbirth and intense suffering and expectation is used. In these verses God speaks through the prophet:

> Ask now, and see, if a male can give birth. Why do I see every man with his hands on his loins, as a woman in childbirth?...Alas! for that day is great, there is none like it.

In this passage, Jeremiah is looking to a time beyond the judgment that was soon to fall on his people. He was referring to the tribulation era. Dr. Randall Price writes of this passage and its imagery:

> On the one hand, the figure is applied to the experience of tribulation because its application to males or to the nation of Israel is tantamount to reducing them to the helpless state of women at the time of birth, something every army hoped their enemy would become (cf. Jeremiah 50:37). On the other hand, the involuntary and uncontrollable nature of birth pangs, as well as their intensification leading ultimately to divine deliverance, well pictured the concept of a time of divine judgment that must run its course until the promise of new life could be experienced.[6]

When Jesus spoke of birth pangs in Matthew 24:8, the imagery used was very clearly that of Jeremiah and other Old Testament prophets. He is saying that the tribulation will be like the intense pain of a woman in childbirth. The pain will be great, but it will end, and with its cessation will come a new era. Note again the comments of Dr. Price:

> The birth pangs are significant in the timing of the Tribulation, as revealed by Jesus in the Olivet discourse (Matthew 24:8). Jesus' statement of the "birth pangs" is specifically that the events of the first half of the Tribulation (vv. 4-7) are merely the "beginning," with the expectation of greater birth pangs in the second half (the "Great Tribulation"). Based on this analogy, the entire period of the seventieth week is like birth pangs. As a woman must endure the entire period of labor before giving birth, so Israel must endure the entire seven-year Tribulation. The time divisions of Tribulation are also illustrated by the figure, for just as the natural process intensifies toward delivery after labor ends, so here the Tribulation moves progressively toward the second advent (vv. 30-31), which takes place "immediately after" the Tribulation ends (v. 29). As there are two phases of the birth pangs (beginning labor and full labor), so the seven years of Tribulation are divided between the less severe and more severe experiences of terrestrial and cosmic wrath, as revealed progressively in the Olivet discourse and the judgment section of Revelation 6–19.[7]

9. How does the Holy Spirit relate to the tribulation?

When believers are raptured just prior to the tribulation (1 Thessalonians 4:16,17) the indwelling presence of the Holy Spirit will also be removed. We see this in 2 Thessalonians 2:6-8 where Paul writes that once the Holy Spirit as a restrainer is removed from the earth, the "man of lawlessness" (Antichrist) will be free to initiate his program:

> And you know what restrains him now, so that in his time he may be revealed. For the mystery of lawlessness is already at work; only he who now restrains will do so until he is taken out of the way. And then that lawless one will be revealed whom the Lord will slay with the breath of His mouth and bring to an end by the appearance of His coming.

That the Holy Spirit, resident in the church, is the restrainer is supported by the fact that it would take God Himself (in this case, the third person of the Trinity) to restrain the Antichrist. Dr. Robert Thomas explains:

> To one familiar with the Lord Jesus' Upper Room Discourse, as Paul undoubtedly was, fluctuation between neuter and masculine recalls how the Holy Spirit is spoken of. Either gender is appropriate, depending on whether the speaker (or writer) thinks of natural agreement (masc. because of the Spirit's personality) or grammatical (neuter because of the noun *pneuma;* see John 14:26; 15:26; 16:13,14).... The special presence of the Spirit as the indweller of saints will terminate abruptly at the *parousia* as it began abruptly at Pentecost. Once the body of Christ has been caught away to heaven, the Spirit's ministry will revert back to what he did for believers during the OT period. His function of restraining evil through the body of Christ (John 16:7-11; 1 John 4:4) will cease similarly to the way he terminated his striving in the days of Noah (Genesis 6:3). At that point the reins will be removed from lawlessness and the Satanically inspired rebellion will begin. It appears that *to katechon* ("what is holding back") was well known at Thessalonica as a title for the Holy Spirit on whom the readers had come to depend in their personal attempts to combat lawlessness (1 Thessalonians 1:6; 4:8; 5:19; 2 Thessalonians 2:13).[8]

The teaching in these verses does not mean, however, that the ministry of the Holy Spirit will be absent during the tribulation. The Holy Spirit will continue to minister, but it will be a much different ministry than Christians experience today. Dr. Ryrie notes, "Just as the omnipresent Spirit worked in behalf of men in Old Testament times, so He will continue to work after the rapture of the Church, even though His work of building the Body of Christ will be finished."[9]

What will be the nature of this ministry and to whom will it be given? In relation to unbelievers, the Spirit will continue to work in bringing about conviction of sin and, in the process, of salvation.

There will be many men and women, Jews and Gentiles, who become Christians during the tribulation, and the Holy Spirit will be active in their salvation (Zechariah 12:10; 13:1; Romans 11:25,26; Revelation 7:9-17). At the beginning of the tribulation, God will seal 144,000 Jewish witnesses, and this sealing entails their salvation and therefore the work of the Spirit (Revelation 7:3,4; 14:4).

According to Acts 2:16-21, which cites Joel 2:28-32 and was partially fulfilled at the day of Pentecost, "EVERYONE WHO CALLS ON THE NAME OF THE LORD WILL BE SAVED." Such a prophetic promise must include the work and ministry of the Holy Spirit. Dr. Walvoord says of this work:

> In view of the natural blindness of the human heart, and the inability of the natural man to understand the gospel sufficiently to believe, apart from the convicting work of the Holy Spirit (John 16:7-11), it must be assumed that there is a continued work of the Holy Spirit in revealing to the lost the way of salvation. This ministry of the Holy Spirit is especially needed in the spiritual darkness which will characterize the tribulation period. We can expect that there will be mighty conviction, especially among Israel, that Christ is indeed the Savior and the Messiah.[10]

Not only will the Holy Spirit be active in relation to unbelievers, but the Spirit will also work in the lives of those who become Christians. While there are few verses from which to discern the complete scope of the Spirit's ministry, it is clear that there will be ministry to believers. There will be preaching of the gospel throughout the world (Matthew 24:14), and many believers will be martyred for their faith. Walvoord notes that "the spiritual victory achieved by the martyrs to the faith in the tribulation could hardly be accomplished apart from the spiritual enablement of the Holy Spirit. The general phenomena of the tribulation make any sort of spiritual achievement unthinkable apart from the power of God."[11]

The ministry to believers will probably be similar to that experienced by some Old Testament saints. Since the Spirit will be removed (2 Thessalonians 2:7), the possibility of a universal indwelling of believers seems unlikely. There will instead be selective indwelling and empowerment to evangelize. Walvoord notes again:

The tribulation period, also, seems to revert back to
Old Testament conditions in several ways; and in the
Old Testament period, saints were never permanently
indwelt except in isolated instances, though a number
of instances of the filling of the Spirit and of empower-
ing for service are found. Taking all the factors into
consideration, there is no evidence for the indwelling
presence of the Holy Spirit in believers in the tribulation.[12]

CHAPTER 13

Can the Antichrist Be Identified?

10. Who is the Antichrist?

The reality of a future leader known as the Antichrist is well attested in the Bible; no serious reader of the Bible can deny his existence. He is more than a symbol of evil or an impersonal force—his entire existence and being opposes the plan of God and the Son of God.

Glimpses of the person and work of the Antichrist are found in both the Old and New Testaments. Although there are many allusions and references to him, two major sections of Scripture focus on the Antichrist: Daniel 7–9 (especially 7:8,24-27 and 9:26,27), and Revelation 10–13 (especially 13:1-10). He is also mentioned in 2 Thessalonians 2:3,4,8 and 1 John 2:18. In Matthew 24, Jesus taught His disciples about the Antichrist. In verses 24:15 and 16, Jesus refers to Daniel 9:27; 11:31; and 12:11, and says, "Therefore when you see the ABOMINATION OF DESOLATION which was spoken of through Daniel the prophet, standing in the holy place...then let those who are in Judea flee to the mountains." (See also Mark 13:14.)

As we might expect from a book filled with prophetic teaching, there are many references to the Antichrist throughout Revelation. John mentions him repeatedly in Revelation: 6:2; 13:1-10; 14:9,11; 15:2; 16:2; 17:3,13; 19:19,20; 20:10. The authors of the biblical text are very clear on his existence and nature—he will be a real person who will manipulate and destroy many people.

The Bible rarely uses the title "Antichrist." However, the apostle John uses the term "antichrist" and "antichrists" in 1 John 2:18,22; 4:3, and 2 John 7. He writes in 1 John 2:18,22:

> Children, it is the last hour; and just as you heard that antichrist is coming, even now many antichrists have arisen; from this we know that it is the last hour....Who is the liar but the one who denies that Jesus is the Christ? This is the antichrist, the one who denies the Father and the Son.

With the exception of 1 John 2:18, a study of each of these passages shows that John is not referring to the Antichrist (which he usually calls "the beast"), but rather to the denial of the person of Christ by contemporaries of his readers. They were like the Antichrist in *kind* but not in *magnitude*. Ultimately, there will only be one Antichrist, but there have been, are, and will be many who are Antichrist-like—who disdain the message of Christianity or teach false doctrine. They live and function in opposition to the gospel of Jesus Christ and therefore represent *in part* that which will be fully manifested in the Antichrist.

11. What other names and titles does he have?

Antichrist

Except for 1 John 2:22, the Bible never specifically refers to this coming leader as *the Antichrist. Antichrist* has been used by students of prophecy throughout church history. It is clearly an appropriate term, for it captures the essence of the person and work of this individual. A.W. Pink says:

> At every point he is the antithesis of Christ. The word "Antichrist" has a double significance. Its primary meaning is one who is *opposed* to Christ; but its secondary meaning is one who is *instead* of Christ....

> Not only does *anti*-christ denote the antagonist of Christ, but it tells of one who is instead of Christ. The word signifies another Christ, a pro-Christ, an *alter christus,* a pretender to the name of Christ. He will seem to be and will set himself up as the true Christ. He will be the Devil's counterfeit.[13]

Scripture does, however, use other titles and phrases to describe and identify him. Among his many and more prominent identifications are the following:

Biblical Titles

- *the little horn:* "While I was contemplating the horns, behold, another horn, a little one, came up among them, and three of the first horns were pulled out by the roots before it; and behold, this horn possessed eyes like the eyes of a man, and a mouth uttering great boasts" (Daniel 7:8).

- *the insolent king:* "In the latter period of their rule, when the transgressors have run their course, a king will arise, insolent and skilled in intrigue" (Daniel 8:23).

- *the prince who is to come:* "Then after the sixty-two weeks the Messiah will be cut off and have nothing, and the people of the prince who is to come will destroy the city and the sanctuary" (Daniel 9:26a).

- *the one who makes desolate; abomination of desolation:* "...on the wing of abominations will come one who makes desolate..." (Daniel 9:27).

  "Therefore when you see the ABOMINATION OF DESOLATION which was spoken of through Daniel the prophet..." (Matthew 24:15).

- *the man of lawlessness:* "Let no one in any way deceive you, for it will not come unless the apostasy comes first, and the man of lawlessness is revealed..." (2 Thessalonians 2:3).

- *the son of destruction:* "...unless the apostasy comes first, and the man of lawlessness is revealed, the son of destruction" (2 Thessalonians 2:3).

- *the lawless one:* "Then that lawless one will be revealed whom the Lord will slay with the breath of His mouth and bring to an end by the appearance of His coming" (2 Thessalonians 2:8).

- *the beast:* "When they have finished their testimony, the beast that comes up out of the abyss will make war with them, and overcome them and kill them" (Revelation 11:7; see also 13:1; 14:9; 15:2; 16:2; 17:3,13; 19:20; 20:10).

- *the despicable person:* "And in his place a despicable person will arise, on whom the honor of kingship has not been conferred, but he will come in a time of tranquility and seize the kingdom by intrigue" (Daniel 11:21).

- *the strong-willed king:* "Then the king will do as he pleases, and he will exalt and magnify himself above every god, and will speak monstrous things against the God of gods; and he will prosper until the indignation is finished, for that which is decreed will be done" (Daniel 11:36).

- *the worthless shepherd:* "For behold, I am going to raise up a shepherd in the land who will not care for the perishing, seek the scattered, heal the broken, or sustain the one standing, but will devour the flesh of the fat sheep and tear off their hoofs. Woe to the worthless shepherd who leaves the flock! A sword will be on his arm and on his right eye! His arm will be totally withered, and his right eye will be blind" (Zechariah 11:16,17).

Counterfeit Christ and Messiah

Some have noted that Satan has never originated anything, except sin; he has always counterfeited God's actions. The Antichrist is no exception. He is Satan's human masterpiece—a false Messiah and forged representation of Jesus who is the true Messiah.

Although the Antichrist will counterfeit many aspects of God's plan, none will be more blatant than his attempt to replace worship of Christ with worship of himself. He will accomplish this through many counterfeit acts:

Building a Temple[14]

Christ: Then say to him, "Thus says the LORD of hosts, 'Behold, a man whose name is Branch, for He will branch out from where He is; and He will build the temple of the LORD'" (Zechariah 6:12).

Antichrist: ...the man of lawlessness is revealed, the son of destruction, who opposes and exalts himself above every so-called god or object of worship, so that he takes his seat in the temple of God, displaying himself as being God (2 Thessalonians 2:3,4).

Making a Peace Covenant

Christ: And I will make a covenant of peace with them; it will be an everlasting covenant with them. And I will place them and multiply them, and will set My sanctuary in their midst forever (Ezekiel 37:26).

Antichrist: And he will make a firm covenant with the many for one week, but in the middle of the week he will put a stop to sacrifice and grain offering; and on the wing of abominations will come one who makes desolate, even until a complete destruction, one that is decreed, is poured out on the one who makes desolate (Daniel 9:27).

Consecration of the Temple

Christ: "And I will shake all the nations; and they will come with the wealth of all nations; and I will fill this house with glory," says the LORD of hosts. "The silver is Mine, and the gold is Mine," declares the LORD of hosts. "The latter glory of this house will be greater than the former," says the LORD of hosts, "and in this place I shall give peace," declares the LORD of hosts (Haggai 2:7-9).

Antichrist: ...the man of lawlessness is revealed, the son of destruction, who opposes and exalts himself above every so-called god or object of worship, so that he takes his seat in the temple of God, displaying himself as being God (2 Thessalonians 2:3,4).

Battle for Israel

Christ: For I will gather all the nations against Jerusalem to battle, and the city will be captured, the houses plundered, the women ravished, and half of the city exiled, but the rest of the people will not be cut off from the city. Then the LORD will go forth and fight against those nations, as when He fights on a day of battle (Zechariah 14:2,3).

Antichrist: And it was given to him to make war with the saints and to overcome them; and authority over every tribe and people and tongue and nation was given to him (Revelation 13:7).

A Temple Presence

Christ: Then I heard one speaking to me from the house, while a man was standing beside me. And He said to me, "Son of man, this is the place of My throne and the place of the soles of My feet, where I will dwell among the sons of Israel forever. And the house of Israel will not again defile My holy name, neither they nor their kings, by their harlotry and by the corpses of their kings when they die" (Ezekiel 43:6,7).

"Behold, I am going to send My messenger, and he will clear the way before Me. And the Lord, whom you seek, will suddenly come to His temple; and the messenger of the covenant, in whom you delight, behold, He is coming," says the LORD of hosts" (Malachi 3:1).

Antichrist: And he will make a firm covenant with the many for one week, but in the middle of the week he will put a stop to sacrifice and grain offering; and on the wing of abominations will come one who makes desolate, even until a complete destruction, one that is decreed, is poured out on the one who makes desolate (Daniel 9:27).

Therefore when you see the ABOMINATION OF DESOLATION which was spoken of through Daniel the prophet, standing in the holy place (let the reader understand) (Matthew 24:15).

The man of lawlessness is revealed, the son of destruction, who opposes and exalts himself above every so-called god or object of worship, so that he takes his seat in the temple of God, displaying himself as being God (2 Thessalonians 2:3,4).

Universal Rule of Peace

Christ: And I will cut off the chariot from Ephraim, and the horse from Jerusalem; and the bow of war will be cut off. And He will speak peace to the nations; and His dominion will be from sea to sea, and from the River to the ends of the earth (Zechariah 9:10).

Antichrist: While they are saying, "Peace and safety!" then destruction will come upon them suddenly like birth pangs upon a woman with child; and they shall not escape (1 Thessalonians 5:3).

The New Testament pictures three satanic persons, often called the "satanic trinity" because of their efforts at counterfeiting God and His plan. These three are Satan, corresponding to God the Father; the Antichrist, juxtaposed to God the Son—Jesus Christ; and the false prophet, who corresponds to God the Holy Spirit.

PROPHECY WATCH

The Antichrist and the false prophet are different individuals. The false prophet "ministers in connection with the first beast as his prophet or spokesman"[15] (see Revelation 16:13; 19:20; 20:10). Revelation 13:11-17 states that the false prophet shares the beastly nature of the Antichrist and he is called another beast:

> And I saw another beast coming up out of the earth; and he had two horns like a lamb, and he spoke as a dragon. And he exercises all the authority of the first beast in his presence. And he makes the earth and those who dwell in it to worship the first beast, whose fatal wound was healed. And he performs great signs, so that he even makes fire come down out of heaven to the earth in the presence of men. And he deceives those who dwell on the earth because of the signs which it was given him to perform in the presence of the beast, telling those who dwell on the earth to make an image to the beast who had the wound of the sword and has come to life. And there was given to him to give breath to the image of the beast, that the image of the beast might even speak and cause as many as do not worship the image of the beast to be killed. And he causes all, the small and the great, and the rich and the poor, and the free men and the slaves, to be given a mark on their right hand, or on their forehead, and he provides that no one should be able to buy or to sell, except the one who has the mark, either the name of the beast or the number of his name.

Dr. Pentecost summarizes the person and activities of the false prophet in 11 works:

1. He is a Jew arising out of the earth, e.g. Palestine (13:11).

2. He is religiously influential (13:11).

3. He is motivated by Satan (13:11).

4. He has a delegated authority (13:12).

5. He promotes worship of the first beast (13:12).

6. He performs signs and miracles (13:13-14).

7. He deceives the unbelieving world (13:14).

8. He promotes idolatrous worship (13:14-15).

9. He has the power of death over people who do not worship the beast (13:15).

10. He has great economic power (13:16-17).

11. He will establish the mark of the beast (13:17).[16]

The false prophet works in conjunction with the Antichrist, who not only represents the epitome of human evil, but will also be the personification of human and satanic evil. The somber remembrance of the Holocaust should be warning enough to those who doubt the future potential of the Antichrist. He may be unknown, but his work is not unimaginable.

Many attempts have been made to identify, label, and describe the Antichrist. Much of this, though finding its source in the biblical text, has diverged significantly from the Bible. Indeed, *any* document or teaching about the Antichrist which places him in events now past is biblically incorrect.

Our own century has brought such leaders as Mussolini, Hitler, Stalin, Gorbachev, Hussein, and many others under the lens of prophetic teachers and soothsayers—some carefully attempting to apply Scripture, some not. Yet, as destructive as these twentieth-century leaders were, none were the final enemy. Misidentifications of the Antichrist throughout church history should be a lesson to contemporary students of prophecy. *Biblical prophecy must be interpreted consistently and carefully, always maintaining a futurist perspective.*

What is perhaps most significant is the *belief* in the person and work of the Antichrist. Although many Christians have been wrong in their identification, *they were not wrong in their anticipation.*

12. What is the nationality of the Antichrist?

A widely held belief throughout the history of the church and today has been the notion that the Antichrist will be of Jewish origin. However, upon closer examination, we find no scriptural basis for such a view.

Arguments for Jewish Origin

Three reasons are often given in support of the argument that Antichrist will be Jewish.[17] First, it is argued that he will be a Jew since the Jews are responsible for the world's problems. Thus, it follows that the greatest problem of history—Antichrist—will also be Jewish. This is the anti-Semitic reason. Since we do not have enough space to give an in-depth refutation of anti-Semitism, suffice it to say that anti-Semitism is unbiblical, and so is any logic that reasons upon such a premise.

Dr. Arnold Fruchtenbaum offers a refutation of the second reason, which he calls "The Logical Reason." He writes:

> Stated in a syllogism, this argument goes as follows:
>
> Major Premise: The Jews will accept the Antichrist as the Messiah.
>
> Minor Premise: The Jews will never accept a Gentile as the Messiah.
>
> Conclusion: The Antichrist will be a Jew.[18]

The difficulties of this argument are many, not the least of which are the two premises. Neither premise can be supported from the Bible. Just because the Jews make a covenant with the Antichrist (Daniel 9:27), it does not follow either textually or logically that they accept him as Messiah (or Antichrist). Second, since they are not accepting him as Messiah, the fact that he is a Gentile peacemaker is irrelevant. Thus, the conclusion does not follow.

An attempt at a scriptural argument reasons that Antichrist will spring forth from the tribe of Dan. Support for this view is inappropriately derived from Genesis 49:17; Deuteronomy 33:22; Jeremiah 8:16; Daniel 11:37; and Revelation 7:4-8. Even though many passages are cited in support of this argument, none of them actually support the notion because they are taken out of context. In reality, only Daniel 11:37 refers to the Antichrist. Even though some people believe that the phrase in Daniel 11:37 "the God of his fathers" (KJV), implies a Jewish apostasy, the phrase is more accurately translated "the gods of his fathers" (NASB). Since Antichrist will be a Gentile, as we will show, the argument is unfounded. Since the original Hebrew supports the NASB translation and not the KJV, Antichrist's apostasy will be Christian and not Jewish.[19]

Arguments for a Gentile Origin

We have seen that the Bible does not teach that Antichrist will be Jewish; however, Scripture does teach that he will be of Gentile descent.

This can first be seen from biblical typology. Most commentators agree that Daniel 11 speaks of Antiochus Epiphanes, a Gentile, who typifies the future Antichrist. Since Antiochus is a Gentile, then so will be Antichrist.

Second, biblical imagery supports a Gentile origin of Antichrist. Scripture pictures Antichrist as rising up out of the sea (Revelation 13:1; 17:15). In prophetic literature, the sea is an image of the Gentile nations. Thus, Antichrist is seen as a Gentile progeny.

Third, the nature of the "times of the Gentiles" supports a Gentile Antichrist (see Luke 21:24). Fruchtenbaum notes:

> It is agreed by all premillennialists that the period known as the Times of the Gentiles does not end until the second coming of Christ. It is further agreed that the Antichrist is the final ruler of the Times of the Gentiles....
>
> If this is so, how then can a Jew be the last ruler at a time when only Gentiles can have the preeminence? To say the Antichrist is to be a Jew would contradict the very nature of the Time of the Gentiles.[20]

Finally, the Bible not only teaches that Antichrist will be Gentile, but it also implies he will be of Roman descent. This is understood from Daniel 9:27, where the one cutting a covenant with Israel represents the revived Roman Empire, since it was the Romans who destroyed Jerusalem and the Temple in A.D. 70. The revived Roman Empire comes from a second phase of the Roman Empire, i.e., "feet partly of iron and partly of clay" (Daniel 2:33,40-45).

13. When will the Antichrist arise?

According to Daniel, the Antichrist will emerge in power during the prophetic milestone known as the "70th week" and after the fulfillment of the previously prophesied "69 weeks." Daniel 9:27 says,

> And he [the Antichrist] will make a firm covenant with the many for one week, but in the middle of the week

> he will put a stop to sacrifice and grain offering; and on
> the wing of abominations will come one who makes
> desolate, even until a complete destruction, one that is
> decreed, is poured out on the one who makes desolate.

We understand this "70th week" to be a future seven-year period known to prophecy students as the tribulation. We believe this era follows the rapture of the church and will be a time of unparalleled suffering and turmoil. The chart and explanation on page 132 provide an overview of the 69 weeks, the 70th week, and Daniel's timetable.

Two words describe the ascent of the Antichrist: unification and subjugation. According to Daniel 7:7,8,23,24, the Antichrist will rise to power after a confederation of 10 nations emerges. This confederation is symbolized as a beast with ten horns and represents a final international political entity. It will be a unique and powerful empire. According to Daniel, "The fourth beast will be a fourth kingdom on the earth, which will be different from all the other kingdoms, and it will devour the whole earth and tread it down and crush it" (7:23).

The Antichrist will forcibly take control of the confederation and will subdue three of the ten members. "As for the ten horns, out of this kingdom ten kings will arise; and another will arise after them, and he will be different from the previous ones and will subdue three kings" (Daniel 7:24). John writes of his ascent in Revelation 13:1, "And he stood on the sand of the seashore. And I saw a beast coming up out of the sea, having ten horns and seven heads, and on his horns were ten diadems, and on his heads were blasphemous names."

Dr. John F. Walvoord has written extensively about this confederation. He notes:

> The prediction that there will be a ten-kingdom stage
> of the revival of the Roman Empire is one of the impor-
> tant descriptive prophecies of the end time. This
> prophecy anticipates that there will be ten countries
> originally related to the Roman Empire that will con-
> stitute the Roman Empire in its revived form. The
> names of these countries are not given, but it can be
> presumed that Italy, the capital country, would be
> included, along with major countries in southern

> Europe and possibly some countries of western Asia
> and northern Africa which were included in the
> ancient Roman Empire. Since the names of the coun-
> tries are not given and there are many more than ten
> countries in the ancient Roman Empire, it leaves some
> flexibility in the fulfillment. The prediction, however,
> requires a political union and then a dictator over the
> ten countries.[21]

Some students of prophecy speculate that the European Economic Community, founded in 1958 and often called the European
Common Market, is the fulfillment of this prophecy. However, to
make such claims is to go beyond the pages of the Bible and doctrinal certainty. Prophecy scholar Dr. Charles H. Dyer reiterates this
uncertainty:

> Is the EEC the ten-nation confederacy predicted in
> Daniel and Revelation? In its present form it is not.
> Twelve nations now form the EEC, and several others
> have applied for membership. The Bible predicts one
> diverse empire ruled by the end-time dictator. This
> empire will be composed of at least ten nations who
> will ally themselves with this ruler. No such alignment
> exists today.[22]

Will this confederation arise before the rapture? Perhaps, but
that is not a necessity. It is possible that the present EEC is a fore-
shadowing and a precursor to the future confederation, which will
crystallize during the tribulation. Dr. Walvoord writes:

> Though Scripture does not date the formation of this
> ten-nation political group, and it could conceivably
> happen even before the rapture of the church, the
> emergence of the leader who will conquer first three
> countries and then all ten is an event that necessarily
> must follow the rapture of the church.[23]

When the Antichrist does emerge, it will be through his skills as
a peacemaker that he will gain acknowledgment and acceptance. As
the head of the multination confederation, he will impose peace on
Israel and the Middle East and will initiate and formulate a covenant
of peace for Israel. Dr. Walvoord writes of this peace:

> When a Gentile ruler over the ten nations imposes a peace treaty on Israel, it will be from superior strength and will not be a negotiated peace treaty, but it apparently will include the necessary elements for such a contract. It will include the fixing of Israel's borders, the establishment of trade relations with her neighbors—something she does not enjoy at the present time, and, most of all, it will provide protection from outside attacks, which will allow Israel to relax her military preparedness. It can also be anticipated that some attempts will be made to open the holy areas of Jerusalem to all faiths related to it.[24]

One significant way the Antichrist will control the population is by a special mark. This "mark of the beast" is mentioned in Revelation 13:16,17; 14:9; and 20:4. According to the first of these passages, everyone will be required to receive the mark or the name of the beast before "buying or selling," that is, before they can conduct any normal daily business. All private and public transactions will require that the parties involved have this mark.[25] Those who do not have it will be subject to great difficulty and persecution. The mark will identify those who worship and follow the Antichrist. The mark "will be a token of the immense power and worldwide authority of the Beast."[26] Dr. Walvoord writes:

> To receive such a mark, the people would have to recognize the world ruler as God and Satan as the supreme deity. Thousands will refuse to do this, and according to Revelation 20:2-4, they will be beheaded. They will be resurrected at the Second Coming to reign with Christ for a thousand years. There is no doubt that with today's technology, a world ruler, who is in total control, would have the ability to keep a continually updated census of all living persons and know day-by-day precisely which people had pledged their allegiance to him and received the mark and which had not.[27]

Although all the specifics and ramifications of the mark are not known, we do know that it will be a symbol of the Antichrist and allegiance to him.

14. What does "666" mean?

In biblical symbolism and numerology, the number 666 is certainly one of the most significant items recorded. We read of this unique number in Revelation 13:16-18:

> And he [the Antichrist] causes all, the small and the
> great, and the rich and the poor, and the free men and
> the slaves, to be given a mark on their right hand, or on
> their forehead, and he provides that no one should be
> able to buy or to sell, except the one who has the mark,
> either the name of the beast or the number of his
> name. Here is wisdom. Let him who has understanding
> calculate the number of the beast, for the number is
> that of a man; and his number is six hundred and sixty-
> six.

Probably no other number in history or in biblical studies has captivated the minds of both Christians and non-Christians as "666." Even those who know nothing of the future plan of God as revealed in the Bible know there is significance to this number. Secular and religious writers, film makers, artists, and cultural critics allude to, portray, and expound upon it. It has been used and abused by evangelicals as well as others and has been the subject of much fruitless speculation. Too often, sincere students of prophecy have tied the number to contemporary technology and its potential in an effort to demonstrate the relevance of their interpretation. Yet to do so is to put the cart before the horse, for prophecy and the Bible do not gain authority or legitimacy because of culture or technology. The Bible is authoritative because it is the Word of God. We must allow the Bible to interpret and define culture and technology; culture and technology must not define and interpret the Bible. What then can we say about this number? After a lifetime of prophetic study, Dr. John Walvoord writes:

> The Bible itself does not interpret the "666." Because
> in some languages the alphabet that is used has
> numerical value, some felt that this pointed to the
> beast as a character out of the past whose name in its
> numerical value would reveal the number "666."
> Accordingly, schemes abounded where many different
> names were suggested.... Though there may be more

light cast on it at the time this prophecy is fulfilled, the passage itself declares that this number is "man's number." In the Book of Revelation the number "7" is one of the most significant numbers indicating perfection. Accordingly, there are seven seals, seven trumpets, seven bowls of the wrath of God, seven thunders, etc. This beast claims to be God, and if that were the case, he should be 777. This passage, in effect, says, No, you are only 666. You are short of deity even though you were originally created in the image and likeness of God. *Most of the speculation on the meaning of this number is without profit or theological significance.* [28]

Dr. Robert L. Thomas wisely notes:

The identity of the person represented by the number 666 should not be a subject of speculation until that person arrives on the earthly scene....It is true that 666 has a secondary implication regarding human limitation, but its primary meaning will be to help Christians of the future recognize the false Christ when he becomes a public figure. [29]

15. What are the final stages of the Antichrist's rule?

Once the Antichrist is in power and his program fully manifested, it will be all-encompassing and intense. He will be active throughout the tribulation, but primarily it is the last half that will be tumultuous. His unprecedented, unparalleled, and unrestrained power will command worldwide attention for a period of 42 months.

While the Antichrist emerges in a political environment and functions initially as a political leader, he also will gradually acquire religious connotations. Eventually he will require that people worship him when he sets up his image in Israel's temple (2 Thessalonians 2:4). John writes,

And the whole earth was amazed and followed after the beast; and they worshiped the dragon, because he gave his authority to the beast; and they worshiped the beast, saying, "Who is like the beast, and who is able to wage war with him?" And there was given to him a mouth speaking arrogant words and blasphemies; and authority to act for forty-two months was given to him. And he opened his mouth in blasphemies against God, to blaspheme His name and His tabernacle, that is, those who dwell in heaven. And it was given to him to make war with the saints and to overcome them; and authority over every tribe and people and tongue and nation was given to him. And all who dwell on the earth will worship him, everyone whose name has not been written from the foundation of the world in the book of life of the Lamb who has been slain (Revelation 13:3b-8).

The prophet Daniel and the apostle Paul teach of his unquenchable thirst for deification. Daniel 11:36,37 says,

Then the king will do as he pleases, and he will exalt and magnify himself above every god, and will speak monstrous things against the God of gods; and he will prosper until the indignation is finished, for that which is decreed will be done. And he will show no regard for the gods of his fathers or for the desire of women, nor will he show regard for any other god; for he will magnify himself above them all.

Paul writes in 2 Thessalonians 2:4 that the Antichrist is one "who opposes and exalts himself above every so-called god or object of worship, so that he takes his seat in the temple of God, displaying himself as being God." Although the Antichrist will primarily be a political figure, the religious aspects of his plan and work will not initially be revealed.

The deification of emperors, kings, and other political leaders has occurred throughout history. Ultimately, it stems from Satan's desire to be like God. This desire for exaltation is first seen in the temptation of Adam and Eve. We read in Genesis 3:4,5, "The serpent said to the woman, 'You surely shall not die! For God knows that in the day you eat from it your eyes will be opened, and you will be like God, knowing good and evil.'"

Such desire for divine power is the epitome of sin and will culminate in the desire of the Antichrist to be worshiped as a god.

Not surprisingly, Revelation 13:2 says that the Antichrist's power is derived from Satan: "And the beast which I saw was like a leopard, and his feet were like those of a bear, and his mouth like the mouth of a lion. And the dragon gave him his power and his throne and great authority." Whatever power he acquires from military or political alliances or from "natural" talents and abilities is secondary and stems ultimately from Satan.

> He may come appearing to be a man of peace, and he may be motivated by pride and a thirst for power. But any success he achieves is due largely to supernatural forces at work behind the scenes. Ultimately he is a pawn in the hand of Satan.[30]

Satanic rebellion against God is referenced throughout the Bible and has been evidenced throughout all of history. The conflict, which began before the creation of the cosmos, will continue until God's final judgment of Satan. The rise and demise of the Antichrist and the tribulation events will be among the final struggles of Satan for physical and spiritual control of the world.

The signal for the last half of the tribulation occurs because the Antichrist's peace treaty, or covenant, will bring only a temporary and superficial peace to the area. It may be effective and reassuring initially, but it will not last. After three-and-a-half years it will shatter and the previous cries of joy will be replaced by cries of anguish. Like all of Satan's works, the proclaimed victory will erode to pain and violence:

> Though the particulars of the covenant are not revealed in Scripture, it apparently will bring great relief to Israel as well as to the whole world. The time of peace is anticipated in the prophecies of Ezekiel, which describe Israel as "a peaceful and unsuspecting people" at that time (38:11). In 1 Thessalonians 5:3 the people are quoted as saying, "Peace and safety," before the Great Tribulation overtakes them.... The peace that Israel enjoyed for three and a half years will tragically turn out to be a false peace and the prelude to her unprecedented time of trouble when two out of three Israelites will perish in the land (Zechariah 13:8).[31]

At some point around the middle of the tribulation, Israel's peace will be challenged by invading armies from the north (Ezekiel

38-39). These armies will attack Israel, challenging both the peace established by the Antichrist and the authority of the Antichrist. However, God will intervene on behalf of Israel, protecting her and decimating the invading armies (Ezekiel 38:19-39:5). This will be accomplished in part by an earthquake (38:19,20), military confusion (38:21), and a plague coupled with hail and fire (38:22).

Following this conflict and the breaking of the covenant with Israel, the Antichrist will declare himself to be the world ruler. This may come as a result of his victory over the invading armies. Dr. Walvoord writes that, "the ruler of the ten-nation confederacy will find himself in a position where he can proclaim himself dictator over the world, and apparently no one will be strong to contend against him. Without a fight on his part, he will therefore rule the world as Satan's tool."[32] His power and might will increase, as will his tyranny, and this will result in a final challenge of his military and political strength, which will culminate in the battle of Armageddon (Revelation 16:14-16). Like so many leaders and rulers before him, the Antichrist will promise peace but wage war. He will engage in a conflict of global consequences—an ultimate "winner take all"—and he will be defeated and destroyed by Jesus Christ (see Psalm 2).

16. What finally happens to the Antichrist?

According to Revelation 19:20, the Antichrist will be captured by Christ and, along with the false prophet, will be among the first to be thrown into the lake of fire (see Revelation 20:14). The Antichrist will be finished in history (unlike Satan who will be bound for 1,000 years and then released and judged after a final rebellion). In all of his actions and attitudes, the Antichrist will indeed be against Christ, *but it will be Christ and not his human enemy who will have the final victory.*

We live in a world where evil is rampant and often appears out of control. We are confronted daily with headlines of tragedy, catastrophe, and inhumanity. Prophetic teaching tells us that God is still on His throne, and He is allowing evil to run its course. However, this will not always be the case. In the past, the focus of redemption revolved around the person and work of Jesus Christ. In the same way in the future, the focus of human evil *will revolve around the person and work of Antichrist.*

There have been many false prophets and teachers. In 1 John 4:3, we read, "and every spirit that does not confess Jesus is not from God; and this is the spirit of the antichrist, of which you have heard that it is coming, and now it is already in the world."

First John 4:1 says, "Beloved, do not believe every spirit, but test the spirits to see whether they are from God; because many false prophets have gone out into the world." How does a believer "test the spirits"? Testing the spirits is not done through a mystical sense that something is "not quite right." Instead, a spirit is tested by evaluating the content of its message by the Word of God. In the case cited in 1 John 4, it related to the person of Christ. Thus, those who taught error in this matter were proven to be false prophets or antichrists.

All false teachers distort the Word of God and the person and work of Jesus Christ. As such, they oppose Christ in the same way (though not to the same degree) as the final Antichrist. In the same sense that John the Baptist was a forerunner of Jesus Christ, so are these false teachers forerunners of the Antichrist (see Matthew 24:5,24; 1 John 2:18,22; 4:3; 2 John 7).

While we may be near, we are not currently living in the time of Antichrist. Knowing God's plan for history in advance gives us as Christians confidence that God will triumph over evil—even the greatest human concentration of evil in the Antichrist.

Biblical teaching regarding the Antichrist is not given to us to make us anxious, but to make us aware that the present and the future are firmly in the grasp of God. We should be concerned about the Antichrist, not just because the Bible speaks of him or out of curiosity, but because he provides present insight into the mystery of lawlessness that is already at work (2 Thessalonians 2:7). The pattern of evil which will be clearly played out in the future and personified in the Antichrist should be our concern, so that we can more skillfully resist evil in the present. Even though a biblical passage or subject may not directly apply to a particular believer today, a thorough knowledge of Scripture gives the saint of God added insight in living faithfully for the Savior.

CHAPTER 14

Does the Tribulation Have a Specific Timetable?

17. Why is the tribulation necessary?

God's basic purpose for the tribulation is that it be a time of judgment, while at the same time holding forth the grace of the gospel, which will precede Christ's glorious 1,000-year reign in Jerusalem from David's throne.

Dr. Arnold Fruchtenbaum divides God's purpose into three aspects.[33]

- *To make an end of wickedness and wicked ones.*

    Isaiah 13:9—"Behold, the day of the LORD is coming, cruel, with fury and burning anger, to make the land a desolation; and He will exterminate its sinners from it."

    Isaiah 24:19-20—"The earth is broken asunder, the earth is split through, the earth is shaken violently. The earth reels to and fro like a drunkard, and it totters like a shack, for its transgression is heavy upon it, and it will fall, never to rise again."

The first purpose for the tribulation is seen to be a punishment in history upon the whole world for its sins against God, in a way similar to that of the global flood in Noah's time (Matthew 24:37-39).

- *To bring about a worldwide revival.*

    This purpose is given and fulfilled in Revelation 7:1-17: During the first half of the tribulation, God will evangelize the world by the means of the 144,000 Jews and thus fulfill the prophecy found in Matthew 24:14.[34]

    Matthew 24:14—"And this gospel of the kingdom shall be preached in the whole world for a witness to all the nations, and then the end shall come."

• *To break the power of the holy people—Israel.*

Finally, the tribulation will be a time in which God, through evil agencies, prepares Israel for conversion and acknowledgment that Jesus is the Messiah, resulting in the second coming of Christ. Fruchtenbaum notes:

> In Daniel 11 and 12, the prophet was given a vision of what conditions will be like for his people (Israel) during the tribulation. Then in Daniel 12:5-7 a question is raised as to how long this period will be allowed to continue.

> Daniel 12:5-7—"Then I, Daniel, looked and behold, two others were standing, one on this bank of the river, and the other on that bank of the river. And one said to the man dressed in linen, who was above the waters of the river, 'How long will it be until the end of these wonders?' And I heard the man dressed in linen, who was above the waters of the river, as he raised his right hand and his left toward heaven, and swore by Him who lives forever that it would be for a time, times, and half a time; and as soon as they finish shattering the power of the holy people, all these events will be completed."

> This passage provides a third goal of the tribulation. It is to break the power or the stubborn will of the Jewish nation. The tribulation will continue and will not end until this happens. So from this, the third purpose of the tribulation can be deduced: God intends to break the power of the holy people in order to bring about a national regeneration.[35]

18. What are the major events of the tribulation?

The seven-year tribulation is divided into two three-and-a-half-year parts. We will look at the major events of each half and events occurring in the middle, knowing that some can be placed in their proper sequence, while other events are harder to place. The chart on page 161 should give a helpful overview.

Events of the First Half of the Tribulation

1. *The seal judgments*—Revelation 6 outlines the seven seal judgments (the seventh contains the trumpet judgments) that kick off the tribulation.[36] The first four seals are also known as the four horsemen of the Apocalypse. These judgments are the beginnings of the wrath of God which is directed at the earth.

2. *The rise of Antichrist and the ten-nation confederacy*—Since the beginning of the tribulation will be marked by the signing of a covenant between Israel and the Antichrist (Daniel 9:26,27), it makes sense that he will come on the scene in the first half of the tribulation. He will be the head of a ten-nation confederacy (Daniel 2:42,44; 7:7,24; Revelation 12:3; 13:1; 17:12,16) that will rule the world during the tribulation.

3. *The ministry of Elijah*—Malachi 4:5,6 says,

> Behold, I am going to send you Elijah the prophet before the coming of the great and terrible day of the LORD. And he will restore the hearts of the fathers to their children, and the hearts of the children to their fathers, lest I come and smite the land with a curse.

The ministry of Elijah, which could be fulfilled through the ministry of the two witnesses, will be one of restoration toward the nation of Israel. Since it will be "before the coming of the great and terrible day of the LORD," it will occur in the first half of the tribulation.

4. *The revival through the 144,000 Jewish evangelists*— Revelation 7 details the call and ministry of 144,000 Jewish evangelists who preach the gospel during the first half of the tribulation.

5. *The trumpet judgments*—Revelation 8 and 9 speak of the trumpet judgments. As with the seal judgments, the seventh trumpet contains the final series of judgments known as the bowl judgments. These judgments focus on nature and include two of the three woe judgments.

6. *The ministry of the two witnesses*—Just as the 144,000 are engaged in world evangelism, the two witnesses are sealed by

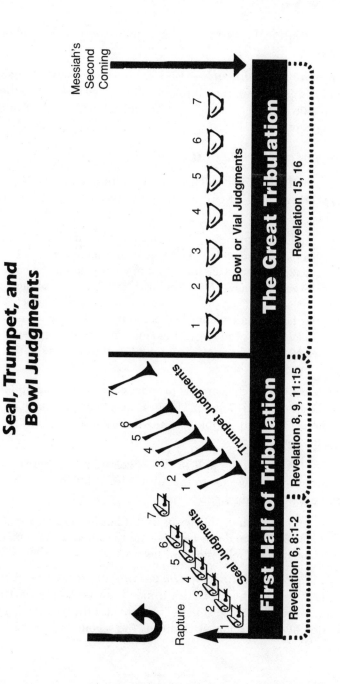

Seal, Trumpet, and Bowl Judgments

Rapture

Seal Judgments
1 2 3 4 5 6 7

Trumpet Judgments
1 2 3 4 5 6 7

Bowl or Vial Judgments
1 2 3 4 5 6 7

Messiah's Second Coming

First Half of Tribulation

Revelation 6, 8:1-2   Revelation 8, 9, 11:15

The Great Tribulation

Revelation 15, 16

God (Revelation 11:3-6) to be a special witness to Jerusalem and Israel.

7. *The false church*—Also known as Ecclesiastical Babylon, it will have great power and influence during the first half of the tribulation (Revelation 17:1-6). The false church will aid the Antichrist in his deception.

Events of the Middle of the Tribulation

1. *The little scroll*—The apostle John is commanded by the interpreting angel to eat the little book (scroll) in Revelation 10:9,11:

> And I went to the angel, telling him to give me the little book. And he said to me, "Take it, and eat it; and it will make your stomach bitter, but in your mouth it will be sweet as honey." And I took the little book out of the angel's hand and ate it, and it was in my mouth sweet as honey; and when I had eaten it, my stomach was made bitter. And they said to me, "You must prophesy again concerning many peoples and nations and tongues and kings."

The content of the scroll is prophecy relating to the middle and second half of the tribulation. Biblical prophecy is considered good (i.e., sweet) by many people, but the message of judgment (i.e., bitter) is hard to take.

2. *The Antichrist is killed*—Revelation 13:3 notes that the seventh head (a reference to the Antichrist) is killed. As we will note later, he is not yet finished.

> And I saw one of his heads as if it had been slain, and his fatal wound was healed. And the whole earth was amazed and followed after the beast.

3. *Satan cast down to the earth from heaven*—Revelation 12:7-9 reveals that Satan himself is cast to the earth from heaven through angelic agency. This provides the basis for an intensification of events upon earth during the second half of the tribulation:

> And there was war in heaven, Michael and his angels
> waging war with the dragon. And the dragon and his
> angels waged war, and they were not strong enough,
> and there was no longer a place found for them in
> heaven. And the great dragon was thrown down, the
> serpent of old who is called the devil and Satan, who
> deceives the whole world; he was thrown down to the
> earth, and his angels were thrown down with him.

4. *The resurrection of the Antichrist*—One of the first things
Satan does on earth after being cast out of heaven is to resurrect the
Antichrist. Revelation 13:3,4 records this episode as the Antichrist
attempts to counterfeit the career of Jesus, the Messiah:

> And I saw one of his heads as if it had been slain, and
> his fatal wound was healed. And the whole earth was
> amazed and followed after the beast; and they wor-
> shiped the dragon, because he gave his authority to the
> beast; and they worshiped the beast, saying, "Who is
> like the beast, and who is able to wage war with him?"

5. *Three kings killed and seven submit*—After his death
and resurrection, Antichrist consolidates his worldwide rule by kill-
ing three of the ten kings, which leads to the other seven submitting
voluntarily. This event provides the political basis from which Antichrist will project his power during the last half of the tribulation:

> As for the ten horns, out of this kingdom ten kings will
> arise; and another will arise after them, and he will be
> different from the previous ones and will subdue three
> kings (Daniel 7:24).

> And the ten horns which you saw are ten kings, who
> have not yet received a kingdom, but they receive
> authority as kings with the beast for one hour. These
> have one purpose and they give their power and
> authority to the beast (Revelation 17:12,13).

6. *Destruction of the false church*—As has often been the
case historically, when a tyrant reaches his goal of total political
control, he destroys those who helped him reach that point. Antichrist now destroys the harlot, Ecclesiastical Babylon, as noted in
Revelation 17:16:

> And the ten horns which you saw, and the beast, these
> will hate the harlot and will make her desolate and
> naked, and will eat her flesh and will burn her up with
> fire.

7. *The death and resurrection of the two witnesses*—
God enables the temporary deception of Antichrist to proceed
further with the death of the two witnesses. During the first half of
the tribulation, the two witnesses were miraculously protected by
God. The Antichrist's deception deepens when God allows him to
murder the two witnesses in Jerusalem—and the whole world
rejoices. However, after three-and-a-half days the two witnesses will
be resurrected and taken to heaven in the sight of all. Fear then grips
those who have followed after the beast:

> And when they have finished their testimony, the
> beast that comes up out of the abyss will make war
> with them, and overcome them and kill them. And
> their dead bodies will lie in the street of the great city
> which mystically is called Sodom and Egypt, where
> also their Lord was crucified. And those from the peo-
> ples and tribes and tongues and nations will look at
> their dead bodies for three and a half days, and will not
> permit their dead bodies to be laid in a tomb. And
> those who dwell on the earth will rejoice over them
> and make merry; and they will send gifts to one
> another, because these two prophets tormented those
> who dwell on the earth. And after the three and a half
> days the breath of life from God came into them, and
> they stood on their feet; and great fear fell upon those
> who were beholding them. And they heard a loud voice
> from heaven saying to them, "Come up here." And
> they went up into heaven in the cloud, and their ene-
> mies beheld them. And in that hour there was a great
> earthquake, and a tenth of the city fell; and seven
> thousand people were killed in the earthquake, and
> the rest were terrified and gave glory to the God of
> heaven (Revelation 11:7-13).

8. *The worship of the Antichrist*—Since the "earth dwellers" prefer the counterfeit over the genuine, they will be deceived
into worshiping the Antichrist as God. In reality, they will be

worshiping Satan. No wonder the Bible is filled with warnings about spiritual deception!

> And I saw one of his heads as if it had been slain, and his fatal wound was healed. And the whole earth was amazed and followed after the beast; and they worshiped the dragon, because he gave his authority to the beast; and they worshiped the beast, saying, "Who is like the beast, and who is able to wage war with him?" (Revelation 13:3,4).

> And all who dwell on the earth will worship him, everyone whose name has not been written from the foundation of the world in the book of life of the Lamb who has been slain (Revelation 13:8).

9. *The false prophet*—This person is a counterfeit of the ministry of the Holy Spirit in that he is temporarily empowered to do false signs, wonders, and miracles which greatly aid the Antichrist's rise to power. False religion is the vehicle of deception for this second beast—the false prophet:

> And I saw another beast coming up out of the earth; and he had two horns like a lamb, and he spoke as a dragon. And he exercises all the authority of the first beast in his presence. And he makes the earth and those who dwell in it to worship the first beast, whose fatal wound was healed. And he performs great signs, so that he even makes fire come down out of heaven to the earth in the presence of men. And he deceives those who dwell on the earth because of the signs which it was given him to perform in the presence of the beast, telling those who dwell on the earth to make an image to the beast who had the wound of the sword and has come to life. And there was given to him to give breath to the image of the beast, that the image of the beast might even speak and cause as many as do not worship the image of the beast to be killed (Revelation 13:11-15).

10. *The mark of the beast (666)*—Another "ministry" of the false prophet will be the administering of the counterfeit seal of the Holy Spirit: the famous mark of the beast, 666. Placement of this

mark on the forehead or right hand will be required to conduct economic transactions during the second half of the tribulation. It should be noted that any person receiving this mark cannot be saved. This mark will not be distributed during the first half of the tribulation, but only during the latter half. Since the meaning of 666 is a mystery, it is not wise to speculate about this until the time in which it is distributed. It is clear that its meaning will be evident to believers during the tribulation:

> And he causes all, the small and the great, and the rich and the poor, and the free men and the slaves, to be given a mark on their right hand, or on their forehead, and he provides that no one should be able to buy or to sell, except the one who has the mark, either the name of the beast or the number of his name. Here is wisdom. Let him who has understanding calculate the number of the beast, for the number is that of a man; and his number is six hundred and sixty-six (Revelation 13:16-18).

11.   *The seven-year covenant broken*—It is not at all surprising that the Antichrist should break his covenant with Israel. Such a move is in keeping with his character. This betrayal will involve Antichrist's military invasion of Israel:

> He will also enter the Beautiful Land, and many countries will fall; but these will be rescued out of his hand: Edom, Moab and the foremost of the sons of Ammon (Daniel 11:41).

> And your covenant with death shall be canceled, and your pact with Sheol shall not stand; when the overwhelming scourge passes through, then you become its trampling place (Isaiah 28:18).

12.   *The abomination of desolation*—Antichrist will not only break his covenant with Israel, but he will also set himself up as God to be worshiped in the rebuilt Jewish temple at the midpoint of the tribulation. This defiling of the third temple is called "the abomination of desolation." This will be a sign to the Jews to flee Jerusalem:

> And he will make a firm covenant with the many for
> one week, but in the middle of the week he will put a
> stop to sacrifice and grain offering; and on the wing of
> abominations will come one who makes desolate, even
> until a complete destruction, one that is decreed, is
> poured out on the one who makes desolate (Daniel
> 9:27).

> Therefore when you see the ABOMINATION OF DESOLA-
> TION which was spoken of through Daniel the prophet,
> standing in the holy place (let the reader understand),
> then let those who are in Judea flee to the mountains
> (Matthew 24:15,16).

> ...who opposes and exalts himself above every so-
> called god or object of worship, so that he takes his
> seat in the temple of God, displaying himself as being
> God (2 Thessalonians 2:4).

13. *The persecution of the Jews*—The second half of the
tribulation will be characterized by an extreme attempt to wipe the
Jews off the face of the earth. Likely, Satan's thinking on this matter
is that if the Jews are exterminated, then God's plan for history will
have been thwarted. Satan might think that this would somehow
prevent the second coming. This persecution is pictured in Revelation 12:1-6. Within the imagery, the woman represents Israel, and
her male child represents Christ:

> And a great sign appeared in heaven: a woman clothed
> with the sun, and the moon under her feet, and on her
> head a crown of twelve stars; and she was with child;
> and she cried out, being in labor and in pain to give
> birth. And another sign appeared in heaven: and
> behold, a great red dragon having seven heads and ten
> horns, and on his heads were seven diadems. And his
> tail swept away a third of the stars of heaven, and
> threw them to the earth. And the dragon stood before
> the woman who was about to give birth, so that when
> she gave birth he might devour her child. And she gave
> birth to a son, a male child, who is to rule all the
> nations with a rod of iron; and her child was caught up
> to God and to His throne. And the woman fled into the

wilderness where she had a place prepared by God, so
that there she might be nourished for one thousand
two hundred and sixty days.

Events of the Second Half of the Tribulation

1. *The bowl judgments*—The bowl judgments are the most
severe series of judgments of the whole tribulation. They occur in
the second half of the tribulation, devastate Antichrist's kingdom,
and prepare the way for the second coming of Christ. The bowl judgments are the result of the prayers of the saints for God to take
revenge on their behalf (Revelation 15:1-8). The bowl judgments are
described in Revelation 16.

2. *The protection of the Jewish remnant*—At the midpoint
of the tribulation the Jews will flee when the Antichrist commits the
abomination of desolation. Apparently these Jews will be protected
in the Jordanian village of Bozrah, known also as Petra. A remnant
will be preserved through this and other means:

> I will surely assemble all of you, Jacob, I will surely
> gather the remnant of Israel. I will put them together
> like sheep in the fold [literally, Bozrah]; like a flock in
> the midst of its pasture they will be noisy with men
> (Micah 2:12).

> Then let those who are in Judea flee to the mountains
> (Matthew 24:16).

> And the woman fled into the wilderness where she had
> a place prepared by God, so that there she might be
> nourished for one thousand two hundred and sixty
> days (Revelation 12:6).

> And the two wings of the great eagle were given to the
> woman, in order that she might fly into the wilderness
> to her place, where she was nourished for a time and
> times and half a time, from the presence of the serpent
> (Revelation 12:14).

3. *The campaign of Armageddon*—The final great war of
history will occur in Israel as prophesied in Daniel 11:40-45; Joel
3:9-17; Zechariah 14:1-3; and Revelation 16:14-16. As the forces of

the Antichrist move against Jerusalem, Jesus Christ will return in His second coming, destroy the Antichrist's forces, and cast the Antichrist and the false prophet into the lake of fire (Revelation 19:11-21).

4. *The conversion of Israel*—Right before the second coming, the people of Israel will be converted to belief in the Messiahship of Jesus and saved from their sins. This will prepare them for their role in the millennial kingdom after the second advent:

> And I will pour out on the house of David and on the inhabitants of Jerusalem, the Spirit of grace and of supplication, so that they will look on Me whom they have pierced; and they will mourn for Him, as one mourns for an only son, and they will weep bitterly over Him, like the bitter weeping over a first-born (Zechariah 12:10).

> For I do not want you, brethren, to be uninformed of this mystery, lest you be wise in your own estimation, that a partial hardening has happened to Israel until the fullness of the Gentiles has come in; and thus all Israel will be saved; just as it is written, "THE DELIVERER WILL COME FROM ZION, HE WILL REMOVE UNGODLINESS FROM JACOB. AND THIS IS MY COVENANT WITH THEM, WHEN I TAKE AWAY THEIR SINS" (Romans 11:25-27).

19. Has the tribulation already occurred?

On the night He was betrayed, Jesus told His disciples, "In the world you have tribulation, but take courage; I have overcome the world" (John 16:33). With these words, Jesus stated that tribulation or hardship would be a continual reality in the lives of those who followed Him throughout the current church age. Christian martyrs throughout the history of the church have certainly proven the veracity of His words.

However, the tribulation of Daniel's seventieth week is a completely different era. The tribulation of God's prophetic plan is much greater and of a different purpose than that of which Jesus spoke in John 16. The tribulation of the future is not the same as the daily trials and struggles of Christians throughout church history. This is not to belittle the pain, hardship, suffering, and even death that those who follow Christ have often endured. Rather, it is to say that the future will bring even greater and more widespread trials which will culminate in the seventieth week. Also, current trials and tribulation are directed against us today by the world (John 15:18-25) as a hardship for following Christ. The tribulation is a time of God's wrath which will come upon the people of the earth to test them (Revelation 3:10; 6:15-17).

Some interpreters of prophecy wish to argue that the tribulation is already past. This view is called "preterism" (Latin for "past") and holds that all prophecies relating to the tribulation are now history and were fulfilled during the first century A.D., usually revolving around events associated with the destruction of Jerusalem in A.D. 70.

Preterism cannot be supported from Scripture for at least two major reasons. First, in order to support the notion of an A.D. 70 fulfillment of the large number of details surrounding the tribulation, preterists must use an unwarranted allegorical interpretative approach. This means that passages such as Matthew 24:30 and Revelation 19:11-21, which have traditionally been interpreted as references to Christ's second coming, must somehow be understood to really represent Christ coming mysteriously through the Roman army which conquered Jerusalem in A.D. 70. Such an approach exceeds the legitimate hermeneutical disagreements over figurative versus normal use of figures of speech and commits the error of spiritualization by supplying a meaning not supported by textual interpretation.

A second major error of preterism is the confusion of judgment and salvation in relation to the nation of Israel. Preterism sees only judgment toward Israel in passages that speak of the tribulation, such as the Olivet Discourse (Matthew 24; Mark 13; Luke 17:20-37; 21:5-36) and Revelation 4–19. Except for Luke 21:20-24, which clearly speaks of the A.D. 70 judgment upon Jerusalem, the rest of the passages picture Israel in a position from which God will deliver them from their enemies through His second coming. Even their allegorical approach to the biblical text cannot hide the clear fact that tribulation passages describe our Lord's salvation of Israel—not His judgment upon them.[37]

20. Are we currently in the tribulation?

Even though believers during the current church age experience trials and tribulation (John 15:18-25; 16:33; 2 Timothy 2:12), these are not the trials of *the* tribulation, from which the church has been promised removal (Revelation 3:10). Thus, we are not currently in the tribulation.

21. Will the tribulation take place in the future?

According to the prophetic timeline of Daniel 9:24-27 and 2 Thessalonians 2, the tribulation will follow the rapture of the church. This event, which is yet future, will terminate the present interval between the sixty-ninth and seventieth weeks of Daniel and will allow the tribulation to begin. Dr. Ryrie writes of this era:

> The Tribulation does not necessarily begin the day the church is taken to meet the Lord in the air. Though I believe that the Rapture precedes the beginning of the Tribulation, actually nothing is said in the Scriptures as to whether or not some time (or how much time) may elapse between the Rapture and the beginning of the Tribulation.

> The Tribulation actually begins with the signing of a covenant between the leader of the "Federated States of Europe" and the Jewish people. This treaty will set in motion the events of the seventieth week (or seven years) of Daniel's prophecy. There is an interval of undetermined length between the first sixty-nine weeks of seven years each and the last or seventieth week of seven years.[38]

Since none of the events of the tribulation have yet taken place (Antichrist's signing a covenant with Israel, the revelation of the Antichrist, the abomination of desolation, the mark of the beast, and so on), then it stands to reason that the tribulation is yet future.

22. Where does the Bible teach a seven-year tribulation?

Belief that the tribulation will last for seven years comes from the prophetic calendar of Daniel 9:24-27, specifically from verse 27:

> And he [the Antichrist] will make a firm covenant with
> the many for one week, but in the middle of the week
> he will put a stop to sacrifice and grain offering; and on
> the wing of abominations will come one who makes
> desolate, even until a complete destruction, one that is
> decreed, is poured out on the one who makes desolate.

The "week" that Daniel writes of is understood by most prophecy scholars to be a "week of years" or seven years. These years follow the interval of the "seven weeks and sixty-two weeks" found in
Daniel 9:25. In Daniel 9:2, Daniel was thinking about the years of
Israel's captivity by the Babylonians. This captivity had been prophesied by Jeremiah as being a period of 70 years:

> "This whole land shall be a desolation and a horror,
> and these nations shall serve the king of Babylon sev-
> enty years. Then it will be when seventy years are
> completed I will punish the king of Babylon and that
> nation," declares the LORD, "for their iniquity, and the
> land of the Chaldeans; and I will make it an everlasting
> desolation" (Jeremiah 25:11,12).

> For thus says the LORD, "When seventy years have
> been completed for Babylon, I will visit you and fulfill
> My good word to you, to bring you back to this place"
> (Jeremiah 29:10).

As Daniel studied the words of Jeremiah and prayed (Daniel 9:3-
19), the angel Gabriel appeared to him revealing the prophetic timetable found in Daniel 9:24-27. The Hebrew term used for "weeks" in
this passage means "sevens" or "units of seven," without specifying
whether it means days, months, or years. In this passage only
"years" fits the timetable since a period of 490 days or 490 months is
historically too short a time span. The 70 weeks must be a period of
490 years (70 × 7). The seventieth week must also therefore be a
period of seven years. Dr. Walvoord writes of this:

> The only system of interpretation, however, that gives
> any literal meaning to this prophecy is to regard the
> time units as prophetic years of 360 days each accord-
> ing to the Jewish custom of having years of 360 days
> with an occasional extra month inserted to correct the
> calendar as needed. The seventy times seven is,

therefore, 490 years with the beginning at the time of "the commandment to restore and rebuild Jerusalem" found in verse 25 and the culmination of 490 years later in verse 27. Before detailing the events between the sixty-ninth seven and the seventieth seven, and the final seven years, Daniel gives the overall picture in verse 24. Careful attention must be given to the precise character of this important foundational prophecy.[39]

The book of Revelation gives a number of time indicators. These include:

- time, times, and half a time (i.e., 3½ years) (Revelation 12:14)
- 1,260 days (Revelation 11:3)
- 42 months (Revelation 11:2; 13:5)

These time indicators, each a different way of indicating three-and-a-half years, reflect the two halves of the seven-year tribulation period of the seventieth week as developed from Daniel 9:24-27.

CHAPTER 15

Does Tribulation Prophecy Impact Us Today?

23. How does Israel relate to the Antichrist and the tribulation?

According to Daniel 9:27, when the Antichrist is revealed (following the rapture), he will make a political covenant or treaty with Israel. When Daniel writes, "and he will make a firm covenant with the many for one week," he understands "the many" to be the nation Israel. That he understands it to be his own people, the Jews, is seen from Daniel 9:24, "Seventy weeks have been decreed for your people and your holy city."

Dr. Walvoord writes of this passage:

> In a word, the prophecy is that there will be a future compact or covenant between a political ruler designated as *the prince that shall come* [KJV] in verse 26 with the representatives of the Jewish people. Such an alliance will obviously be an unholy relationship and ultimately to the detriment of the people of Israel, however promising it may be at its inception.[40]

Although we do not know the details of this covenant, it will be one which will bring some measure of peace and stability to Israel for the first three-and-a-half years of the tribulation. As the Antichrist transforms himself from primarily being a political leader to the added role of religious leader, his relationship with Israel will deteriorate. He will not only stop the Jewish sacrificial system and worship of God, but in his blasphemy he will demand to be worshiped. This will culminate in his desecration of the temple. The result of this act will be the inauguration of horrible persecution for Israel and the Jews.

One of the major reasons for the tribulation is to prepare Israel for her conversion. Thus, both Israel as a nation and a people will experience the manifestations of evil during this era. In fact, many of the events of the tribulation revolve around Israel. Geographically and spiritually, Israel is at center stage during the tribulation.

24. How do Gentiles and believers relate to the tribulation?

Because the tribulation is worldwide in its scope, all people or nations will be affected. As during the flood of Noah's time, there will be no escape. Thus, the Gentiles will be judged for their treatment of Israel and their rejection of Jesus as the Lord and Savior of humanity. However, multitudes of Gentiles will come to faith in Christ during the tribulation:

> After these things I looked, and behold, a great multi-
> tude, which no one could count, from every nation and
> all tribes and peoples and tongues, standing before the
> throne and before the Lamb, clothed in white robes,
> and palm branches were in their hands; and they cry
> out with a loud voice, saying, "Salvation to our God
> who sits on the throne, and to the Lamb" (Revelation
> 7:9,10).

Prior to the beginning of the tribulation, Jesus Christ will appear in the clouds and both dead and living believers will be raptured or "caught up" to Him. The central passage for this is found in 1 Thessalonians 4:16,17:

> For the Lord Himself will descend from heaven with a
> shout, with the voice of the archangel, and with the
> trumpet of God; and the dead in Christ shall rise first.
> Then we who are alive and remain shall be caught up
> together with them in the clouds to meet the Lord in
> the air, and so we shall always be with the Lord.

When the rapture occurs, the church as we know it today will be gathered to the Lord and, therefore, will not be present on earth during Antichrist's reign and the tribulation. This is confirmed by Paul in 1 Thessalonians and John in Revelation. Paul encourages Christians to "wait for His Son from heaven, whom He raised from the dead, that is Jesus, who rescues us from the wrath to come" (1 Thessalonians 1:10). Paul continues in 1 Thessalonians 5:1-11 to describe the tribulation era and related events. He assures his readers that the church will not endure this time, "for God has not

destined us for wrath, but for obtaining salvation through our Lord
Jesus Christ, who died for us, that whether we are awake or asleep,
we may live together with Him" (1 Thessalonians 5:9,10).

This preservation from the tribulation or "wrath to come" is
reiterated by John who records the Lord's words: "Because you have
kept the word of My perseverance, I also will keep you from the hour
of testing, that hour which is about to come upon the whole world, to
test those who dwell upon the earth" (Revelation 3:10).

The church as the body of Christ will not be present during the
tribulation. Dr. Walvoord writes:

> The nature of the tribulation, if Scriptures relating to it
> are interpreted normally and literally, gives no basis
> for the idea that the church, the body of Christ, the
> saints of this present age, will be forced to remain on
> earth through it. According to the Scriptures, it is spe-
> cifically the time of Jacob's trouble (Jeremiah 30:7)
> and coincides with the last seven years of Israel's pro-
> gram as outlined in Daniel 9:24-27....The fact is most
> significant that the terms normally used of the church
> and which set it apart as distinct from saints of previ-
> ous ages are never found in any tribulation
> passage....That there is reference to Israel, to saints,
> to saved Israelites, and to saved Gentiles does not
> prove that the church is in this period as these terms
> are general terms, not specific.[41]

Although the church is not present during the tribulation, there
will be men and women who come to a saving knowledge of Jesus
Christ. There will be redeemed individuals living on earth during the
tribulation. Dr. Walvoord notes:

> The elect or the saved of the tribulation period are
> composed of both Jews and Gentiles who turn to
> Christ for salvation. During the early part of the period
> between the rapture and the second coming of Christ,
> there is some religious freedom as indicated by the res-
> toration of Jewish sacrifices. With the beginning of the
> great tribulation, however, this freedom is abruptly
> ended, and Jewish sacrifices cease. All who oppose the
> deification and worship of the world dictator are sub-
> ject to persecution. Both Jew and Christian become

the objects of this satanic oppression, and many are martyred. The elect are delivered by the return of Christ at the close of the tribulation period.[42]

We read in Revelation 6:9-11:

And when He broke the fifth seal, I saw underneath the altar the souls of those who had been slain because of the word of God, and because of the testimony which they had maintained; and they cried out with a loud voice, saying, "How long, O Lord, holy and true, wilt Thou refrain from judging and avenging our blood on those who dwell on the earth?" And there was given to each of them a white robe; and they were told that they should rest for a little while longer, until the number of their fellow servants and their brethren who were to be killed even as they had been, should be completed also.

These verses describe the fifth seal judgment and presuppose prior events happening on earth. The fact that verse 9 speaks of martyrs implies that they are believers who were killed early in the tribulation because of their faith.

There is also the witness of the 144,000 Jews described in Revelation 7:1-8. Dr. Ryrie writes of these people:

They are Jews from each of the twelve tribes, and they do some particular service for God. Whether the seal placed on them [Revelation 7:3] is a visible mark or characteristic of some kind is neither stated nor implied in the text. A seal need not be visible to be real (Ephesians 4:30). It is principally a guarantee of ownership and security. Both these ideas are involved in the sealing of this group. These people are owned by God, which means that they are redeemed. They are kept secure by God, which may mean He protects them from their enemies on earth while they complete their service for Him.[43]

Following the rapture there will still be Bibles, religious literature, and many people who knew the gospel before the rapture but had not yet converted to Christianity. These materials will be used, and many previously evangelized unbelievers will come to faith in

Jesus Christ. It is through these means and these people, in addition to the ministry of the 144,000, that there will be Christians during the tribulation. We read in Revelation 14:4 that the 144,000 "have been purchased from among men as first fruits to God and to the Lamb." This is further confirmation that there will be many new believers during this time. And just as in the early days of the faith, many will be martyred because of their beliefs.

Is End-Time Study Really Important?

We look forward to the coming times because God included it in His Word. Remember, the study of God's Word is always important and needs to be handled with great care. Regardless of the type of passages studied, whether covenant or chronology, poetry, parable, or prophecy, all are to be diligently studied and applied. "All Scripture is inspired by God and profitable for teaching, for reproof, for correction, for training in righteousness; that the man of God may be adequate, equipped for every good work" (2 Timothy 3:16,17).

The tribulation is important because, in a sense, Satan is unmasked and we see his ultimate intentions and purposes. Such an understanding of his plan, if properly applied, can aid the believer today in spiritual warfare. For example, we note that during the tribulation, Satan uses religion in a false and deceptive way. This stands as a warning for us today.

Much of what we see today and have seen in the past is a forerunner of that which will come. For example, the current impulse toward globalism should not be surprising for those who are aware of what the Bible teaches. Because our Sovereign God has foreordained such events, we should take comfort from the fact that He is in control. This future time of evil is the full development of humanity's sinful nature in conjunction with Satan's rebellious plan. Yet both will be brought under the judgment of a righteous and omnipotent God.

Human history has been filled with personal, national, and international tragedy and despair. In every century, every empire, and every era there have been multiple manifestations of original sin, the fall, and satanic activity. Passages of biblical prophecy (and other portions of Scripture) clearly teach that the future will bring a specific period of increased trauma and tragedy during which terror and tribulation will be both intense and international. The tribulation and Antichrist era will last for seven years and, following the battle of Armageddon, will culminate in the second coming of the Lord Jesus Christ to establish His millennial kingdom and reign on earth.

We believe that this tribulation era of destruction and persecution will follow the rapture of the church. However, such a belief does not alleviate contemporary Christians of daily responsibilities, evangelism, discipleship, or holy living. Tribulation is certain, but so is triumph. Concerning the tribulation, it is not the living of *those* days about which we need to be concerned; rather, it is the living of *these* days. "Therefore be careful how you walk, not as unwise men but as wise, making the most of your time, because the days are evil" (Ephesians 5:16,17).

As believers, we are to focus our primary energies and witness on proclaiming the certainty of salvation through our risen Lord. As men and women of biblical faith, we are confident of our future and dedicated to sharing God's Word and the majesty of a living Savior.

PART 4

Armageddon and the Middle East

A Glimpse of the Future

Throughout history countless battles, campaigns, and wars have been waged across the earth. Some have been limited in scope; others have been global. Armies have fought because of land and leaders, love and loyalty, for causes that have been just and, more often, unjust. The pain, suffering, and death inflicted from these conflicts and ones in our own day are beyond measure.

The Bible tells us that the future will also be filled with war. There is one major prophetic conflict that has captured the attention of Christians and non-Christians throughout the centuries—Armageddon. This event is prophesied to be the most catastrophic and devastating occurrence in human history. Whether or not people believe it will really happen, they readily identify with the magnitude of its symbolism. It is directly and indirectly spoken of in literature, movies, propaganda, political debates, sermons, and cultural commentaries. Everyone, it seems, has some notion or vague idea about it. Some of the ideas are biblical; many are not.

There is only one place to find accurate information about Armageddon—the Bible. In its prophetic pages we also discover the events that will precede and follow this final war of world history. Although we aren't given all the details, we are provided with an overall glimpse of God's plans for the future.

Why does the Bible speak of Armageddon? Because it affirms God's sovereignty over history and reminds us that there is a divine purpose and plan that will not be thwarted. God will one day right all wrongs, judge all evil, and establish a universal reign of righteousness. The hope of Christians throughout the centuries will be realized with the second coming of Jesus Christ and the defeat of those who oppose Him at Armageddon. It is because of this hope that we study prophecy, waiting for the fulfillment of God's promises.

CHAPTER 16

What Does the Bible Say About Armageddon?

1. Where does the Bible teach about the conflict?

We read of Armageddon in Daniel 11:40-45; Joel 3:9-17; Zechariah 14:1-3; and Revelation 16:14-16. This great battle will occur in the final days of the tribulation. John tells us that the kings of the world will be gathered together "for the war of the great day of God, the almighty" in a place known as Har-Magedon (Revelation 16:14,16). The site for the converging of the armies is the plain of Esdraelon, around the hill of Megiddo. This area is located in northern Israel about 20 miles south-southeast of Haifa.

According to the Bible, great armies from the east and the west will gather on this plain. The Antichrist will respond to threats to his power from the south. He will also move to destroy a revived Babylon in the east before finally turning his forces toward Jerusalem. For hundreds of years Babylon, located in present-day Iran, was one of the world's most important cities. According to Revelation 14:8; 16:9; and 17–18, it will again arise in the last days as a powerful religious, social, political, and economical city. As the Antichrist and his armies move on Jerusalem, God will intervene and Jesus Christ will return. The Lord will destroy the armies, capture the Antichrist and the false prophet, and cast them into the lake of fire (Revelation 19:11-21).

When the Lord returns, the power and rule of the Antichrist will come to an end. Dr. Charles Dyer writes of this event:

> Daniel, Joel, and Zechariah identify Jerusalem as the site where the final battle between Antichrist and Christ will occur. All three predict that God will intervene in history on behalf of His people and will destroy the Antichrist's army at Jerusalem. Zechariah predicts that the battle will end when the Messiah returns to earth and His feet touch down on the Mount of Olives. This battle concludes with the second coming of Jesus to earth.... The battle is over before it even begins.[1]

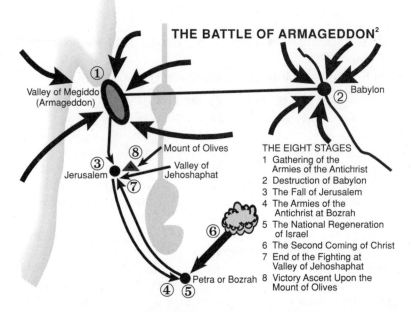

THE BATTLE OF ARMAGEDDON[2]

Valley of Megiddo
(Armageddon)

Babylon

Mount of Olives

Jerusalem

Valley of
Jehoshaphat

Petra or Bozrah

THE EIGHT STAGES
1 Gathering of the
   Armies of the Antichrist
2 Destruction of Babylon
3 The Fall of Jerusalem
4 The Armies of the
   Antichrist at Bozrah
5 The National Regeneration
   of Israel
6 The Second Coming of Christ
7 End of the Fighting at
   Valley of Jehoshaphat
8 Victory Ascent Upon the
   Mount of Olives

The battle of Armageddon—actually at Jerusalem—will be the most anticlimactic combat in history. As John describes the armies mustered on both sides, we expect to witness some epic struggle between good and evil. Yet no matter how mighty someone on earth is, that individual is no match for the power of God.

2. Will Armageddon be a real battle?

Armageddon prophecy is not literary allegory or myth. Armageddon will be a real event of tragic proportions for those who oppose God. It will be a converging of actual military forces in the Middle East on some of the most contested land of all time—a land that has never known lasting peace. It is also a spiritual battle between the forces of good and evil. It will conclude with divine intervention and the return of Jesus Christ.

3. Where will Armageddon start?

As noted earlier, the armies will converge on the plain of Esdraelon, around the hill of Megiddo. John writes in Revelation

16:16, "And they gathered them together to the place which in Hebrew is called Har-Magedon." This area is located in northern Israel about 20 miles south-southeast of Haifa and 50 miles north of Jerusalem. The area was the scene of many battles in Old Testament times. For instance, Judges 4 records it as the area of Barak's conflict with the Canaanites, and it was also the area of Gideon's battle with the Midianites recorded in Judges 7.

However, Armageddon is not the site of the final battle or of the actual fighting. It is, rather, a place where the forces will assemble as they prepare for this tumultuous and terrible conflict. It is a staging area where final preparations are made. Dr. Arnold Fruchtenbaum writes:

> It should be noted that the passage [Revelation 16:12-16] says nothing of a battle in this valley for no fighting will take place here. The Valley of Jezreel, guarded by the mountain of Megiddo, will merely serve as the gathering ground for the armies of the Antichrist. Armageddon will play the same role that England played in the closing conflicts of World War II. The allied forces gathered their armies together in England but that is not where the final battle took place. The final battle began on the beaches of Normandy, France, on "D" Day. Armageddon will also serve as the gathering place with the battle beginning elsewhere.[3]

4. When will the conflict of Armageddon occur?

Though there is often mention of the battle in today's popular culture, it will not take place tomorrow, next month, or next year. Many prophetic events have already been fulfilled, including the birth, death, and resurrection of Jesus Christ 2,000 years ago. Many other events, such as the rapture of the church, the seven-year tribulation, the second coming of Christ, and the millennial kingdom are yet to come. The prophecies related to these events will be fulfilled as certainly as were the events of the past. However, they will also be brought to fruition in accordance with God's specific timing. There is a chronology and sequence to His plan. (According to God's plan there are several major events which will transpire before the campaign of Armageddon commences. The next major event is the rapture of the church spoken of in 1 Thessalonians 4:13-18 and elsewhere.)

Conflicts, battles, and wars around the globe are part of our daily headlines. Lasting peace in the Middle East is a commendable and desirable goal, but, according to the Bible, it is a dream that will not be attained in our day. There will be more conflicts in the Middle East and around the world, but these are not to be associated with Armageddon because some prophesied events must precede this battle.

We believe that Armageddon is a military conflict that occurs *after* the rapture and at the end of the seven-year tribulation.[4] It is our understanding that the Armageddon conflict will be the culmination of the Antichrist's reign, and it will end with the second coming of Jesus Christ and the destruction of the Antichrist and his forces.

Armageddon is the last major event on the prophetic timeline before the establishment of the millennial kingdom, Christ's 1,000-year reign on earth. Armageddon is not an event that people should desire or anticipate with joy because it will bring death and destruction. It is, however, a definite military conflict that will not, and cannot, be avoided by any amount of negotiation.

5. Is Armageddon a single battle or a campaign?

The detailed sequence of events and the terms used in relation to Armageddon suggest that it will be a campaign or series of battles. While it is not inappropriate to speak of it as the "final battle," or to use other similar language, technically we should probably refer to it as a campaign or the war of Armageddon. The Greek word *polemos,* translated "war" in Revelation 16:14, usually signifies an extended war or campaign. A single battle or fight is normally referred to by the word *mache*. An example of a passage where both terms are used is found in James 4:1, where James writes of interpersonal conflict: "What is the source of quarrels [*polemos*] and conflicts [*mache*] among you? Is not the source your pleasures that wage war [*strateuomai*] in your members?"

Armageddon's battles will not occur in a single day. One of the last phases of Armageddon is three days in duration. The battles are carried out over a wide geographic area to the north and south of Jerusalem and as far east as Babylon.

CHAPTER 17

What Is the Course of the Campaign?

6. What is the sequence and content of the stages of Armageddon?

Although the sequence of events is not found in one specific verse, detailed study of all the biblical passages pertaining to Armageddon reveals a very complex campaign. One of the most thorough studies of the campaign is that of Dr. Arnold Fruchtenbaum, who has divided the campaign into eight stages.[5] Although other plans can just as readily be proposed, his evaluation seems to be the most logical and comprehensive. Dr. Fruchtenbaum writes:

> The two climactic events of the Great Tribulation are the Campaign of Armageddon and the second coming of Jesus Christ. A considerable amount of data is given about this time period in the Scriptures. One of the greatest difficulties in the study of eschatology is placing these events in chronological sequence in order to see what exactly will happen in the Campaign of Armageddon....The Campaign of Armageddon can be divided into eight stages, and this in turn will facilitate an understanding of the sequence of events.[6]

Each of these eight stages serves a distinct purpose in the overall campaign. Each stage builds in anticipation and intensity until the climax at the second coming of Christ.

Stage 1: The Antichrist's Allies Assemble

The primary biblical reference to this first stage is Revelation 16:12-16:

> And the sixth angel poured out his bowl upon the great river, the Euphrates; and its water was dried up, that the way might be prepared for the kings from the east. And I saw coming out of the mouth of the dragon and out of the mouth of the beast and out of the mouth of the false prophet, three unclean spirits like frogs; for

> they are spirits of demons, performing signs, which go
> out to the kings of the whole world, to gather them
> together for the war of the great day of God, the
> Almighty. ("Behold, I am coming like a thief. Blessed is
> the one who stays awake and keeps his garments, lest
> he walk about naked and men see his shame.") And
> they gathered them together to the place which in
> Hebrew is called Har-Magedon.

The assembling of the armies begins at the same time as the
divine judgment of the sixth bowl. At this time the Euphrates River
will be dried up, making it faster and easier for the armies of the
"kings from the east" to assemble. In the Bible, "east" refers to the
region of Mesopotamia (Assyria and Babylon), and the drying up of
the river will make it easier for the forces of the Antichrist to assemble out of Babylon, which is his capital. The armies joining him will
be those of the seven remaining kings out of the ten described in
Daniel 7:24-27 and Revelation 17:12,13. Their goal will be the final
destruction of the Jews.

Writing of the satanic powers behind this coalition, Dr. Fruchtenbaum states:

> The gathering for this final campaign against the Jews
> is clearly the work of the counterfeit trinity. All three
> members of the counterfeit trinity are involved: the
> dragon, or Satan who is the counterfeit father; the
> Prophet who is the counterfeit son; and the False
> Prophet who is the counterfeit holy spirit. The sum-
> mons will be reinforced by demonic activity to make
> sure that the nations will indeed cooperate in assem-
> bling their armies together. These demonic messen-
> gers will be empowered to perform signs in order to
> assure compliance and defeat any reluctance to fall
> into line on the part of the other kings.[7]

Stage 2: Babylon Destroyed

In this stage, the activity shifts from the gathering armies of the
Antichrist to the destruction of Babylon [present-day Iran]. While
the Antichrist is with his armies at Armageddon, his capital city will
be attacked and destroyed. In the Old Testament, Babylon was both
the place of Israel's captivity and the originating site of idolatry.

Known also as Shinar (Genesis 10:10; 11:2; Daniel 1:2; Zechariah 5:11), Babylon will be a worldwide economic and religious center of activity during the tribulation (Revelation 17–18).

Two of the key passages regarding Babylon's future destruction are found in Jeremiah 50–51 and Revelation 18 (see also Isaiah 13–14). In these chapters we read of a future destruction of the city and nation, one that looks far beyond its first destruction in 539 B.C. In Jeremiah 50:1-10, divine judgment is pronounced against Babylon, and then, in verses 11-16, the fall of Babylon is pictured. The warfare will be intense and the destruction will be massive. We read in these verses:

> Because you are glad, because you are jubilant, O you who pillage My heritage, because you skip about like a threshing heifer and neigh like stallions, your mother will be greatly ashamed, she who gave you birth will be humiliated. Behold, she will be the least of the nations, a wilderness, a parched land, and a desert. Because of the indignation of the LORD she will not be inhabited, but she will be completely desolate; everyone who passes by Babylon will be horrified and will hiss because of all her wounds. Draw up your battle lines against Babylon on every side, all you who bend the bow; shoot at her, do not be sparing with your arrows, for she has sinned against the LORD. Raise your battle cry against her on every side! She has given herself up, her pillars have fallen, her walls have been torn down. For this is the vengeance of the LORD: take vengeance on her; as she has done to others, so do to her. Cut off the sower from Babylon, and the one who wields the sickle at the time of harvest; from before the sword of the oppressor they will each turn back to his own people, and they will each flee to his own land (Jeremiah 50:11-16).

A few verses later the description of the destruction continues:

> "Against the land of Merathaim, go up against it, and against the inhabitants of Pekod. Slay and utterly destroy them," declares the LORD, "and do according to all that I have commanded you. The noise of battle is in the land, and great destruction. How the hammer

190 Armageddon and the Middle East

of the whole earth has been cut off and broken! How Babylon has become an object of horror among the nations! I set a snare for you, and you were also caught, O Babylon, while you yourself were not aware; you have been found and also seized because you have engaged in conflict with the LORD. The LORD has opened His armory and has brought forth the weapons of His indignation, for it is a work of the Lord GOD of hosts in the land of the Chaldeans. Come to her from the farthest border; open up her barns, pile her up like heaps and utterly destroy her, let nothing be left to her. Put all her young bulls to the sword; let them go down to the slaughter! Woe be upon them, for their day has come, the time of their punishment" (Jeremiah 50:20-27).

According to Isaiah 13:19 and Jeremiah 50:40, the destruction will be as devastating and complete as was that of Sodom and Gomorrah. Once the attack and destruction are finished, Babylon will be uninhabitable and will never again be rebuilt (Revelation 18:21-24).

Who will come against the Antichrist, and what forces will contest his authority and power? According to Jeremiah 50:9 and 50:41,42, the attackers will be an alliance of forces from north of Babylon.

> For behold, I am going to arouse and bring up against Babylon a horde of great nations from the land of the north, and they will draw up their battle lines against her; from there she will be taken captive. Their arrows will be like an expert warrior who does not return empty-handed (Jeremiah 50:9).

> Behold, a people is coming from the north, and a great nation and many kings will be aroused from the remote parts of the earth. They seize their bow and javelin; they are cruel and have no mercy. Their voice roars like the sea, and they ride on horses, marshalled like a man for the battle against you, O daughter of Babylon (Jeremiah 50:41,42).

Although the Antichrist will be a world ruler, his control will not be so absolute as to preclude rebellion or opposition (Daniel 11:41). He will try, but it will be tactically impossible. The destruction will come as divine punishment for Babylon's long history of antagonism and evil against the people of Israel, and the result will be the razing of the city. "Because Babylon has ruled the entire world ruinously, God will now destroy her that had destroyed so many."[8]

> "But I will repay Babylon and all the inhabitants of Chaldea for all their evil that they have done in Zion before your eyes," declares the LORD. "Behold, I am against you, O destroying mountain, who destroys the whole earth," declares the LORD, "and I will stretch out My hand against you, and roll you down from the crags and I will make you a burnt out mountain. And they will not take from you even a stone for a corner nor a stone for foundations, but you will be desolate forever," declares the LORD (Jeremiah 51:24,25).

Although Babylon will be destroyed, the victors will not necessarily know that they are acting on behalf of God and fulfilling His prophetic plan. Their motives will be personal and political rather than prophetic. When Babylon is destroyed, the Antichrist will not be present in the city. He will be told of its destruction by messengers (Jeremiah 50:43; 51:31,32).

The attack will be swift, but there will be some warning or opportunity for Jews who are living in Babylon to flee from the city (Jeremiah 50:6-8,28; 51:5,6). Even in these last days, God will preserve a remnant of His people. These refugees are to go to Jerusalem and tell them of the city's destruction and their escape (Jeremiah 51:10,45,50; Revelation 18:4,5).

The destruction of Babylon will occur at the same time the nation of Israel begins to turn to God for spiritual renewal and regeneration (Jeremiah 31:31-34; 50:19,20). According to Revelation 18:1-3, after Babylon's destruction it will become a place of demonic habitation. Because of its political and economic prominence there will be great confusion, chaos, and despair over Babylon's destruction. The leaders and rulers who aligned themselves with the Antichrist, the merchants and those who prospered because of Babylon, and those who transported and moved commercial goods throughout the world will all be greatly affected by Babylon's fall and will lament their losses (Revelation 18:9-18).

Stage 3: Jerusalem Falls

Although the Antichrist's capital will have been destroyed in the second phase of the campaigning, his forces will not have been lost. Rather than moving eastward to confront the attackers of his capital, the Antichrist will move south against Jerusalem. We read of this move in Zechariah 12:1-3 and 14:1,2:

> The burden of the word of the LORD concerning Israel. Thus declares the LORD who stretches out the heavens, lays the foundation of the earth, and forms the spirit of man within him, "Behold, I am going to make Jerusalem a cup that causes reeling to all the peoples around; and when the siege is against Jerusalem, it will also be against Judah. And it will come about in that day that I will make Jerusalem a heavy stone for all the peoples; all who lift it will be severely injured. And all the nations of the earth will be gathered against it."

> Behold, a day is coming for the LORD when the spoil taken from you will be divided among you. For I will gather all the nations against Jerusalem to battle, and the city will be captured, the houses plundered, the women ravished, and half of the city exiled, but the rest of the people will not be cut off from the city.

The Antichrist's forces will sweep down to Jerusalem, and once again the city will fall into Gentile control. Although there will be a temporary resurgence of Jewish strength and stiff resistance, as described in Zechariah 12:4-9 and Micah 4:11–5:1, Jerusalem will fall. The losses on both sides will be enormous, but the Antichrist's forces will prevail initially. However, these passages teach the eventual victory of Israel through the Messiah.

Stage 4: The Antichrist Moves South Against the Remnant

In the fourth stage, the campaign shifts into the desert and mountains, probably to a location about 80 miles south of Jerusalem to the area of Bozrah/Petra. At the beginning of the second half of the tribulation, after the Antichrist breaks his treaty with

Israel (Daniel 9:27; Matthew 24:15), many of the Jews will flee into the desert for safety. This activity will be a fulfillment of the words and exhortations of Jesus in Matthew 24:16-31. In verse 16 Jesus says of those who see the abomination of desolation: "Then let those who are in Judea flee to the mountains." This flight for life is also described in Revelation 12:6,14.

After Jerusalem is captured, the Antichrist will move south in an attempt to destroy those who fled in the previous three-and-a-half years. In Micah 2:12 we read of God's gathering and protection of this remnant: "I will surely assemble all of you, Jacob, I will surely gather the remnant of Israel. I will put them together like sheep in the fold; like a flock in the midst of its pasture they will be noisy with men." The area normally associated with this part of the campaign is that of Mount Seir, about 30 miles south of the lower end of the Dead Sea. Two specific sites in that area are possibilities for the location of the fleeing Jews: Bozrah and Petra.[9] In Isaiah 33:13-16 we read of the gathering of the Jews in this area during the last half of the tribulation. In Jeremiah 49:13,14 we read of the gathering of the armies in Bozrah to destroy them. As the Antichrist's forces gather in the rugged wilderness, the fourth phase will come to an end, and the last few days of the campaign will begin.

Stage 5: The Regeneration of Israel

The campaign of Armageddon will culminate in the second coming of Christ. But before Christ returns there will be a confession of Israel's national sin (Leviticus 26:40-42; Deuteronomy 4:29-31; 30:6-8; Jeremiah 3:11-18; Hosea 5:15), and a pleading for the Messiah to return (Isaiah 64; Zechariah 12:10; Matthew 23:37-39). This will come as the armies of the Antichrist are gathered to destroy the Jews in the wilderness. According to Hosea 6:1-3, there will be a call issued by the Jewish leaders for the nation to repent. The nation will respond positively and repentance will take place for two days. Dr. Fruchtenbaum writes:

> The leaders of Israel will finally recognize the reason why the tribulation has fallen on them. Whether this will be done by the study of the Scriptures, or by the preaching of the 144,000, or via the Two Witnesses (the third sign of Jonah to which the Jews of Jerusalem had already responded), or by the ministry of Elijah, is

not clearly stated. Most likely there will be a combination of these things. But the leaders will come to a realization of the national sin in some way. Just as the Jewish leaders once led the nation to the rejection of the Messiahship of Jesus, they will then lead the nation to the acceptance of His Messiahship by issuing the call of Hosea 6:1-3. The confession of Israel's national sin will last for two days as the entire nation becomes regenerated and saved.[10]

The people of Israel will confess their sins with the words of Isaiah 53:1-9 and will be saved, fulfilling the prophecy of Romans 11:25-27:

For I do not want you, brethren, to be uninformed of this mystery, lest you be wise in your own estimation, that a partial hardening has happened to Israel until the fullness of the Gentiles has come in; and thus all Israel will be saved; just as it is written, "The Deliverer will come from Zion, He will remove ungodliness from Jacob. And this is My covenant with them, when I take away their sins."

The pleading for the return of the Messiah will be done in the wilderness as well as in Jerusalem, thus, the prophecy of Joel 2:28-32 will be fulfilled. At this same time, Zechariah 13:2-6 states that false prophets who have arisen during the tribulation and led Israel astray will be executed. Tragically, according to Zechariah 13:7-9, two-thirds of the Jewish population will have been killed during the tribulation. The remaining one-third will confess their sins, and God will answer their pleas for the return of the Messiah. This pleading is spoken of in Isaiah 64:1-12, as well as Psalms 79 and 80. "Only by faith in the Son of Man can Israel be regenerated. Only by calling upon the name of the Lord can Israel be saved spiritually. Only by the return of the Son of Man can Israel be saved physically."[11]

The fifth stage will come to completion on the third day of Israel's confession and prayer for Messiah's return. In the sixth stage, God will answer them, fulfilling biblical prophecy and the hope of the ages.

Stage 6: The Second Coming of Jesus Christ

In the sixth stage the prayers of the Jews are answered. Jesus Christ will return to earth in the clouds, in the same manner in which He departed (Matthew 24:30; Acts 1:9-11). The fact that Jesus returns first to the mountain wilderness of Bozrah is seen from Isaiah 34:1-7; 63:1-6; Habakkuk 3:3; and Micah 2:12,13. At His second coming, Jesus Christ, the Messiah, will enter battle with the Antichrist's forces, fighting not with human assistance, but with the word of His mouth. He will miraculously defeat them.

According to Jude 14–15 and Revelation 19:11-16, Jesus will return with an angelic army and with the church saints who had been raptured prior to the tribulation. From the verses in Revelation, it is clear that the second coming will bring destruction to the enemies of Jesus Christ:

> And I saw heaven opened; and behold, a white horse, and He who sat upon it is called Faithful and True; and in righteousness He judges and wages war. And His eyes are a flame of fire, and upon His head are many diadems; and He has a name written upon Him which no one knows except Himself. And He is clothed with a robe dipped in blood; and His name is called The Word of God. And the armies which are in heaven, clothed in fine linen, white and clean, were following Him on white horses. And from His mouth comes a sharp sword, so that with it He may smite the nations; and He will rule them with a rod of iron; and He treads the wine press of the fierce wrath of God, the Almighty. And on His robe and on His thigh He has a name written, "KING OF KINGS, AND LORD OF LORDS."

Stage 7: The Final Battle

In the seventh phase, Jesus the Messiah will fight alone on Israel's behalf, destroying the Antichrist and those who have come against the nation and persecuted it. In this phase the Antichrist will be slain by the true Christ (Habakkuk 3:13; 2 Thessalonians 2:8). "Among the very first casualties will be the Antichrist himself. Having ruled the world with great power and spoken against the true Son of God, the counterfeit son will be powerless before Christ."[12]

Beginning at Bozrah and moving back to Jerusalem and the Kidron Valley (also known as the Valley of Jehoshaphat), Jesus, the Messiah and King of the Jews, will miraculously engage and destroy the Antichrist's forces (Joel 3:12,13; Zechariah 14:12-15; Revelation 14:19,20).

Stage 8: The Ascent to the Mount of Olives

With the destruction of the Antichrist and his forces complete, the campaign will be over. Jesus will go and stand on the Mount of Olives in a symbolic victory ascent. When He does so, there will be a number of cataclysmic events that will bring the tribulation to an end. As described in Zechariah and Revelation:

> Then the LORD will go forth and fight against those nations, as when He fights on a day of battle. And in that day His feet will stand on the Mount of Olives, which is in front of Jerusalem on the east; and the Mount of Olives will be split in its middle from east to west by a very large valley, so that half of the mountain will move toward the north and the other half toward the south (Zechariah 14:3,4).

> And the seventh angel poured out his bowl upon the air; and a loud voice came out of the temple from the throne, saying, "It is done." And there were flashes of lightning and sounds and peals of thunder; and there was a great earthquake, such as there had not been since man came to be upon the earth, so great an earthquake was it, and so mighty. And the great city was split into three parts, and the cities of the nations fell. And Babylon the great was remembered before God, to give her the cup of the wine of His fierce wrath. And every island fled away, and the mountains were not found. And huge hailstones, about one hundred pounds each, came down from heaven upon men; and men blasphemed God because of the plague of the hail, because its plague was extremely severe (Revelation 16:17-21).

The supernatural calamities that come upon the world at this time, including the greatest earthquake the world has known, correspond to the seventh bowl judgment. As a result of the earthquake,

Jerusalem will split into three areas and the Mount of Olives will split into two parts, creating a valley. This is the means of escape from the earthquake for the Jewish inhabitants of the city (Zechariah 14:4,5).

In addition to the earthquake there will be a tremendous hailstorm and a blackout with an eclipse or darkening of the sun and moon (Joel 3:14-16; Matthew 24:29). With the subsiding of these events, the campaign of Armageddon and the tribulation will finally end. It is fitting that such worldwide catastrophes accompany the global judgment and Christ's second coming.

7. Is there any relationship between the "200 million" of Revelation 9:16 and Armageddon?

Many people have the mistaken idea that the conflict of Armageddon will entail battle with an army of the Antichrist consisting of 200 million troops. It is further held by some that this army will probably be Chinese. The "200 million" is derived from Revelation 9:16. The Chinese army idea is based on a reported claim by China that it can field such an army, coupled with the "kings of the east" mentioned in Revelation 16:12. However, a careful reading of the texts in question shows that the army of 200 million is demonic rather than human and that the events are two separate events. The force of 200 million is *not* part of Armageddon and is *not* Chinese or any other nationality.

The "200 million" is found in the midst of the description of the sixth trumpet judgment of Revelation 9:13-21. This judgment occurs just prior to the middle of the tribulation, three-and-a-half years *before* the conflict of Armageddon, which occurs during the sixth and seventh *bowl* judgments (Revelation 16). Attempts to put the two events together confuse the judgments and chronology of Revelation and the tribulation.

The "200 million" is better understood to be demonic because it is led by four fallen angels (Revelation 9:14,15). Revelation 9:17 also describes this army as something other than human: "And this is how I saw in the vision the horses and those who sat on them: the riders had breastplates the color of fire and of hyacinth and of brimstone; and the heads of the horses are like the heads of lions; and out of their mouths proceed fire and smoke and brimstone." If we look at Joel 1:15–2:11 in conjunction with Revelation 9:13-21, we are given a very descriptive image of the sixth trumpet judgment. This army

Tribulation Judgments from Revelation

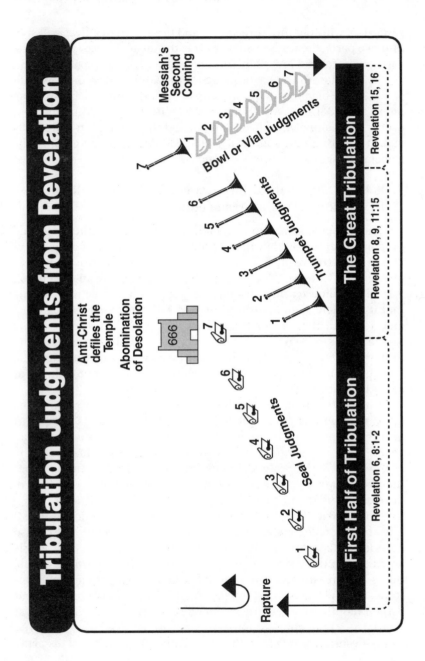

comes from the "bottomless pit," not from a human source. (See Revelation 9:2.) Additionally, "east" in the Bible always refers to Mesopotamia (today: eastern Syria and northern Iraq, between the Tigris and Euphrates Rivers) and, therefore, when they arise in preparation for Armageddon, the "kings of the east" will come from that region rather than China or elsewhere.[13]

It is unfortunate that there has been so much popularization of the "200 million Chinese theory." Such popularization focuses on the sensational rather than the sincere and can detract from profitable study of prophecy and the Bible. Dr. Fruchtenbaum writes:

> Sensationalism has had a field day with this figure, resulting in some fantastic speculation. In order for this speculation to stand, the 200 million figure must be pulled out of its context. The speculation all rests on current events. Communist China once declared that they can field an army of 200 million. Without even so much as questioning the truthfulness of this assertion, many have concluded that the 200 million must involve a Chinese invasion of the Middle East. The context just will not allow for this.[14]

Without doubt, Armageddon will involve large armies and vast amounts of military resources. Those resources are not, however, the same as found in Revelation 9.

8. What are the circumstances leading up to Armageddon?

As with many human events, there are two purposes for Armageddon: a divine intent and a human rationale. The divine purpose for Armageddon is judgment in preparation for the 1,000-year reign of Christ on earth. The satan-inspired human purpose is to once-and-for-all eliminate the Jews.

The Divine Purpose

All history and future events are ultimately the outworking of the decree of the Triune God. Nothing takes place that He did not actively plan. Throughout history, the battle has raged between God and Satan, good and evil, although usually not realized by humanity. The war of Armageddon is the culmination of a series of events that climax in this final act. Dr. Paul Feinberg explains:

Almost every passage that gives us the biblical story shows this supernatural factor at work. In Revelation 16:12-16, the New Testament passage in which we see the word "Armageddon," John sees three evil spirits that look like frogs come out of the mouth of the dragon. These evil spirits went out to the kings of the whole earth to bring them to Armageddon. Great deceptive power was given to these demon spirits so that they could perform miraculous signs. In Zechariah, it is God who says that He will make Jerusalem a burden to all the nations of the world (12:3), and that it is He who will gather all the nations to this city (14:2)....The nations have hated God and His people Israel. Now the nations are brought supernaturally to the valley of Jehoshaphat so that God can enter into judgment against the nations (Joel 3:1-3).[15]

The divine purpose for Armageddon is that it will serve as a venue by which God will judge His enemies. Since both satanic and human opposition is focused on God's elect nation of Israel, they are brought to that location so that God may bring down their foolish schemes of rebellion. The psalmist records God's response of laughter at the puny human plans to overthrow Him at Armageddon:

Why are the nations in an uproar, and the peoples devising a vain thing? The kings of the earth take their stand, and the rulers take counsel together against the LORD and against His Anointed: "Let us tear their fetters apart, and cast away their cords from us!" He who sits in the heavens laughs, the Lord scoffs at them. Then He will speak to them in His anger and terrify them in His fury: "But as for Me, I have installed My King upon Zion, My holy mountain" (Psalm 2:1-6).

The Human Purpose

The demented human perspective leading to the final march to Jerusalem appears to be motivated by efforts to solve what the majority of the population believes to be the source of the world's problems—the Jews. As we follow the buildup to Armageddon in Revelation (11–18), the persecution of Israel begins at the midpoint of the tribulation and culminates in the worldwide gathering of armies in Israel.

9. What military forces or nations will be involved in Armageddon?

Scripture indicates that all the nations of the world will be gathered in their war against Israel. This is a fitting climax to the tribulation—the whole world in rebellion against heaven (except for a remnant of believers). Dr. Feinberg explains:

> Not only will this war involve the whole land of Israel, but the Bible teaches that all the nations of the world will also become embroiled in it (Zechariah 12:3; 14:2; Revelation 16:14). These nations quite clearly will form four power blocks or alliances: nations to the south of the land of Palestine; a confederacy from the West; armies from the East (Revelation 16:12);...and finally, nations from the north of the land of Israel (Ezekiel 38, 39; Daniel 11:40-45).

> When the Bible speaks of all the nations of the whole world, does this mean that every country in existence today will do battle in Armageddon? Obviously not. Just within the last decade, we have seen some nations come and go. None of us can say for sure just what nations will be in existence at the time this prophecy is fulfilled. Will the nations of the Western Hemisphere— the U.S., Canada, and Mexico—be a part of this final conflict? They are not mentioned by name anywhere in the Bible. This does not mean that they will not be in existence, but neither would any prophecy be falsified by their absence.[16]

Scripture emphasizes the kings of the east who take a prominent role in the military buildup in preparation for the war of Armageddon. "And the sixth angel poured out his bowl upon the great river, the Euphrates; and its water was dried up, that the way might be prepared for the kings from the east" (Revelation 16:12). One reason why there is an emphasis on the eastern powers could be because this is where the largest masses of population reside. Not only does this include Middle Eastern nations such as Iran, Iraq, and Saudi

Arabia, but even more remote nations such as India, China, Japan, Korea, and so on. Dr. Feinberg tells us:

> Other nations named specifically as participants in this conflict include: Ammon (Jeremiah 9:26; Ezekiel 25:1-7; Daniel 11:41); Assyria (Isaiah 14:24-27); Egypt (Isaiah 19, 20; Ezekiel 29, 30; Daniel 11:41); Libya (Daniel 11:43); Moab (Isaiah 15, 16); and Syria (Isaiah 17), to name just a few. There is also the possibility that Babylon (Isaiah 13, 14, 21) will be rebuilt. Ancient Babylon is modern Iraq and part of Iran. The Bible speaks of its absolute destruction, and this seems never to have occurred historically. While we do not know exactly what nations will be in existence at the time of Armageddon, the Bible states clearly that all those nations which do survive until eschatological times will participate in the meeting at Megiddo.[17]

10. Is Armageddon the only military conflict during the tribulation?

When we consider the fact that, in essence, the whole tribulation will be a war between God and His opponents—Satan, the fallen angels, and mankind—it should not be surprising that there will be a great number of military conflicts throughout. With so much conflict, it would not be incorrect to see the tribulation period characterized as a world war.

There are some wars and battles that are specifically mentioned in the Bible in addition to Armageddon. Some of the military conflicts include the Battle of Gog and Magog (Ezekiel 38–39); Jerusalem being surrounded by armies at the midpoint of the tribulation (Daniel 9:27; Matthew 24:15-23); various battles involving the Antichrist's consolidation of global power (Daniel 8:23-27); a battle between the Antichrist and the king of the South (Daniel 11:40-45); and a battle of the armies of the Antichrist at Bozrah (Jeremiah 49:13,14; Micah 2:12). In such a general climate characterized by military conflict, it is not hard to imagine that there will be other battles not specifically mentioned in the Bible. As Matthew 24:6 says, this will be a time of "wars and rumors of wars."

11. What impact will the conflict of Armageddon have on Christians?

After the rapture of the church and the beginning of the tribulation there will many individuals who will come to faith in Jesus Christ. Throughout the seven-year tribulation many of these Christians will be persecuted and martyred for their faith and for their resistance to the Antichrist. Among these will be those who refuse to take the mark of the beast described in Revelation 13:16-18. Some Christians will probably die in the conflict of Armageddon also.

Though Armageddon will be a time of great death, destruction, and devastation, it will also be a sign to Christians that the end of the tribulation is near. It is for this reason that we find the comforting parenthetical statement by Jesus in verse 15 of the discussion of Armageddon in Revelation 16:12-16:

> Behold, I am coming like a thief. Blessed is the one
> who stays awake and keeps his garments, lest he walk
> about naked and men see his shame.

The imagery is that of taking the clothes of the guard caught sleeping on duty, leaving him naked and disgraced. Jesus is saying believers are not to be like this. Rather, they are to understand the signs and the times. This is the same teaching found in Matthew 24:32-51 and Luke 21:5-36. Christians are encouraged to continue in their faith and to hold on physically and spiritually for a short time longer, for when the armies begin to gather, the return of the Lord and the end is near.

12. What impact will the conflict of Armageddon have on Jerusalem?

Jerusalem will experience both war and peace during the tribulation. It has always been a city whose daily life swings as a pendulum between these two conditions. In the tribulation, the pendulum will swing even faster. In the first half of the tribulation there will be peace in the city, although other disasters from the seal and trumpet judgments of Revelation 6, 8, and 9 will befall it.

At some point during the tribulation, Israel will experience the fighting and events of Ezekiel 38–39, where armies from Gog and Magog will come against the nation. These forces will be destroyed by God through natural disasters and internal dissension (Ezekiel 38:17-23).

In the second half of the tribulation the city will experience war and fighting, especially at the end when the battle of Armageddon ensues. According to Zechariah 14:1-3, armies will be fighting in Jerusalem on the very day of the second coming of Christ:

> Behold, a day is coming for the LORD when the spoil taken from you will be divided among you. For I will gather all the nations against Jerusalem to battle, and the city will be captured, the houses plundered, the women ravished, and half of the city exiled, but the rest of the people will not be cut off from the city. Then the LORD will go forth and fight against those nations, as when He fights on a day of battle.

Under attack, Jerusalem will receive supernatural strength and the city will be victorious:

> In that day the LORD will defend the inhabitants of Jerusalem, and the one who is feeble among them in that day will be like David, and the house of David will be like God, like the angel of the LORD before them. And it will come about in that day that I will set about to destroy all the nations that come against Jerusalem (Zechariah 12:8,9).

Whether one believes that Armageddon will be a single battle or a campaign that encompasses days or even years, the battle will affect Jerusalem. Ultimately the security of the city will be assured only by the return of Christ—but not before the city is attacked and many people flee. Future victory in Jerusalem is certain . . . but so is combat.

13. What impact will the conflict of Armageddon have on Babylon?

In the course of developments relating to Armageddon, Babylon will be destroyed. Revelation 16 indicates that the final two bowl judgments are related to Babylon and Armageddon. The sixth bowl judgment is poured out "upon the great river, the Euphrates; and its water was dried up, that the way might be prepared for the kings from the east" (verse 12) that they may be gathered "together to the place which in Hebrew is called Har-Magedon" (verse 16). In conjunction with the sixth, the seventh bowl judgment follows with the judgment of Babylon (Revelation 16:17-21). Revelation 16:19 describes this judgment: "And the great city was split into three parts, and the cities of the nations fell. And Babylon the great was remembered before God, to give her the cup of the wine of His fierce wrath."

Babylon, God's ancient enemy, will meet her Waterloo in conjunction with the war of Armageddon. Destroyed in one hour and gone forever will be political, religious, and commercial Babylon. Frankly, for believers, it should be a day we look forward to. Finally God will make right the wrongs of Babylon:

> For this reason in one day her plagues will come, pestilence and mourning and famine, and she will be burned up with fire; for the Lord God who judges her is strong. And the kings of the earth, who committed acts of immorality and lived sensuously with her, will weep and lament over her when they see the smoke of her burning, standing at a distance because of the fear of her torment, saying, "Woe, woe, the great city, Babylon, the strong city! For in one hour your judgment has come" (Revelation 18:8-10).

CHAPTER 18

What Else Do We Know About Armageddon?

14. How does Armageddon relate to Israel's conversion?

Armageddon relates significantly to Israel's conversion and, in a very real way, is a major cause for her conversion. Scripture teaches that when Jerusalem is surrounded by the armies of the Antichrist and the world, who are poised to destroy Israel, the wayward nation will recognize that Jesus of Nazareth is truly their long-awaited Messiah. Notice what the Lord said through His prophet Zechariah:

> "Behold, I am going to make Jerusalem a cup that causes reeling to all the peoples around; and when the siege is against Jerusalem, it will also be against Judah. And it will come about in that day that I will make Jerusalem a heavy stone for all the peoples; all who lift it will be severely injured. And all the nations of the earth will be gathered against it.

> "In that day," declares the LORD, "I will strike every horse with bewilderment, and his rider with madness. But I will watch over the house of Judah, while I strike every horse of the peoples with blindness. Then the clans of Judah will say in their hearts, 'A strong support for us are the inhabitants of Jerusalem through the LORD of hosts, their God.' In that day I will make the clans of Judah like a firepot among pieces of wood and a flaming torch among sheaves, so they will consume on the right hand and on the left all the surrounding peoples, while the inhabitants of Jerusalem again dwell on their own sites in Jerusalem.

> "The LORD also will save the tents of Judah first in order that the glory of the house of David and the glory of the inhabitants of Jerusalem may not be magnified above Judah. In that day the LORD will defend the inhabitants of Jerusalem, and the one who is feeble among them in that day will be like David, and the house of David will be like God, like the angel of the

LORD before them. And it will come about in that day that I will set about to destroy all the nations that come against Jerusalem. And I will pour out on the house of David and on the inhabitants of Jerusalem, the Spirit of grace and of supplication, so that they will look on Me whom they have pierced; and they will mourn for Him, as one mourns for an only son, and they will weep bitterly over Him, like the bitter weeping over a first-born.

"In that day there will be great mourning in Jerusalem, like the mourning of Hadadrimmon in the plain of Megiddo. And the land will mourn, every family by itself; the family of the house of David by itself, and their wives by themselves; the family of the house of Nathan by itself, and their wives by themselves; the family of the house of Levi by itself, and their wives by themselves; the family of the Shimeites by itself, and their wives by themselves; all the families that remain, every family by itself, and their wives by themselves. In that day a fountain will be opened for the house of David and for the inhabitants of Jerusalem, for sin and for impurity" (Zechariah 12:2–13:1).

It is clear that Armageddon is the historical context in which Israel is converted. It is Israel's conversion that leads the Jews to call upon their newly found Messiah for the second coming (Matthew 23:39) so they may be physically rescued from the Antichrist's efforts to exterminate their race (Romans 10:13,14).

15. How does the Antichrist relate to Armageddon?

The Antichrist is soundly in the middle of the battle of Armageddon. He is the primary human involved in conceiving, planning, and executing the campaign.

After Babylon is destroyed (Revelation 16–18), the Antichrist is furious at the Lord of Heaven. With revenge in his heart he turns his fury toward Israel and God's people, the Jews (Daniel 11:38,39). As he waits in Israel for all his armies to arrive (Daniel 11:45) for his attack upon Jerusalem, his anger is likely building. His wrath has directed him exactly where God intends him to be. Now our Lord is ready for the action to begin, as recorded in Joel:

208 Armageddon and the Middle East

> Proclaim this among the nations: prepare a war; rouse the mighty men! Let all the soldiers draw near, let them come up! Beat your plowshares into swords, and your pruning hooks into spears; let the weak say, "I am a mighty man." Hasten and come, all you surrounding nations, and gather yourselves there. Bring down, O LORD, Thy mighty ones. Let the nations be aroused and come up to the valley of Jehoshaphat, for there I will sit to judge all the surrounding nations. Put in the sickle, for the harvest is ripe. Come, tread, for the wine press is full; the vats overflow, for their wickedness is great. Multitudes, multitudes in the valley of decision! For the day of the LORD is near in the valley of decision. The sun and moon grow dark, and the stars lose their brightness. And the LORD roars from Zion and utters His voice from Jerusalem, and the heavens and the earth tremble. But the LORD is a refuge for His people and a stronghold to the sons of Israel. Then you will know that I am the LORD your God, dwelling in Zion My holy mountain. So Jerusalem will be holy, and strangers will pass through it no more (3:9-17).

It will be on this day in history, during the battle of Armageddon, that the Antichrist will be captured by Jesus Christ and His human and angelic army. The beast (as the book of Revelation refers to the Antichrist) is taken and thrown forever into the lake of fire.

> And I saw an angel standing in the sun; and he cried out with a loud voice, saying to all the birds which fly in midheaven, "Come, assemble for the great supper of God; in order that you may eat the flesh of kings and the flesh of commanders and the flesh of mighty men and the flesh of horses and of those who sit on them and the flesh of all men, both free men and slaves, and small and great."

> And I saw the beast and the kings of the earth and their armies, assembled to make war against Him who sat upon the horse, and against His army. And the beast was seized, and with him the false prophet who performed the signs in his presence, by which he deceived those who had received the mark of the beast and

those who worshiped his image; these two were thrown alive into the lake of fire which burns with brimstone. And the rest were killed with the sword which came from the mouth of Him who sat upon the horse, and all the birds were filled with their flesh (Revelation 19:17-21)

At the end of Armageddon, the Antichrist's day of victory will be turned into everlasting defeat.

16. How does Jesus Christ relate to Armageddon?

Christ is the star of the Armageddon show. He stands the satanic intent of crushing Israel at Armageddon on its head by returning to rescue His newly converted people. Revelation 19:11-16 describes Christ's grand return to the stage of earth history. At Armageddon the hero is not hard to spot because He shows up riding a white horse:

And I saw heaven opened; and behold, a white horse, and He who sat upon it is called Faithful and True; and in righteousness He judges and wages war. And His eyes are a flame of fire, and upon His head are many diadems; and He has a name written upon Him which no one knows except Himself. And He is clothed with a robe dipped in blood; and His name is called The Word of God. And the armies which are in heaven, clothed in fine linen, white and clean, were following Him on white horses. And from His mouth comes a sharp sword, so that with it He may smite the nations; and He will rule them with a rod of iron; and He treads the wine press of the fierce wrath of God, the Almighty. And on His robe and on His thigh He has a name written, "KING OF KINGS, AND LORD OF LORDS."

In the early 1970s there was a cartoon in a Christian publication that depicted Armageddon. The drawing included a five-star general standing on a hill overlooking a military battle taking place in the valley below. This was clearly Armageddon. Looking through his binoculars, the general's attention was focused on the battle below. The general's aide was simultaneously nudging his commander and looking up and pointing at the sky. In the sky was a classic depiction of Christ's return on a white horse with His heavenly armies following.

The caption had the aide telling the general something like, "Sir! I think the direction of the battle is about to change!" What an understatement! Christ's role in Armageddon will be to not only turn the battle against the Antichrist, but also transition history from the horrors of the tribulation to the blessings of the millennial kingdom.

At Armageddon, Christ will disrupt the flow of events by returning in judgment in preparation for His glorious 1,000-year reign upon planet Earth. Like a child awaking from a nightmare to find that he is really safe, so will be the rescue of God's people (Matthew 24:29-31). The turmoil of Armageddon and the Middle East becomes a long-awaited peace. Christ finally brings the long prophesied "shalom" of the Bible to rule in the hearts of His people, and, at this time, to rule in the human affairs of His people. He brings the world to a new beginning.

17. Where does the Bible teach that Jesus will return to the Mount of Olives?

In the first chapter of Acts we read of the ascent of Jesus from the Mount of Olives after the resurrection and the 40 days with the disciples. As the disciples stood watching the ascent, two angels appeared to them telling them that Jesus would return to the same location: "Men of Galilee, why do you stand looking into the sky? This Jesus, who has been taken up from you into heaven, will come in just the same way as you have watched Him go into heaven" (Acts 1:11). Jesus' first-century departure was prefigured in the sixth century B.C. when Ezekiel watched the glory of God depart from Israel's temple and descend from the Mount of Olives.

The return of Christ, or the second coming, was prophesied by Zechariah almost six hundred years earlier in Zechariah 14:4: "And in that day His feet will stand on the Mount of Olives, which is in front of Jerusalem on the east; and the Mount of Olives will be split in its middle from east to west by a very large valley, so that half of the mountain will move toward the north and the other half toward the south." Since Christ delivered His great prophetic discourse on His second coming from the Mount of Olives, it is clearly implied that His return will be at the same location (Matthew 24–25). This will be Christ's victory ascent after defeating the Antichrist and his forces. (This coming should not be confused with the rapture, which occurs seven years earlier and is recorded in 1 Thessalonians 4:14-17. These two comings are separate and distinct events.)[18]

18. What happens after Armageddon?

Armageddon culminates in the second coming of Jesus Christ to the earth and the destruction of the forces of the Antichrist. This will conclude the 7-year tribulation. There will then be a 75-day transition period between the tribulation and the 1,000-year reign of Jesus Christ upon the earth known as the millennium.[19] In this interim period, the image of the Antichrist that was set up in the temple at the middle of the tribulation will be removed after 30 days (Daniel 12:11). According to Revelation 19:20, the Antichrist and the false prophet will be cast into the lake of fire at this point. Since the Antichrist was killed at the second coming of Christ, he will be resurrected for this punishment. Satan will also be bound at this time for the duration of the millennium (Revelation 20:1-3). During this time, Jewish survivors of the tribulation will be judged (Ezekiel 20:34-38), as well as living Gentiles and the nations who persecuted the Jews during the tribulation (Joel 3:1-3; Matthew 25:31-46). This will also be the time of the resurrection of Old Testament saints (Isaiah 26:19; Daniel 12:2) and the resurrection of tribulation saints (Revelation 20:4-6).

Following this interval will be the millennial kingdom of Jesus Christ as foretold in passages such as Isaiah 2:2-4; Ezekiel 37:1-13; 40–48; Micah 4:1-7; and Revelation 20.[20] In Psalm 2:6-9, the psalmist tells of the yet future reign of Jesus Christ:

> But as for Me, I have installed My King upon Zion, My holy mountain. I will surely tell of the decree of the LORD: He said to Me, "Thou art My Son, today I have begotten Thee. Ask of Me, and I will surely give the nations as Thine inheritance, and the very ends of the earth as Thy possession. Thou shalt break them with a rod of iron, Thou shalt shatter them like earthenware."

An earthly kingdom with a physical presence and rule by the Messiah-King is foretold throughout the Bible. This promise was not fulfilled in the first coming of Jesus Christ (when He did what only He could do—die on the cross to pay for sin) because, though offered, the kingdom was rejected by Israel and, thus, it was postponed until the second coming of Christ. Revelation 5 says that Christ is worthy to receive this kingdom, and in Revelation 11:15 we are told that the prophecies will yet be fulfilled. The millennium is a transitional period in God's program; it is the beginning of the eternal rule of God in the kingdom, which will pass into the eternal state. It is "the consummating link between history and the eternal order."[21] History and current events are moving toward a final era that will be the pinnacle of God's plan. Dr. David Larsen, citing the French theologian René Pache, writes:

> If history culminated with cataclysm and judgment, the Second Coming of Christ in power would be only "a walk through the ruins." The stone which becomes a mountain will "fill all the earth" (Daniel 2:35). "They will reign on earth" is the promise (Revelation 5:10). The venue of the Kingdom is to be on earth before we come to the final expression of the Kingdom in "the new heaven and the new earth" (2 Peter 3:13; Revelation 21–22).[22]

The millennium will be followed by the final judgment and the eternal state. At this point, Armageddon will be an event 1,000 years old, and the horrors of it will be replaced by the joys of eternal worship and eternal life. (We cover the millennium in greater detail in Part 5.)

19. Do the events of Ezekiel 38–39 relate to Armageddon?

The two chapters of Ezekiel 38–39 prophesy a great campaign and battle in the Middle East, but there is not unanimous agreement by prophecy scholars on when it occurs. Within premillennialism there are at least six views on the timing of the events in these chapters. Each view has some strengths and objections to it.[23] The views regarding the timing of these chapters are as follows:

1. Before the tribulation begins (but not necessarily before the rapture)

2. At the midpoint of the tribulation

3. At the end of the tribulation and as part of Armageddon

4. Throughout the second half of the tribulation (chapter 38 at the midpoint and chapter 39 at the end)

5. After the tribulation but prior to the millennium

6. At the end of the millennium

There are several details of these chapters that differ from accounts of Armageddon in Revelation that lead us away from strict identification of it with Armageddon. Fruchtenbaum summarizes these:

> First, in Ezekiel there are definite allies mentioned and they are limited in number while other nations stand in opposition. In the Campaign of Armageddon all nations are allied together against Jerusalem without exception. Secondly, the Ezekiel invasion comes from the north, but the Armageddon invasion comes from the whole earth. Thirdly, the purpose of the Russian [38:6] invasion is to take spoil; the purpose of the Armageddon Campaign is to destroy all the Jews. Fourthly, in the Ezekiel invasion there is a protest against the invasion; in the Armageddon Campaign there is no protest since all the nations are involved. Fifthly, the Ezekiel invasion is destroyed through convulsions of nature; the Armageddon invasion is destroyed by the personal second coming of Jesus Christ. Sixthly, the Ezekiel invasion is destroyed on the mountains of Israel; the Armageddon Campaign is destroyed in the area between Petra and Jerusalem. Seventh, the Russian invasion takes place while Israel is living securely in the land; but the Armageddon Campaign takes place while Israel is in flight and in hiding.[24]

Two of the major issues that any view must address is that of the seven months to bury the dead from the battle (Ezekiel 39:12-14) and the seven years of burning the weapons (Ezekiel 39:9,10). In the second half of the tribulation the Jews are fleeing and being persecuted; therefore, the burying of the dead is a problem. Also, of the six major views, only the first one doesn't place some of the burning of the weapons beyond the seven-year tribulation and into the millennium. (In the case of the sixth view, into the eternal state, which makes no sense.) For some, the issue of weapons in the millennium is not an issue but is seen as fitting with other statements such as beating swords into plowshares and spears into pruning hooks (Isaiah 2:4; Micah 4:3).[25]

Proponents of each view are trying to put the pieces of this portion of the prophetic puzzle together. To do so, there must be consistent interpretation of the various texts and proper identification of all the various elements in the chapters. Though not necessarily controversial, the chapters are detailed, and there has been much legitimate speculation about the details. Many interpreters opt to place these chapters at the end of the tribulation (and associate them with Armageddon) or beginning at the middle of the tribulation and carrying through to the end. However, Dr. Fruchtenbaum holds the view that the events are prior to the tribulation but not necessarily prior to the rapture. Such a view allows the possibility (though not necessity) of a significant lapse between the rapture and the beginning of the tribulation, which comes with the signing of the seven-year covenant (Daniel 9:27). There are several strong points to be made in support of this view. First, the nation of Israel today is populated by Jews and other peoples from many nations (Ezekiel 38:8,12). Second, the Jews dwell securely (Ezekiel 38:11,14), even though not always peacefully. Third, this view allows for the seven years and seven months with no difficulty.[26] While some have tried to argue that such a view destroys the doctrine of imminency in relation to the rapture, such is not the case, for, as he points out, "stating that something must precede the tribulation is *not* the same as stating that it must precede the rapture unless it is further stated that the rapture begins the tribulation. However, the act that begins the tribulation is not the rapture but the signing of the seven year covenant."[27]

Whichever view one holds, there is the certainty that these chapters will yet be fulfilled and that at least one and very likely two great military campaigns will occur in the Middle East in the coming years. It doesn't appear that the events of Ezekiel 38–39 relate to Armageddon.

20. Why must Armageddon occur?

From a human perspective, Armageddon will be a horrible war of mass destruction. It will be the culmination of the greatest time of terror the world has known. Wouldn't it be better for all of this not to happen? Dr. Charles Ryrie writes:

> Why must there be such a time as this? There are at least two reasons: First, the wickedness of man must be punished. God may seem to be doing nothing about evil now, but someday He will act. A second reason is that man must, by one means or another, be prostrated before the King of kings and Lord of lords. He may do so voluntarily now by coming to Christ in faith and receiving salvation. Later he will *have* to do so, receiving only condemnation.[28]

21. How do current events in the Middle East relate to Armageddon?

Current events in the Middle East do not relate directly to the next prophetic *event* on God's calendar—the rapture of the church. However, they do relate, prophetically, to the next *phase* of history, which is the tribulation. Since the seven-year tribulation will climax in the battle of Armageddon in the Middle East, then events occurring today are preparatory for the tribulation and can be tracked as setting the stage for the future. Dr. John Walvoord explains:

> The world today is like a stage being set for a great drama. The major actors are already in the wings waiting for their moment in history. The main stage props are already in place. The prophetic play is about to begin....All the necessary historical developments have already taken place.[29]

These major situations that are true now, and that were not true 50 years ago, point to the conclusion that the rapture itself may be very near because the stage has been set for events that will follow the rapture.

> All areas of prophecy combine in the united testimony that history is preparing our generation for the end of the age.
>
> In each area of prophecy a chronological checklist of important prophetic events can be compiled. In each list, in regard to the church, the nations, or

Israel, the events of history clearly indicate that the world is poised and ready for the Rapture of the church and the beginning of the countdown to Armageddon.[30]

Earlier, Dr. Walvoord noted:

Never before in history have all the factors been present for the fulfillment of prophecy relating to end-time religious trends and events. Only in our generation have the combined revival of Israel, the formation of a world church, the increasing power of Muslim religion, the rise of the occult, and the worldwide spread of atheistic philosophy been present as a dramatic setting for the final fulfillment of prophecy. As far as world religion is concerned, the road to Armageddon is already well prepared, and those who will travel to their doom may well be members of our present generation.[31]

CHAPTER 19

Why Does Armageddon Matter?

22. Why should I be concerned about Armageddon?

As a Christian living before the rapture of the church and before the conflict of Armageddon, the perspective is very different from the one that new believers will have after the rapture. We will not experience either the tribulation or the campaign of Armageddon; they may experience both. Yet Armageddon is important for us, not because we are to be "Christian Chicken Littles," who panic and say that the end is near, but because we are to be discerning students of the Bible who realize that God has a plan for the world and history is "going somewhere."

God has told us some of the future through biblical prophecy. We do not know the future fully, but we know with certainty that God is presently working in the lives of people and the events of each day. Through past and present events, God is working to set the stage for the final act of world history. It is an act in which Jesus Christ will reign supreme, and Armageddon is one scene in that closing act.

As Christians we should also express concern about Armageddon because of the devastation and death that will occur. The biblical glimpses of the conflict should serve as a catalyst for evangelism, obedience, and prayer—for believers and nonbelievers. For those who do not know Jesus Christ, the future in this world and the next will be tragic. Armageddon serves as a warning of the coming judgment and an encouragement to seek a personal relationship with Jesus Christ—the Messiah and Savior.

23. How should I pray for Jerusalem and the Middle East?

Journalists, diplomats, politicians, and historians frequently use the phrase "peace and prosperity." However, from a biblical perspective, "peace and *salvation*" is correct. We should pray daily for peace in the Middle East so that the gospel and the message of Jesus Christ can spread unimpeded (1 Timothy 2:1-4). Recognizing God's prophetic plan, we should also pray for the salvation of all people who inhabit that region.

The pain, pride, prejudice, and politics of the Middle East are very real. The suffering has been immense and the solutions are elusive. Yet the prophecies are as real as the problems, and the solution rests ultimately in the Scripture and the Savior.

As we await the return of Jesus Christ, Jerusalem's Messiah-King, we should heed the words of King David:

> Pray for the peace of Jerusalem: "May they prosper who love you. May peace be within your walls, and prosperity within your palaces." For the sake of my brothers and my friends, I will now say, "May peace be within you" (Psalm 122:6-9).

24. What is the hope for the future?

The hope for the Christian continues to be the return of the Lord Jesus Christ for His own in the rapture. Titus 2:13 admonishes believers to be "looking for the blessed hope and the appearing of the glory of our great God and Savior, Christ Jesus." In the interim, we are to be faithful to Him, to proclaim the gospel of salvation to all who will listen, and to "do good to all men, and especially those who are of the household of the faith" (Galatians 6:10). Christians are not pessimistic about the future; rather, we are realistic and know that, regardless of tomorrow's headlines, our hope and our destiny is in Christ Jesus, the final victor.

The Great Battle That Never Was

Armageddon will be the last great world war of history. It will take place in Israel in conjunction with the second coming of Christ. The Bible is very clear that it is a certain and cataclysmic event yet to come. According to the Bible, great armies from the east and the west will gather and assemble to strike a final blow against Israel. There will be threats to the power of the Antichrist from the south, and he will also move to destroy a revived Babylon in the east before finally turning his forces toward Jerusalem. As he and his armies move on Jerusalem, God will intervene and Jesus Christ will return to rescue His people, Israel. The Lord and His angelic army will destroy the armies, capture the Antichrist and the false prophet, and cast them into the lake of fire (Revelation 19:11-21).

In a sense, Armageddon is a battle that never really takes place. That is, it does not take place in accordance with its human intent to gather the armies of the world to execute the Antichrist's solution to the "Jewish problem." This is why Jesus Christ chooses this moment in history for His return to earth. He will thwart the Antichrist's attempted annihilation of the Jews and destroy the armies of the world who have been gathered for that purpose. It seems only fitting, in light of mankind's bloody legacy, that the return of Christ should be precipitated by worldwide military conflict against Israel. History is moving toward Armageddon.

PART 5

The Millennium

The Mountain of the House of the Lord

"Thy kingdom come. Thy will be done, on earth as it is in heaven." Countless times every day for almost 2,000 years, Christians around the globe have voiced this prayer modeling the one Jesus gave to His disciples as recorded in Matthew 6:9-13 and Luke 11:2-4. What are we asking for with these words?

Throughout its history, the world has known many kingdoms, dynasties, and empires. They have risen and fallen, blowing across the pages of history like leaves on an autumn day. Some have been spectacular and adorned with splendor, others have enslaved and slaughtered their populations. Regardless of how we remember them, they all share the same common denominator—human leaders. Even in our own day, many think that if we could just get the right people into political office, then humanity would be free to reach its full potential.

There are many views of history and its relation to the future. Some people see it as cyclical, others look back wishfully to a "golden age." Some say it is progressing according to "laws of nature," others say it is digressing by those same laws. To all of this, the Bible gives a clear and certain answer to the questions of the future. History and human events *are* going somewhere and there will be a glorious future kingdom. The prayers of Christians will be answered and God Himself, in the person of Jesus Christ, the second member of the Trinity, will reign and rule on earth for 1,000 years in the millennial kingdom. The best is yet to come!

Human history is sandwiched between two paradises. The first paradise began in the garden of Eden, but the fall into sin brought the pain and sorrow of God's curse. Humanity was given the mandate of developing the garden into the city of God. Instead of the New Jerusalem, the result was Babylon and the kingdom of man. With Christ's intervention into history (first in humility, next in glory), humankind will yet return to paradise, this time in a city—New Jerusalem.

History in our own day is moving toward the establishment of God's victory and rule upon earth through Jesus Christ and His people. But what are the details? What does the Bible teach about the coming millennium? Actually the Bible has a great deal to say about this subject. Let's examine its teachings together.

CHAPTER 20

What Is the Millennium?

1. Where does the Bible teach about the millennium?

If you look in an English translation of the Bible concordance for the word *millennium*, you will probably be disappointed. There are many Bible passages that teach about the millennium even though the word itself is not mentioned. The millennium is a biblical doctrine and theological concept derived from many passages. Like many English theological terms, millennium is derived from Latin. It refers to the length of time that the Bible says the Messiah's kingdom will last upon earth before the end of history.

> The English word *millennium* comes from the Latin word *mille,* meaning "thousand." The Greek word for millennium comes from *chilias,* meaning "a thousand," and *annus,* meaning "year." The Greek term is used six times in the original text of the twentieth chapter of Revelation to define the duration of Christ's kingdom on earth prior to the destruction of the old heavens and the old earth. Therefore, the word millennium refers to the thousand years of Christ's future reign on earth that will precede eternity.[1]

Numerous Old Testament passages speak of a future time of true peace and prosperity for the righteous followers of God under the benevolent physical rule of Jesus Christ on earth. Zechariah 14:9 tells of this time, saying, "And the LORD will be king over all the earth; in that day the LORD will be the *only* one, His name the *only* one." The passage then continues in verses 16-21 to describe some of the millennial conditions. Even though the Bible speaks descriptively throughout about the millennial kingdom, it was not until the final book—Revelation—that the length of His kingdom is revealed.

Isaiah also foretold of this future era:

> Now it will come about that in the last days, the mountain of the house of the LORD will be established as the chief of the mountains, and will be raised above the

hills; and all the nations will stream to it. And many peoples will come and say, "Come, let us go up to the mountain of the LORD, to the house of the God of Jacob; that He may teach us concerning His ways, and that we may walk in His paths." For the law will go forth from Zion, and the word of the LORD from Jerusalem. And He will judge between the nations, and will render decisions for many peoples; and they will hammer their swords into plowshares, and their spears into pruning hooks. Nation will not lift up sword against nation, and never again will they learn war (Isaiah 2:2-4).

Several chapters later, he again writes of the millennium:

And the wolf will dwell with the lamb, and the leopard will lie down with the kid, and the calf and the young lion and the fatling together; and a little boy will lead them. Also the cow and the bear will graze; their young will lie down together; and the lion will eat straw like the ox. And the nursing child will play by the hole of the cobra, and the weaned child will put his hand on the viper's den. They will not hurt or destroy in all My holy mountain, for the earth will be full of the knowledge of the LORD as the waters cover the sea (Isaiah 11:6-9).

Other extensive Old Testament passages include: Psalm 2:6-9; Isaiah 65:18-23; Jeremiah 31:12-14,31-37; Ezekiel 34:25-29; 37:1-13; 40–48; Daniel 2:35; 7:13-14; Joel 2:21-27; Amos 9:13-14; Micah 4:1-7; and Zephaniah 3:9-20. These verses are only a few of the scores of prophetic passages found regarding this subject before the first coming of Christ. Prophecy scholar David Larsen summarizes these texts succinctly noting, "The whole bulk of Old Testament prophecy points to the establishment of a kingdom of peace upon earth when the law will go forth from Mount Zion."[2]

The New Testament also gives significant witness to this coming kingdom because continuity with the Old Testament vision of a future millennial kingdom is maintained. It is the millennial kingdom that Jesus spoke of during the Passover meal before being betrayed and crucified:

And when He had taken a cup and given thanks, He gave it to them, saying, "Drink from it, all of you; for this is My blood of the covenant, which is poured out for many for forgiveness of sins. But I say to you, I will not drink of this fruit of the vine from now on until that day when I drink it new with you in My Father's kingdom" (Matthew 26:27-29; see also Mark 14:25; Luke 22:18).

The most extensive New Testament passage regarding the millennium is Revelation 20, in which John describes a chronological sequence—the binding, rebellion, and judgment of Satan in the millennium. Some prophecy scholars also hold that Revelation 21:9-27 describes the New Jerusalem during the millennium. This is not likely since it refers to the eternal state which is supported by the sequential development of the text from the millennium in Revelation 20 to the eternal state in Revelation 21. Yet others hold a mediating position and see the passage as teaching the eternal habitation of resurrected saints during the millennium.[3]

The future kingdom of God will have two distinct phases, the millennium and the eternal state. However, the overwhelming emphasis of the Bible is upon the 1,000-year reign of Christ in His future kingdom known as the millennium. The millennium is a biblical reality that is yet to be realized. According to the Bible, life on earth will get better—but not before it gets worse in an era known as the seven-year tribulation.

2. How do we know it's really 1,000 years?

There is no textual reason to reject the position of a literal 1,000-year kingdom as described in Revelation 20:2-7. Six times in this passage the number 1,000 appears, underscoring the significance and literalness of the number. While many interpreters want to see this passage as symbolic, consistent interpretation will lead readers to the conclusion that the passage must refer to a future literal 1,000 years.[4] Any effort to argue against a literal understanding of 1,000 in Revelation 20 must be done on a textual basis, not simply because it offends one's *a priori* sense of what history should be like. It is the Bible that tells us what to believe about the future, thus, any view must be based upon literary indicators from the biblical text.

PROPHECY WATCH

Writing against the view of some interpreters who want to understand the 1,000 and other numbers in Revelation as symbols only, Dr. Roy Zuck argues correctly:

> But are all the numbers he mentions to be taken as symbols? Do they not have meaning as ordinary, literal numbers: If 7, 42, and 1260 are not to be taken literally, then what about the reference to the 2 witnesses in 11:3? And if 1,000 means simply a large number, then what about the reference to 7,000 people in verse 13? On what basis do we say that 7,000 does not mean a literal 7,000: And if 1,000 is a large indefinite number, do the references to 4 angels (7:1) and 7 angels (8:6) mean simply small numbers? If these numbers in the Book of Revelation have no normal, literal numerical value, then what has happened to the principle of normal, grammatical interpretation? How can we say that 144,000 is a symbolic number, when 7:5-8 refers specifically to 12,000 from each of 12 tribes in Israel?[5]

If we are going to maintain consistency and a normal, grammatical, and historical perspective as we approach this passage, we must see it as a literal 1,000 years. Any other interpretation will ultimately break down and create more confusion and interpretive problems. After an extensive and detailed study of this passage, New Testament scholar Dr. Harold Hoehner writes,

> Therefore, the most natural way to take the 1,000 years is literally. Its denial came about because it was depicted as a time of overindulgence of the flesh and because the allegorical interpretation of Scripture had become the dominant school of thought. The denial of a literal 1,000 years is not because of the exegesis of the text but a predisposition brought to the text....In examining Revelation 20, the most natural interpretation is to take the 1,000 years literally.[6]

Even though the millennium is taught throughout the whole of the Bible, the interpretation of this passage is important. Non-premillennialists try to insist, as Nathaniel West notes, "numbers don't count."[7] If it is understood literally, then it assures a premillennial understanding of this passage and the whole of Scripture.

The phrase "a thousand years" occurs six times within the narrative of Revelation 20. This genre is not poetic; it is prose nonfiction, a kind of autobiography. Revelation 20:4-5 contains a vision and 20:6 its interpretation. In both vision and interpretation a thousand years is mentioned. The vision (20:4-5) is in the aorist tense in the original Greek, but the interpretation is in the future tense.[8] This means that 20:6 is an interpretation of 20:4-5, and one does not use a symbol to explain a symbol. The explanation in verse 6 would make no sense if it were not literal.

Because a literal understanding of the 1,000 years leads to premillennialism, antipremillennialists offer speculative guesses as to what it could mean. For example:

> The proper understanding of the thousand-year time frame in Revelation 20 is that it is representative of a long and glorious era and is not limited to a literal 365,000 days. The figure represents a perfect cube of ten, which is the number of quantitative perfection.[9]

Premillennialists do not limit God; He is the one who determines the times and the seasons. History, by its nature, is limited by time and characterized by a sequence of events. The 1,000 years are merely the conclusion of history and a warm-up for God's reign into eternity. The Bible says that Christ's reign on earth will be 1,000 years—not a perfect cube of ten. Such an approach to the text is an example of pulling ideas out of thin air with no textual basis for support. It is significant to note:

> The hope of the 1,000 years' kingdom did not originate with John. Plainly enough, it appears as an already given, steadfast, and of itself a well-grounded, matter of expectation, familiar and needing only to be named, something peculiar and of the highest importance, and woven as closely as possible into the whole web of the Christian life....The Seer...found this term, the 1,000 years, already extant, and assumed that his readers were not unacquainted with it. He retained an expression already in common use....A point undoubtedly common to both Jewish and Christian apocalyptics, is

the period of blessedness on earth, called the 1,000
years.[10]

Indeed, we find in Jewish literature written before the book of
Revelation that some Jews speculated that the Messiah's kingdom
would be 1,000 years in length.[11] Such speculation was turned to
fact with the Holy Spirit's giving of Revelation 20 to the apostle John.

Those who deny a literal 1,000 years are also forced to an unnat-
ural understanding of John's reference to two resurrections. If there
are two resurrections, then premillennialism is assured since this
would mean that one would occur before the 1,000 years and the
second at the end—instead of a single resurrection at the end of current history. Henry Alford shows that such a view cannot be a valid
explanation of Scripture.

> If in a passage where two resurrections are mentioned,
> where certain ["souls came to life"] at the first, and the
> rest of the ["dead came to life"] only at the end of a
> specified period after the first,—if in such a passage
> the first resurrection may be understood to mean spir-
> itual rising with Christ, while the second means literal
> rising from the grave;—then there is an end of all sig-
> nificance in language, and Scripture is wiped out as a
> definite testimony to any thing. If the first resurrection
> is spiritual, then so is the second, which I suppose
> none will be hardy enough to maintain: but if the sec-
> ond is literal, then so is the first, which in common
> with the whole primitive Church and many of the best
> modern expositors, I do maintain, and receive as an
> article of faith and hope.[12]

Numbers do count! Sequential counting is basic to their purpose
and nature. They count all throughout the book of Revelation, especially in chapter 20. Therefore, there will be a literal and, thus,
future 1,000-year reign of Christ on earth.

3. Will the millennium be in heaven or on earth?

The millennial kingdom of Christ will be an earthly kingdom in
which Christ will reign from Jerusalem and all of the specifics of the
"land promise" to Abraham (Genesis 12:7) will be fulfilled (Ezekiel
47–48). That the kingdom is earthly is seen from many biblical pas-

sages, among them Isaiah 11 and Zechariah 14:9-21. The millennium will bring about the complete fulfillment of God's biblical covenants with Israel (the Abrahamic, Davidic, Palestinian, and New Covenants).[13]

The millennium and millennial kingdom is more than the rule of God in the hearts of men and women. It is also distinct from the eternal state. Dr. Walvoord writes:

> A righteous reign of Christ on earth is of course precisely what one would have expected from previous study of the Abrahamic covenant with its promises to the earth, the Davidic covenant relative to the Son of David reigning on the throne forever, and the many promises pertaining to Israel's regathering and reestablishment in their ancient land. The theocratic kingdom, therefore, of which the prophets spoke is an earthly kingdom which can find its fulfillment only in a literal reign of Christ upon the earth.[14]

4. Have Christians always believed in the millennium?

In the first centuries of the church's history there was a clear belief in the millennium. Until the rise of the dominance of Latin as the church's primary language in the fourth century, Greek was commonly used. The early church called millennialism by the Greek term for 1,000—*chiliasm.*

While the study and understanding of biblical prophecy was not as detailed as it would be in later centuries, there was unequivocal belief in the millennium. Prominent church historian Philip Schaff concurs:

> The most striking point in the eschatology of the ante-Nicene age is the prominent chiliasm, or millennarianism, that is the belief of a visible reign of Christ in glory on earth with the risen saints for a thousand years, before the general resurrection and judgment. It was indeed not the doctrine of the church embodied in any creed or form of devotion, but a widely current opinion of distinguished teachers, such as Barnabas, Papias, Justin Martyr, Irenaeus, Tertullian, Methodius, and Lactanius....[15]

With the rise of allegorical interpretation, especially under Augustine, millennialism was largely (though not totally) abandoned in the West until Protestants began to revive it in the late 1500s as they increasingly applied a literal hermeneutic and read the early church fathers. Schaff notes:

> Origen opposed chiliasm as a Jewish dream, and spiritualized the symbolical language of the prophets.... The apocalyptic millennium he [Augustine] understood to be the present reign of Christ in the Catholic church, and the first resurrection, the translation of the martyrs and saints to heaven, where they participate in Christ's reign....From the time of Constantine and Augustine chiliasm took its place among the heresies....[16]

We must always remember that first and foremost, the validity of any teaching or doctrine comes not from the acceptance or denial of the teaching in history, but from the Bible. A doctrine is not true (or false) because a majority of professing Christians have believed it throughout history. A doctrine is true because the Bible says it is true.[17]

CHAPTER 21

What Is the Purpose of the Millennium?

5. Why is the millennium necessary?

In Psalm 2:6-9, the psalmist tells of the yet future reign of Jesus Christ:

> But as for Me, I have installed My King upon Zion, My holy mountain. I will surely tell of the decree of the LORD: He said to Me, "Thou art My Son, today I have begotten Thee. Ask of Me, and I will surely give the nations as Thine inheritance, And the very ends of the earth as Thy possession. Thou shalt break them with a rod of iron, Thou shalt shatter them like earthenware."

An earthly kingdom with a physical presence and rule by the Messiah-King is foretold throughout the pages of the Bible. This promise was not fulfilled in the first coming of Jesus Christ because, though offered, the kingdom was rejected by Israel. Revelation 5 says that Christ is worthy to receive this kingdom, and in Revelation 11:15 we are told that the prophecies will yet be fulfilled. Dr. Charles Ryrie writes:

> Why is an earthly kingdom necessary? Did He not receive His inheritance when He was raised and exalted in heaven? Is not His present rule His inheritance? Why does there need to be an earthly kingdom? Because He must be triumphant *in the same arena* where He was seemingly defeated. His rejection by the rulers of this world was on this earth (1 Corinthians 2:8). His exaltation must also be on this earth. And so it shall be when He comes again to rule this world in righteousness. He has waited long for His inheritance; soon He shall receive it.[18]

The millennium is a transitional period in God's program. It is the beginning of the eternal rule of God in the kingdom, which will pass into the eternal state. It is "the consummating link between history and the eternal order."[19] History and current events are moving toward a final era that will be the pinnacle of God's plan. Dr. David Larsen, citing the French theologian René Pache, writes:

> If history culminated with cataclysm and judgment, the Second Coming of Christ in power would be only "a walk through the ruins." The stone which becomes a mountain will "fill all the earth" (Daniel 2:35). "They will reign on earth" is the promise (Revelation 5:10). The venue of the Kingdom is to be on earth before we come to the final expression of the Kingdom in "the new heaven and the new earth" (2 Peter 3:13; Revelation 21–22).[20]

6. Does the millennium occur right after Christ's second coming?

Careful reading of the Bible reveals that there is a 75-day interval between the tribulation and the millennium during which time judgments of the Antichrist, false prophet, and Gentiles will take place (Matthew 25:31-46). Also at this time will be the resurrection of Old Testament saints and the martyred tribulation saints (see 1 Corinthians 15:20-24). This interval comes at the end of the tribulation, after the second coming of Jesus Christ and the Armageddon conflict. According to Daniel 12:11,12 mention is made of 1,290 days from the midpoint of the tribulation:

> And from the time that the regular sacrifice is abolished, and the abomination of desolation is set up, there will be 1,290 days. How blessed is he who keeps waiting and attains to the 1,335 days!

An extra 30 days are added to the normal three-and-a-half years (1,260 days) giving a total of 1,290 days. Note that Daniel then says, "How blessed is he who keeps waiting and attains to the 1,335 days." The extra 30 days added to the 45 days (1,335–45=1,290) comes to a total of 75 days. This will likely be the time in which the sheep and goat judgment of Matthew 25:31-46 takes place. This also might be additional time for setting up the millennium after the devastation of the tribulation.

7. What are the major events and who are the key personalities of the millennium?

From the midpoint of the tribulation, the "abomination of desolation" as described in Daniel 9:27; Matthew 24:15; and 2 Thessalonians 2:4, until the end of the tribulation there will be three-and-a-half years or 1,260 days until the end of the tribulation. The additional 75 days recorded in Daniel 12:11,12 is an interval between the end of the tribulation and the beginning of the millennium.[21]

The major events of the millennium are:

- the binding of Satan (Revelation 20:1-3)
- the final restoration of Israel to include,
    —regeneration (Jeremiah 31:31-34)
    —regathering (Deuteronomy 30:1-10; Isaiah 11:11–12:6; Matthew 24:31)
    —possession of the Land (Ezekiel 20:42-44; 36:28-38)
    —reestablishment of the Davidic throne (2 Samuel 7:11-16; 1 Chronicles 17:10-14; Jeremiah 33:17-26)
- the righteous reign of Jesus Christ (Isaiah 2:3,4; 11:2-5)
- the loosing and final rebellion of Satan at the end of the millennium (Revelation 20:7-10)
- the great white throne judgment and the second resurrection or judgment of unbelieving dead (Revelation 20:11-15)

As seen in passages above, the major figures of the millennium are Jesus Christ and Israel. Satan will be bound and the church and the nations (Gentiles) will be present and active, but the focus of prophetic revelation is on Israel and Christ—the Messiah-King. Israel's prominence is required in order to facilitate a literal fulfillment of her many Old Testament promises by the Lord. All of the redeemed of God will participate in the worship, blessings, and glories of the millennial kingdom as they prepare for life in the eternal state.

8. What happens at the end of the millennium?

At the end of the 1,000-year reign of Christ on earth, there will be one final rebellion by Satan and his forces. Just as prophesied in

Revelation 20, Satan will be loosed at the end of the millennium and will rebel against the millennial reign of Christ.

> And when the thousand years are completed, Satan will be released from his prison, and will come out to deceive the nations which are in the four corners of the earth, Gog and Magog, to gather them together for the war; the number of them is like the sand of the seashore. And they came up on the broad plain of the earth and surrounded the camp of the saints and the beloved city, and fire came down from heaven and devoured them. And the devil who deceived them was thrown into the lake of fire and brimstone, where the beast and the false prophet are also; and they will be tormented day and night forever and ever (Revelation 20:7-10).

In one final grasp for power and human allegiance, Satan will manifest his true nature (as he has done throughout all of history) and attempt to seize the throne of God. Dr. Walvoord writes of this attempted *coup d'état:*

> The thousand years of confinement will not change Satan's nature, and he will attempt to take the place of God and receive the worship and obedience that is due God alone. He will find a ready response on the part of those who have made a profession of following Christ in the Millennium but who now show their true colors. They will surround Jerusalem in an attempt to capture the capital city of the kingdom of David as well as of the entire world. The Scriptures report briefly, "But fire came down from heaven and devoured them."[22]

According to Revelation 20:10, Satan's termination will be swift but everlasting. He will be cast into the lake of fire joining the Antichrist and the false prophet, who is the Antichrist's lieutenant (Revelation 13:11-18). The fact that the Antichrist and false prophet are placed in the lake of fire at the second coming, prior to the millennium, demonstrates the fact that they are finished in history. The lake of fire is the final form of hell from which, once placed there, no one ever leaves. This is why Satan is bound in the bottomless pit at the start of the millennium—because he will make one more appearance upon the stage of history before he is once and for all consigned to the lake of fire.

The judgment of Satan is then followed by the judgment of the unbelieving dead, known as the great white throne judgment (Revelation 20:11-15). These judgments form the bridge between the millennium and the eternal state as described in Revelation 21–22. They are the final events of the millennium and conclude with the passing away of the present heavens and earth (Matthew 24:35; Mark 13:31; Luke 16:17; 21:33; 2 Peter 3:10). John writes,

> And I saw a new heaven and a new earth; for the first heaven and the first earth passed away, and there is no longer any sea (Revelation 21:1).

9. Why will Satan be loosed at the end of the millennium?

It seems somewhat strange that Satan, once bound, would be loosed again to rebel. This activity provides to all of the created order the supreme illustration of sin and its consequences. Satan will not change, and some humans, even when in a pristine environment, will manifest the sin nature acquired at the fall in the Garden of Eden in Genesis 3.

> The question may fairly be asked why Satan will be loosed at this time. The Bible does not explain this, but it will be a demonstration of the incurable wickedness of Satan and the fact that even a thousand years' confinement have not changed his rebellion against God. It will support the concept that punishment must be eternal because wicked natures do not change. The judgment on the people who join Satan in rebellion will be a demonstration of the wickedness of human hearts, which will be rebellious in spite of living in an almost perfect environment where there is full knowledge of God and full revelation of the glory of Jesus Christ.[23]

History does not merely include the human dimension, it also involves the angelic as well. In the classic demonstration of interplay between the satanic and human drama, Satan makes his encore upon the stage of history by providing fallen humanity what it lacked during the millennium. One last time, Satan serves to embolden rebellious humanity into a deceived mob who amazingly think they can prevail in a confrontation against God Almighty. Finally, through the agency of a recently released Satan, all unbelievers "come out of the closet," and once "outed" are swiftly and finally judged by God, along with Satan.

CHAPTER 22

When Will the Millennium Occur?

10. Don't some people think we are now in the millennium?

Many theologians have taught that the present age is the millennium. They reason that Christ brought in the Kingdom (a spiritual kingdom) at His first advent and it will continue until the second coming. After Christ's return, they believe that we will go directly into the eternal state without a literal, personal reign of Christ upon earth. These are the perspectives of amillennialism and postmillennialism (see Questions 15 and 16 in this section). Even if there were a spiritual phase of the kingdom in the present age, which we do not believe, it would still be impossible to substitute present spiritual characteristics for the many physical and earthly aspects of the Messiah's future kingdom.

The Bible does not teach that the millennium is a totally perfect state. Isaiah 2:4; 11:4; 65:20; and Zechariah 12–14 all teach that there will be sin in the millennium.

> No longer will there be in it an infant who lives but a few days, or an old man who does not live out his days; For the youth will die at the age of one hundred and the one who does not reach the age of one hundred shall be thought accursed. And they shall build houses and inhabit them; they shall also plant vineyards and eat their fruit. They shall not build, and another inhabit, they shall not plant, and another eat; for as the lifetime of a tree, so shall be the days of My people, and My chosen ones shall wear out the work of their hands. They shall not labor in vain, or bear children for calamity; For they are the offspring of those blessed by the LORD, and their descendants with them (Isaiah 65:20-23).

Isaiah 65:20-23 indicates there will also be long life as the norm, childbirth, economic development, and death. Such characteristics do not fit heaven where there is no birth or death, while other aspects, such as an expanded life span, do not correspond to present life. Such a time refers to the millennium, which is a future era of history between our current age and eternity. Thus, it is unreasonable to attempt to equate the "1,000 years" found six times in Revelation 20 with the present age.

11. How does the rapture relate to the millennium?

The rapture and the millennium are two distinct events separated by the seven-year tribulation known as Daniel's "seventieth week" as found in Daniel 9:24-27. At the rapture (described most clearly in 1 Thessalonians 4:13-18), Christians will be "caught up" or raptured to meet Jesus Christ in the air. They will be physically removed from the earth during the tribulation. A seven-year period of great upheaval will ensue as the Antichrist rises to power and is ultimately defeated at Armageddon when Jesus Christ returns at the second advent. It is after this second return and the judgments following it that the millennial kingdom will be inaugurated and Christ will rule for 1,000 years. Thus, it is the second coming that immediately precedes the start of the millennium, not the rapture of the church.

12. How does the tribulation relate to the millennium?

The tribulation is the seven-year period of time following the rapture and coming prior to the establishment of the millennial kingdom. It is the "seventieth week of Daniel" described in Daniel 9:24-27 and it has a threefold purpose: to make an end of sinfulness (Isaiah 13:9; 24:19,20), to bring about worldwide revival (Revelation 17:1-17), and to break the will of the Jewish nation (Daniel 12:5-7; Ezekiel 20:34-38).[24]

Like the rapture, the tribulation is part of God's overall prophetic plan and will be accomplished as specified in the Bible and in accordance with His timing. It precedes the millennium and will show human history at its worst, in contrast to the following 1,000 years which will be human history at its best.

The tribulation relates to the millennium in that both are part of the day of the Lord. The tribulation is the judgment phase that prepares Israel and humanity for the 1,000-year reign of Christ's righteous rule upon earth. In order for righteousness to rule, it must be preceded by judgment of sin. The day of the Lord refers to a time when the Lord will visibly interject Himself into history. During the current "times of the Gentiles" the Lord rules history through His invisible providence.

13. How does the second coming of Christ relate to the millennium?

The second coming, and its accompanying judgments, occur just prior to the inauguration of the millennium. Just as Noah's flood was a bridge from the old world to the new, so the second coming will be the cataclysmic hinge between our current era and the tribulation to the radically new conditions of the millennium. The two events are closely tied together as the second coming "sets the ball in motion" for the millennium to follow. Regarding the relation of these two events, Dr. Walvoord observes:

> The millennial kingdom is a major part of the second coming of Christ. It includes the destruction of the armies gathered against God in the Holy Land (Revelation 19:17,21), the capture of the Beast and the False Prophet and their being cast into the lake of fire (v. 20), the binding of Satan (20:1-3), and the resurrection of the martyred dead of the Tribulation to reign with Christ a thousand years (vv. 4-6). A literal interpretation of Revelation 20:4-6 requires that Christ reign on earth for a thousand years following his second coming.[25]

Both the second coming and the millennium are clearly prophesied in the Bible. They are an integral part of God's plan for the future, and though they are different in purpose, they fall chronologically close on God's prophetic schedule.

14. What's the difference between the millennium and the eternal state?

The millennium and the eternal state are two separate phases of the kingdom of God. The millennium precedes the eternal state. Dr. Fruchtenbaum writes:

> The millennium itself is only one thousand years long. However, according to the promises of the Davidic

Covenant, there was to be an eternal dynasty, an eternal kingdom and an eternal throne. The eternal existence of the dynasty is assured because it culminates in an eternal person: the Lord Jesus Christ. But the eternal existence of the throne and kingdom must also be assured. The millennial form of the kingdom of God will end after one thousand years. But the kingdom of God in the sense of God's rule will continue into the Eternal Order. Christ will continue His position of authority on the Davidic throne into the Eternal Order.[26]

The millennium is the precursor of the eternal state. It will be different than life as we know it today, but will still fall short of the absolute perfection of the eternal state. We read in Revelation 21:1–22:5 that the eternal state will entail the passing away of the old order and the creation of the New Jerusalem and new heavens and earth.

When comparing the two periods of time we observe the following contrasts:

- The millennium is associated with the continuum of human history, while the eternal state is not.

- The millennium is the apex of human history, because sin is still present though restrained through Christ's rule, while heaven in the eternal state is totally void of all sin.

- The millennium will focus worship on Jesus Christ, the second person of the Trinity, while during the eternal state direct fellowship with God the Father, the first person of the Trinity, will be a reality for the first time in history.

- The millennium will be a time in which resurrected believers and nonresurrected humans will routinely commingle in history, while the eternal state will consist of only resurrected people.

- The millennium will still be a time in history when humans come into existence and will trust or reject Christ as their Savior, while the eternal state will be a time in which no one else will ever be added to the human race and everyone's destiny will be frozen, locked into saved or lost for eternity.

There will be many differences between the millennium and the eternal state, and both will differ greatly from our current historical era.

15. What does premillennialism teach about the millennium?

Premillennialism, and specifically pretribulationism, is the view or system of eschatology (doctrine of the last things) that is presented throughout this book. It holds that there will be a future literal millennium or 1,000-year reign of Jesus Christ upon the earth following the events of the rapture, tribulation, and second coming. There are several forms of premillennialism which differ as to how the rapture relates to the tribulation (pretribulationism, midtribulationism, posttribulationism, partial rapture, pre-wrath rapture), but all teach that the millennium is 1,000 literal years and follows Christ's second advent.

Premillennialism

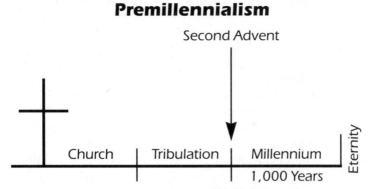

Dispensational premillennialists hold that Israel and the church are two separate and distinct entities throughout all of history, including the millennium. Covenant premillennialists hold that in the Old and New Testament eras, Israel and the church were the same, but in the millennium they will be separate.

It is our belief that premillennialism is the interpretive system that most consistently follows a grammatical-historical-contextual approach to interpreting the whole of Scripture, especially the prophetic portions. This approach has historically been called literal interpretation, since literal means according to the letters. Literal interpretation is the approach to literature that attempts to understand it on the basis of what the text says, as opposed to interpreting the text in light of a key idea or thought that is not actually stated in the text, but believed to yield a deeper meaning. This approach is called allegory or spiritualization.

The most widely used form of allegorical interpretation in our day is the practice of replacing Israel with the church in many biblical passages, especially in the Old Testament. Because there are no literary reasons in the passages in question for such a substitution, this approach has to be viewed as allegorical interpretation. When literal interpretation is followed, then premillennialism will also follow. Amillennialism and postmillennialism have always had to resort to allegorical interpretation at many points in order to sustain their views.

16. What does amillennialism teach about the millennium?

Amillennialism is the view or system of eschatology (doctrine of the last things) that holds that there is no literal earthly millennium. Amillenialists believe that the millennium is spiritual. Some believe that the spiritual kingdom is present during the current era of the church. Other amillennialists believe that the present spiritual reign of God's kingdom consists of the influence that the church exerts through its many worldwide ministries. Another form teaches that the millennium is composed of the reign of all dead Christians in heaven. Still a fourth kind believes that the millennium is equal to the eternal state that will commence at the second coming, for example, the new heavens and new earth equal the millennium.

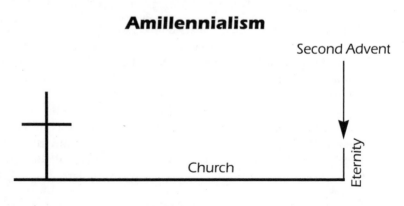

Amillennialism

Second Advent

Church

Eternity

Amillennialism teaches that from the ascension of Christ in the first century until His second coming (no rapture) both good and evil will increase in the world as God's kingdom parallels Satan's kingdom. When Jesus Christ returns, the end of the world will occur with a general resurrection and general judgment of all people. It is essentially a spiritualization of the kingdom prophecies.

Amillennialism was not present in the earliest church. (At least there is no positive record of its existence.) It appears to have developed as a result of its opposition to premillennial literalism and then evolved into a positive system. Amillennialism came to dominate the church when the great church father and theologian Augustine (354–430) abandoned premillennialism for amillennialism. It would probably be safe to say that amillennialism has been the most widely held view for much of the church's history, including most Protestant reformers of the fifteenth and sixteenth centuries. Dr. Ryrie writes of amillennialism:

> One of the popular reasons for preferring amillennialism over premillennialism contrasts the premillennial concept of fulfillment in an earthly kingdom (usually the adjective carnal is placed with this phrase) with the amillennial concept of fulfillment of Old Testament prophecies in the church in this age (and usually the adjective spiritual is put with this phrase). Thus the system which emphasizes the spiritual church rather the carnal kingdom is to be preferred. When I hear or read this argument, I want to ask, since when is the church only spiritual and the kingdom only carnal? The church (look around) has carnal people in it, and the kingdom will have many spiritual facets to it. Spiritual and carnal characterize both the church and the future kingdom.[27]

Always, of course, the conclusive evidence for the truth of a doctrine is not historical but exegetical.

17. What does postmillennialism teach about the millennium?

Postmillennialism is the view or system of eschatology (doctrine of the last things) that teaches that the current age is the millennium.

(It is not necessarily a thousand years.) Postmillennialists believe that the kingdom will gradually be extended through the preaching of the gospel, the eventual conversion of a majority of people, not necessarily all, and the progressive growth of righteousness, prosperity, and development in every sphere of life as this growing majority of Christians struggle to subdue the world for Christ. After Christianity has dominated the world for a long time, Christ will return. Like amillennialism, there will be a general resurrection, destruction of this present creation, and entry into the eternal state.

Postmillennialism

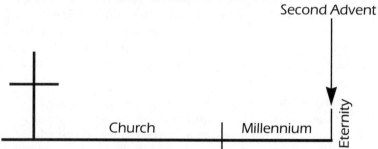

Postmillennialists differ from premillennialism and amillennialism in that they are optimistic that this victory will be realized without the need for a cataclysmic return of Christ to impose righteousness, but rather will result from the faithful application of the present process.

Postmillennialism did not really develop into a distinct system of eschatology until after the Reformation. Prior to that time, there was development of various elements that later were included in the theological mix of modern postmillennialism. But it is safe to say that postmillennialism was the last major millennial position to develop.

John Walvoord notes that there are two principle types of postmillennialism:

> Stemming from Whitby, these groups provided two types of postmillennialism which have persisted to the twentieth century: (1) a Biblical type...finding its material in the Scriptures and its power in God; (2) the evolutionary or liberal theological type which bases its

proof on confidence in man to achieve progress through natural means. These two widely separated systems of belief have one thing in common, the idea of ultimate progress and solution of present difficulties.[28]

Postmillennialism was the dominant view of the millennium in America during much of the nineteenth century, but virtually became extinct up until the 1960s. The last 25 years have witnessed an upsurge in postmillennialism in some conservative arenas through the Christian Reconstruction movement.

CHAPTER 23

What Are the Characteristics of the Millennium?

18. What will the millennium be like physically?

The millennial kingdom will bring about harmony in all of creation. Some of the most graphic portrayals of the millennial kingdom are found in the prophecies of Isaiah. In chapters 11 and 35, Isaiah provides extensive comment on the physical aspects of the kingdom.

Ever since the fall of Adam and Eve in the garden of Eden, humanity and the rest of creation have been under the judgment and ramifications of original sin. The pollution of sin has affected all of humanity and creation. The apostle Paul reminds us of that which we experience daily when he declares in Romans 8:22, "For we know that the whole creation groans and suffers the pains of childbirth together until now." However, during the millennium there will be a partial lifting of the curse and ramifications of original sin. There will still be death and the complete effects of the Fall will not be lifted until the creation of the new heaven and new earth in the eternal state after the millennium (Revelation 22:3).

In Isaiah 35:1,2, we read of some of the effects of the millennium on the environment:

> The wilderness and the desert will be glad, and the Arabah will rejoice and blossom; like the crocus it will blossom profusely and rejoice with rejoicing and shout of joy. The glory of Lebanon will be given to it, the majesty of Carmel and Sharon. They will see the glory of the LORD, the majesty of our God.

There will be abundant rainfall in areas that today are known for their dryness, and therefore there will be plenty of food for animals.

> Then He will give you rain for the seed which you will sow in the ground, and bread from the yield of the ground, and it will be rich and plenteous; on that day your livestock will graze in a roomy pasture. Also the

> oxen and the donkeys which work the ground will eat salted fodder, which has been winnowed with shovel and fork (Isaiah 30:23-24).

> And the scorched land will become a pool, and the thirsty ground springs of water; in the haunt of jackals, its resting place, grass becomes reeds and rushes (Isaiah 35:7).

As part of nature and the created order, animal life will also be affected. The predatory instincts and carnivorous appetites will cease in animals. The distinctions between "tame" and "wild" will be erased as all creatures will live in harmony.

> And the wolf will dwell with the lamb, and the leopard will lie down with the kid, and the calf and the young lion and the fatling together; and a little boy will lead them. Also the cow and the bear will graze; their young will lie down together; and the lion will eat straw like the ox (Isaiah 11:6,7).

Physical conditions for people will also be drastically changed for the better. Just as in the days before the flood of Noah, people will live much longer and the birthrate will increase again because the tribulation will be completed.

> No longer will there be in it an infant who lives but a few days, or an old man who does not live out his days; for the youth will die at the age of one hundred and the one who does not reach the age of one hundred shall be thought accursed (Isaiah 65:20).

> O people in Zion, inhabitant in Jerusalem, you will weep no longer. He will surely be gracious to you at the sound of your cry; when He hears it, He will answer you. Although the Lord has given you bread of privation and water of oppression, He, your Teacher will no longer hide Himself, but your eyes will behold your Teacher (Isaiah 30:19,20).

Many physical infirmities and health concerns will also be eradicated.

PROPHECY WATCH

> And on that day the deaf shall hear words of a book, and out of their gloom and darkness the eyes of the blind shall see (Isaiah 29:18).

> And no resident will say, "I am sick"; the people who dwell there will be forgiven their iniquity (Isaiah 33:24).

The absence of sickness and deformity along with the increased life spans will create less variation between those in the millennium with mortal bodies and those with resurrected bodies.

> It must be remembered that not all participants in the millennial kingdom will have earthly, mortal bodies. Millions of believers from the Old Testament era, the Church Age, and the Tribulation will have resurrected, immortal bodies. But there is no reason to think that these two groups will not be relating to one another and interacting with each other during the Millennium. The resurrected Lord Jesus had no problems teaching and fellowshipping with His disciples during the forty days after His resurrection.[29]

In the midst of this enhanced environment and increased level of health, there will be an overall effect of increased prosperity as poverty, injustice, and disease cease. Jeremiah 31:12-14 describes the prosperity that citizens of the millennial kingdom will experience:

> And they shall come and shout for joy on the height of Zion, and they shall be radiant over the bounty of the LORD—over the grain, and the new wine, and the oil, and over the young of the flock and the herd; and their life shall be like a watered garden, and they shall never languish again. Then the virgin shall rejoice in the dance, and the young men and the old, together, for I will turn their mourning into joy, and will comfort them, and give them joy for their sorrow. And I will fill the soul of the priests with abundance, and My people shall be satisfied with My goodness, declares the LORD.

Dr. Walvoord summarizes the tremendous physical conditions writing:

> Widespread peace and justice, spiritual blessing, and abundance of food will result in a general era of prosperity such as the world has never known (Jeremiah 31:12; Ezekiel 34:25-27; Joel 2:21-27; Amos 9:13,14). The many factors which produce poverty, distress, and unequal distribution of goods will to a great extent be nonexistent in the millennium. Labor problems which now characterize the world will be solved, and everyone will receive just compensation for his labors (Isaiah 65:21-25; Jeremiah 31:5).[30]

Unfortunately, even in the midst of such pristine conditions, there will ultimately be human rebellion. Because the complete effects of the Fall will not be erased, there will be a final revolt against the righteous government of Jesus Christ. This will occur at the end of the millennium when Satan is briefly released from bondage just prior to his final judgment and destruction (Revelation 20:7-10). Dr. Walvoord observes:

> Taken as a whole, the social and economic conditions of the millennium indicate a golden age in which the dreams of social reformists through the centuries will be realized, not through human effort but by the immediate presence and power of God and the righteous government of Christ. That mankind should again fail under such ideal circumstances and be ready to rebel against Christ at the end of the millennium is the final answer to those who put faith in the inherent goodness of man.[31]

19. What will the millennium be like politically?

The government and politics of the millennial kingdom will focus on the benevolent reign of Jesus Christ as Israel's Messiah-King. It will be a theocracy centered in Jerusalem (Isaiah 2:1-4), where Jesus will reign as both Messiah and King of Israel, thus fulfilling the promises and prophecies of the Davidic covenant (2 Samuel 7:12-16). God's covenant with David guaranteed David's dynasty, throne, and kingdom would continue forever. When Jesus Christ returns at the end of the tribulation, He will reestablish the Davidic throne in His personal rule as described by the prophet Jeremiah:

> "Behold, the days are coming," declares the LORD,
> "when I shall raise up for David a righteous Branch;
> and He will reign as king and act wisely and do justice
> and righteousness in the land. In His days Judah will
> be saved, and Israel will dwell securely; and this is His
> name by which He will be called, 'The LORD our righ-
> teousness.' Therefore behold, the days are coming,"
> declares the LORD, "when they will no longer say, 'as
> the LORD lives, who brought up the sons of Israel from
> the land of Egypt,' but, 'as the LORD lives, who brought
> up and led back the descendants of the household of
> Israel from the north land and from all the countries
> where I had driven them.' Then they will live on their
> own soil" (Jeremiah 23:5-8).

The reign of Jesus Christ will fulfill the well-known prophecy of
Isaiah 9:6,7.

> For a child will be born to us, a son will be given to us;
> and the government will rest on His shoulders; and His
> name will be called Wonderful Counselor, Mighty God,
> Eternal Father, Prince of Peace. There will be no end to
> the increase of His government or of peace, on the
> throne of David and over his kingdom, to establish it
> and to uphold it with justice and righteousness from
> then on and forevermore. The zeal of the Lord of hosts
> will accomplish this.

Other significant passages describing Christ's reign over Israel
include Psalm 2; Jeremiah 33:20-26; Ezekiel 34:23-25; 37:23,24;
and Luke 1:32,33. These and other passages provide ample specific
evidence that the kingdom promised to David will be fully realized in
the future.

Christ's rule will also extend to the Gentiles and all nations
throughout the world. We know from Psalm 2:6-9 that Christ will
rule over the entire earth, and in Daniel 7:14 we are again told of
Christ's universal rule.

> But as for Me, I have installed My King upon Zion, My
> holy mountain. I will surely tell of the decree of the
> LORD: He said to Me, "Thou art My Son, today I have
> begotten Thee. Ask of Me, and I will surely give the

nations as Thine inheritance, and the very ends of the
earth as Thy possession. Thou shalt break them with a
rod of iron, Thou shalt shatter them like earthenware"
(Psalm 2:6-9).

And to Him was given dominion, glory and a kingdom,
that all the peoples, nations, and men of every language might serve Him. His dominion is an everlasting
dominion which will not pass away; and His kingdom
is one which will not be destroyed (Daniel 7:14).

One of the major consequences of the righteous and benevolent
rule of Christ will be the extension of peace throughout the world.
Throughout its history the world has been plagued with war and its
effects. There has been no lasting peace and every portion of the
globe has suffered from the destruction of war. Only in the millennium will the words of Micah's prophecy finally come true even
though many have sought to apply them already.

And He will judge between many peoples and render
decisions for mighty, distant nations. Then they will
hammer their swords into plowshares and their spears
into pruning hooks; nation will not lift up sword
against nation, and never again will they train for war.
And each of them will sit under his vine and under his
fig tree, with no one to make them afraid, for the
mouth of the LORD of hosts has spoken (Micah 4:3,4).

True peace and true prosperity will ultimately be realized in the
millennial kingdom. Those things which have been so elusive and
fading throughout human history will be realized only in the reign
and timing of the Lord Jesus Christ.

20. What will the millennium be like spiritually?

Spiritual life in the millennial kingdom will be an experience
unlike any previous era for the redeemed because of the presence of
the exalted King—the Lord Jesus Christ. Dr. Walvoord writes:

The glorious presence of Christ in the millennial scene
is of course the center of worship and spirituality. The
many Scriptures bearing on this theme which cannot
in any reasonable sense be applied to the present age

nor limited to heaven point to the millennial kingdom of Christ on earth. The glory of Christ is further revealed in all aspects of the millennium and affects the spiritual life of the human race to an extent never realized in previous dispensations.[32]

Living daily in the personal and physical presence of Jesus Christ will have enormous manifestations in the lives of believers. Isaiah has said that "the earth will be full of the knowledge of the LORD as the waters cover the sea" (Isaiah 11:9). The knowledge and worship of Christ will be global and unimpeded. There will be no persecution, no secret gatherings or underground assemblies, and no religious censorship. According to Revelation 20:1-3, Satan and his demonic forces will be bound and rendered inactive until the end of the millennium. His removal will greatly enhance the spiritual condition of the world, which would otherwise be impeded and attacked.

The millennium will be an era of great spiritual awareness, sensitivity, and activity for both Christians and the restored nation of Israel. For Israel, the new covenant will be in effect with the resulting conditions prophesied in passages such as Isaiah 59:20,21; Jeremiah 31:31-34; 32:37-40; Ezekiel 16:60-63; and 37:21-28. In the most familiar of these passages, Jeremiah 31:31-34, the Lord speaks through the prophet saying:

> "Behold, days are coming," declares the LORD, "when I will make a new covenant with the house of Israel and with the house of Judah, not like the covenant which I made with their fathers in the day I took them by the hand to bring them out of the land of Egypt, My covenant which they broke, although I was a husband to them," declares the LORD. "But this is the covenant which I will make with the house of Israel after those days," declares the LORD, "I will put My law within them, and on their heart I will write it; and I will be their God, and they shall be My people. And they shall not teach again, each man his neighbor and each man his brother, saying, 'Know the LORD,' for they shall all know Me, from the least of them to the greatest of them," declares the Lord, "for I will forgive their iniquity, and their sin I will remember no more."

Just as in the present age, the ministry of the Holy Spirit will be present and will indwell all believers (Ezekiel 36:27; 37:14). In addition to the indwelling of the Holy Spirit, the filling of the Spirit will also be evidenced and experienced (Isaiah 32:15; 44:3; Ezekiel 39:29; Joel 2:28,29). But, unlike the present age, evangelism will not be needed because everyone will know about the Lord. This is a clear evidence that our current age is not to be equated to the millennium, because the world needs the gospel message through evangelism as never before.

Spiritual conditions in the kingdom are perhaps best seen in the characteristics of righteousness, obedience, holiness, truth, and the fullness of the Holy Spirit.[33] Although these attributes are present today, in the millennial kingdom they will be intensified and expanded. Among the numerous passages portraying these conditions are the following:

Righteousness

> I bring near My righteousness, it is not far off; and My salvation will not delay. And I will grant salvation in Zion, and My glory for Israel (Isaiah 46:13).

> My righteousness is near, My salvation has gone forth, and My arms will judge the peoples; the coastland will wait for Me, and for My arm they will wait expectantly (Isaiah 51:5).

> Instead of bronze I will bring gold, and instead of iron I will bring silver, and instead of wood, bronze, and instead of stones, iron. And I will make peace your administrators, and righteousness your overseers.... Then all your people will be righteous; they will possess the land forever, the branch of My planting, the work of My hands, that I may be glorified (Isaiah 60:17,21).

> To grant those who mourn in Zion, giving them a garland instead of ashes, the oil of gladness instead of mourning, the mantle of praise instead of a spirit of fainting. So they will be called oaks of righteousness, the planting of the LORD, that He may be glorified.... For as the earth brings forth its sprouts, and as a garden

causes the things sown in it to spring up, so the Lord
GOD will cause righteousness and praise to spring up
before all the nations (Isaiah 61:3,11).

Open the gates, that the righteous nation may enter,
the one that remains faithful (Isaiah 26:2).

Obedience

All the ends of the earth will remember and turn to the
LORD, and all the families of the nations will worship
before Thee (Psalm 22:27).

"But this is the covenant which I will make with the
house of Israel after those days," declares the LORD, "I
will put My law within them, and on their heart I will
write it; and I will be their God, and they shall be My
people" (Jeremiah 31:33).

Holiness

The captain of fifty and the honorable man, the
counselor and the expert artisan, and the skillful
enchanter. And I will make mere lads their princes
and capricious children will rule over them...And a
highway will be there, a roadway, and it will be called
the "highway of holiness." The unclean will not
travel on it, but it will be for him who walks that way,
and fools will not wander on it. No lion will be there,
nor will any vicious beast go up on it; these will not
be found there. But the redeemed will walk there,
and the ransomed of the LORD will return, and come
with joyful shouting to Zion, with everlasting joy
upon their heads. They will find gladness and joy,
and sorrow and sighing will flee away (Isaiah 3:3,4;
35:8-10).

Then you will know that I am the LORD your God,
dwelling in Zion My holy mountain. So Jerusalem will
be holy, and strangers will pass through it no more
(Joel 3:17).

Truth

> Lovingkindness and truth have met together; righteousness and peace have kissed each other. Truth springs from the earth; and righteousness looks down from heaven (Psalm 85:10,11).

> Thus says the LORD, "I will return to Zion and will dwell in the midst of Jerusalem. Then Jerusalem will be called the City of Truth, and the mountain of the LORD of hosts will be called the Holy Mountain" (Zechariah 8:3).

Fullness of the Holy Spirit

> And it will come about after this that I will pour out My Spirit on all mankind; and your sons and daughters will prophesy, your old men will dream dreams, your young men will see visions. And even on the male and female servants I will pour out My Spirit in those days (Joel 2:28,29).

The clearest expression of the spiritual characteristics of the millennial kingdom is found in the worship and activity in the millennial temple. Jesus Christ will be reigning on earth in Jerusalem and the millennial temple will be present and functioning as described in Ezekiel 40–46. Dr. Benware writes of the universal worship of Christ at the millennial temple:

> This worship will no doubt be of a quality and depth never before seen on earth, as righteous Jews and Gentiles gladly come to Jerusalem to praise the great Savior King (e.g. Isaiah 2:2-4; 11:9-10; Ezekiel 20:40-41;40:1-46:24; Zechariah 14:16). And with the glory of the Lord once again present in the temple, the scene of worship will be best described by the word *awesome*. Jerusalem will be like a spiritual magnet drawing people to worship and praise the Lord.[34]

21. What is the millennial temple?

The millennial temple will be the fourth and final temple in Israel's history. The first temple, also known as Solomon's temple, is described in 1 Kings 5–8 and was destroyed in 586 B.C. The second temple, also known as Zerubbabel's temple and Herod's temple, is described in Ezra 3:7–6:18. It was the temple of Jesus' time and was destroyed by the Romans in A.D. 70. The third temple, the tribulation temple, will be in existence during the tribulation (Daniel 9:26,27;11:31;12:11; 2 Thessalonians 2:4; Revelation 11:1,2) but will be destroyed at the end of the tribulation at Christ's second advent.

The millennial temple (Ezekiel 40–46; Isaiah 2:2,3; 56:7) will be the center from which the worship of Jesus Christ will be focused during the millennium. It will exist in Jerusalem throughout the 1,000-year reign of Christ. Its purpose is seen, in part, in Ezekiel 37:26-28:

> And I will make a covenant of peace with them; it will be an everlasting covenant with them. And I will place them and multiply them, and will set My sanctuary in their midst forever. My dwelling place also will be with them; and I will be their God, and they will be My people. And the nations will know that I am the LORD who sanctifies Israel, when My sanctuary is in their midst forever.

According to Zechariah 6:11-13, Jesus Christ will be originator of the temple, perhaps bringing it into existence at the second advent. The millennial temple will bear witness that God has always intended that His chosen people, Israel, serve as a priestly nation to the other nations of the world. In the millennial temple, all that was prescribed and initiated in the Old Testament ceremonial and ritual activities will come to completion and their fullest meaning.[35]

22. Why will there be sacrifices in the millennial temple?

One aspect of the millennial temple described in Ezekiel 40–46, especially 43:13-27, has given many prophecy students pause for reflection—the purpose and role of future sacrifices. At least four other Old Testament prophets join Ezekiel in affirming a sacrificial system in a millennial temple (Isaiah 56:7; 66:20-23; Jeremiah 33:18; Zechariah 14:16-21; Malachi 3:3,4).

If we accept the literal interpretation of a millennial sacrificial system, then are we contradicting passages such as Hebrews 7:26,27 and 9:26, which teach that Jesus Christ was the perfect and final sacrifice for sin? Premillennial scholars have fully recognized the issues at hand here. Dr. John F. Walvoord has noted this concern and has written:

> The only real problem in connection with a future literal temple is not the question as to whether such a temple could be built in the millennium, but the fact that this would indicate also a literal interpretation of the temple ritual and sacrifices.... The question is naturally raised why the sacrifices should be observed in the millennium if the sacrifice of Christ once for all fulfilled the typical expectation of the Old Testament sacrificial system. While other objections are also made of a lesser character, it is obvious that this constitutes the major obstacle, not only to accepting the sacrificial system but the possibility of the future temple in the millennium as well.[36]

There are at least two legitimate solutions to this question. First, many students and teachers of prophecy have noted that the sacrifices may function as a memorial to the work of Christ. Dr. Jerry Hullinger has summarized this view writing:

> According to this view the sacrifices offered during the earthly reign of Christ will be visible reminders of His work on the cross. Thus, these sacrifices will not have any efficacy except to memorialize Christ's death. The primary support for this argument is the parallel of the Lord's Supper. It is argued that just as the communion table looks back on the Cross without besmirching its glory, so millennial sacrifices will do the same.[37]

This view does not, however, completely resolve all the concerns. Ezekiel says that the sacrifices are for atonement rather than a memorial (Ezekiel 45:15,17,20). Therefore, a second solution to the question of "why" is that the sacrifices are for ceremonial purification. Rather than merely a memorial view, Dr. Hullinger suggests:

> ...a solution that maintains dispensational distinctives, deals honestly with the text of Ezekiel, and in no way demeans the work Christ did on the cross. This study suggests that animal sacrifices during the millennium

will serve primarily to remove ceremonial uncleanness and prevent defilement from polluting the temple envisioned by Ezekiel. This will be necessary because the glorious presence of Yahweh will once again be dwelling on earth in the midst of a sinful and unclean people.[38]

Dr. Hullinger concludes by saying:

Because of God's promise to dwell on earth during the millennium (as stated in the New Covenant), it is necessary that He protect His presence through sacrifice.... It should further be added that this sacrificial system will be a temporary one in that the millennium (with its partial population of unglorified humanity) will last only one thousand years. During the eternal state all inhabitants of the New Jerusalem will be glorified and will therefore not be a source of contagious impurities to defile the holiness of Yahweh.[39]

The presence and purpose of sacrifices as understood above, neither diminishes the work of Christ, nor violates the normal and "literal" interpretation of the prophetic passages. Although there will be sacrifices, the focus of all worship will remain on the person and work of the Savior.

The sacrifices of the millennial temple will not be a return to the Mosaic law, since the law has forever been fulfilled and discontinued through Christ (Romans 6:14,15; 7:1-6; 1 Corinthians 9:20,21; 2 Corinthians 3:7-11; Galatians 4:1-7; 5:18; Hebrews 8:13; 10:1-14). Instead, as Dr. Arnold Fruchtenbaum notes:

There will be a sacrificial system instituted in the Millennium that will have some features similar to the Mosaic system, along with some new laws. For that very reason, the sacrificial system of the Millennium must not be viewed as a reinstitution of the Mosaic system, because it is not. It will be a new system that will contain some things old and some things new and will be instituted for an entirely different purpose.[40]

CHAPTER 24

Who Will Be in the Millennium?

23. Who enters the millennium?

Only the redeemed will enter the millennium. At the end of the tribulation, the unsaved and those who have aligned themselves with the Antichrist will be destroyed. There will then follow the judgment of the Gentiles (or nations) and the judgment of Israel. The judgment of the Gentiles will allow the believers to enter the coming kingdom, and nonbelievers will be cast into the lake of fire (Matthew 25:31-46). The judgment of Israel will be similar in that those Jews who accept Jesus as Messiah will enter the kingdom, and those who do not will be cast into the lake of fire (Ezekiel 20:37,38).

Also in the kingdom will be tribulation believers who died during the tribulation and all those who were raptured at the time of Christ's appearing before the tribulation. Dr. Pentecost writes of those who enter the millennial kingdom:

> The earthly theocratic kingdom, instituted by the Lord Jesus Christ at His second advent, will include all the saved of Israel and the saved Gentiles, who are living at the time of His return. Scripture makes it very clear that all sinners will be cut off before the institution of the Kingdom....In the record of the judgment of the nations (Matthew 25:35) it is revealed that only the saved enter the kingdom. In the parable of the wheat and tares (Matthew 13:30,31) and in the parable of the good and bad fish (Matthew 13:49,50) it is shown that only the saved go into the kingdom.[41]

24. What about infants and children?

The Bible does not specifically address the issue of tribulation children and infants entering the millennium. We know that people who are believers will enter and people who are not, will not enter. We also know that children will be born in the millennium and will need to face the issue of accepting or rejecting Jesus Christ as they mature. Thus, there will be children in the millennium, though not all of our questions are answered directly. Dr. Walvoord writes of the children of those who enter the millennium that they,

> will be subject to the later decision regarding their salvation. Likewise children who are born in the millennial reign will face decisions about salvation as they grow up. As the Millennium unfolds, there will come into existence a large number of people who will merely profess salvation without having the reality. This will explain the evil in the Millennium and also the final rebellion at the end.[42]

25. How does Jesus Christ relate to the millennium?

Isaiah 11:1-5 foretells of the Messiah who will come from the family of David and rule the nation Israel with righteousness and absolute justice. This passage is a clear prophecy of the reign of Jesus Christ during the millennium.

> Then a shoot will spring from the stem of Jesse, and a branch from his roots will bear fruit. And the Spirit of the LORD will rest on Him, the spirit of wisdom and understanding, the spirit of counsel and strength, the spirit of knowledge and the fear of the LORD. And He will delight in the fear of the LORD, and He will not judge by what His eyes see, nor make a decision by what His ears hear; but with righteousness He will judge the poor, and decide with fairness for the afflicted of the earth; and He will strike the earth with the rod of His mouth, and with the breath of His lips He will slay the wicked. Also righteousness will be the belt about His loins, And faithfulness the belt about His waist.

Jesus Christ will be the focal point of all activity during the millennium. It will be His reign and His kingdom. That which was rejected at the time of His first coming will now be accepted and fully realized as He reigns on earth for 1,000 years. Dr. Walvoord writes:

> In keeping with the announced purpose of God to put a man on David's throne who could rule forever, Jesus Christ will come back to assume this throne. At the present time he is in heaven awaiting this time of tri-

umph over his enemies (Psalm 110:1,2). As the One risen from the dead (Acts 2:29-36), he is qualified to sit on the throne of God forever and without successors. His reign over the house of Israel will be from Jerusalem (Isaiah 2:1-4), and from the same location he will also reign as King of Kings and Lord of Lords over the entire earth (Psalm 72:8-11, 17-19).[43]

The reign of Christ during the millennium is best understood by recognizing its characteristics. Christ's reign will be:

- *Universal*—Daniel 2:35; 7:14,27; Micah 4:1,2; Zechariah 9:10

- *Righteous and just*—Isaiah 3:5-11; 25:2-5; 29:17-21; Micah 5:5,6,10-15; Zechariah 9:3-8

- *Full of the Spirit*—Isaiah 11:2,3

- *A unified government*—Ezekiel 37:13-28

- *Decisive with any outbreak of sin*—Psalm 2:9; 72:1-4; Isaiah 11:4; 29:20,21; 65:20; 66:24; Jeremiah 31:29,30; Zechariah 14:16-21

- *An eternal reign*—Daniel 7:14,27

26. How does David relate to the millennium?

Prophecy scholars are divided in their interpretation of Ezekiel 34:23,24. The passage reads as follows:

> Then I will set over them one shepherd, My servant David, and he will feed them; he will feed them himself and be their shepherd. And I, the LORD, will be their God, and My servant David will be prince among them; I, the LORD, have spoken.

Are the references in this passage to be understood as literally referring to a resurrected David serving as a subordinate ruler under the reign of Christ, or are the references to David a literary device actually meaning Jesus Christ as the greater Son of David? We know that David (along with other Old Testament saints) will be in the millennial kingdom having been resurrected and received his immortal body at the time of Christ's return after the tribulation (Daniel

12:1,2). Also, Jeremiah 30:9 speaks of the resurrection of David. We know that Christ will be assisted in His rule by the twelve apostles (Matthew 19:28), the church (Revelation 5:10), and others (Isaiah 32:1; Jeremiah 30:21; Luke 11:19-27). Regardless of the interpretation one takes on Ezekiel 34:23,24, it seems extremely probable that David will have a significant role in the daily affairs of the millennial kingdom.

27. How does Israel relate to the millennium?

Israel and Jerusalem will have a very special role in the millennium. The millennium is the occasion for the final physical and spiritual restoration of Israel. This restoration is described in Ezekiel 37 and is summarized in verses 21,22:

> And say to them, "Thus says the Lord GOD, Behold, I will take the sons of Israel from among the nations where they have gone, and I will gather them from every side and bring them into their own land; and I will make them one nation in the land, on the mountains of Israel; and one king will be king for all of them; and they will no longer be two nations, and they will no longer be divided into two kingdoms."

Israel and Jerusalem will truly be a holy land and a holy city. The prophet Isaiah writes:

> But be glad and rejoice forever in what I create; for behold, I create Jerusalem for rejoicing, and her people for gladness. I will also rejoice in Jerusalem, and be glad in My people; and there will no longer be heard in her the voice of weeping and the sound of crying. No longer will there be in it an infant who lives but a few days, or an old man who does not live out his days; for the youth will die at the age of one hundred and the one who does not reach the age of one hundred shall be thought accursed. And they shall build houses and inhabit them; they shall also plant vineyards and eat their fruit. They shall not build, and another inhabit, they shall not plant, and another eat; for as the lifetime of a tree, so shall be the days of My people, and My chosen ones shall wear out the work of their hands. They

shall not labor in vain, or bear children for calamity;
for they are the offspring of those blessed by the Lord,
and their descendants with them" (Isaiah 65:18-23).

The restoration of Israel will include regeneration, regathering, possession of the land, and reestablishment of the Davidic throne.[44] There are several other features of the restoration that will accompany the events listed above. According to Jeremiah 3:18 and Ezekiel 37:15-23, the nation will be reunited so that its previous twofold division of Israel and Judah will be eliminated. As a nation, it will become the center of Gentile attention (Isaiah 14:1,2; 49:22,23; Zephaniah 3:20; Zechariah 8:23) and it will enjoy all of the physical and spiritual conditions noted earlier (Isaiah 32:16-20; 35:5-10; 51:3; 55:12,13; 61:10,11).[45]

It is difficult to underestimate the significance and role of the redemption and restoration of Israel in the millennium. David Larsen writes:

> In Greek philosophy, especially Plato, we find a deep antipathy to the physical, as for instance that the body is the prison of the soul. The Hebrews were by contrast an earthly people because God pronounced good the physical order He created. Hence matter is good but it has been defiled and debased by human sin. The created order needs and will obtain redemption (Romans 8:18ff.). Christ will rule for 1,000 years with Jerusalem His earthly center. This is the golden age the prophets foretold. Thus we are not surprised that the earthly reign of Christ has a Jewish cast.[46]

28. How do the Gentiles relate to the millennium?

There is no question that the Gentiles participate in the millennial kingdom and its blessings, some in natural bodies and the rest in resurrected bodies. The rule of Christ will be worldwide and encompass all nations. However, the primary focus of the millennial kingdom will be on the Jews, God's chosen people. Paul says of the future Jewish role, "If their transgression be riches for the world and their failure be riches for the Gentiles, how much more will their fulfillment be!" (Romans 11:12). Many of the prophecies which mention the Gentile nations surrounding Israel are given in the context of

Israel's exaltation during the millennium. With the second coming of Christ, the times of the Gentiles will come to an end and the focus of history will again turn to the Jews. Dr. Walvoord writes of the nations in the millennium:

> Although the pattern of Gentile prophecy and fulfillment is largely one of judgment upon their unbelief and blasphemous rebellion against God, it is another token of the grace of God that, in addition to His program for Israel and the church, the body of Christ, countless Gentiles in the Old Testament period as well as in the tribulation and millennium will come to know Jesus Christ and His saving grace, and accordingly will be qualified to participate as individuals in the blessings which God has ordained for those who love Him. The majestic purpose of God for the nations is therefore crowned with this happy note of the triumph of grace in those among the Gentiles who turn to Jesus Christ.[47]

29. How does the church relate to the millennium?

At the rapture, the church will be removed from the earth and will be present with Christ throughout the tribulation. The church will be judged for rewards in the judgment following the second coming of Christ and will then participate in the blessings of the millennial kingdom (Romans 14:10-12; 1 Corinthians 3:11-16; 4:1-5; 9:24-27; 2 Corinthians 5:10,11; 2 Timothy 4:8).

In Matthew 19:28, Jesus told His disciples that they would join Him in the kingdom and reign over the 12 tribes of Israel. Also, in 2 Timothy 2:12, Paul writes, "If we endure, we shall also reign with Him." From Revelation 20:4, we know that martyred saints from the tribulation will also participate in Christ's reign. Two verses later, in Revelation 20:6, all those who were part of the first resurrection are said to reign with Christ.

Since heaven is above the earth, some have suggested that the church's heavenly role as the Bride of Christ is higher than any earthly role, including Israel's place as head over the nations. Perhaps the matter is better understood as each heading up their respective but equal spheres—Israel the earthly and the church the heavenly. Nevertheless, the primary purpose of the millennium is the restoration of Israel and Christ's rule over it, although the church as the Bride of Christ is not absent from millennial activities.

CHAPTER 25

Why Does the Millennium Matter?

30. Why should I be concerned about the millennium?

The Bible, especially the New Testament, places great emphasis on the future. Specifically, Christians should live in the present age in light of the future. The millennium is part of God's overall prophetic plan for humanity and creation. How we live during this life, to some extent, determines our specific role during this 1,000-year time in history. Believers who are not aware of this may miss an opportunity to prepare for the future in this life.

In this current age, God's rule of His creation is perhaps best described as an invisible, behind the scenes control. It is a time when He allows mankind to follow the path of his sin more freely than during the millennium, while still holding out the gracious opportunity of the gospel. Because the millennium will be a time in which righteousness will be vindicated and practiced, we should not be tempted to pursue a desperate course when things do not appear headed toward God's righteous ways. In the midst of such darkness, believers can hold forth more brightly the light of the day—the millennium.

As we seek to understand the riches of God's Word and the details contained in it, we cannot avoid its prophetic content. The believer's hope and destiny is irrevocably tied to Jesus Christ. He is our sure and certain hope and therefore His kingdom and His reign will have an incomprehensible effect on Christians. Because He lives, we too shall live and worship Him in the millennial kingdom.

31. How does the millennium affect me today?

In a world filled with chaos, despair, corruption, violence, and rampant evil, the certainty of the millennium offers assurance that God's prophetic program has not been abandoned. Christ will rule the world with righteousness and justice. Evil will be judged and believers of all ages will worship Jesus Christ in His presence. God knows the future and controls the future. Because of this, Christians today need not have anxiety or fear from the headlines. Our "blessed hope" is Jesus Christ (Titus 2:13); therefore, we are to be active in these days before our Lord's return proclaiming the gospel of Jesus Christ

(2 Corinthians 5:11). We need not fear, for His kingdom will certainly come. We need to boldly proclaim to all who will listen, the saving message of our Lord and Savior Jesus Christ, the coming Messiah-King.

His Kingdom Will Come

In his work *The Interpretation of Prophecy*, Dr. Paul Lee Tan writes that "when discussing the millennium, the literal interpreter, encounters a peculiar hardship, not of searching for, but of sifting through mountains of millennial prophecies."[48] He is correct, for there are scores of biblical passages proclaiming the reality of the millennial kingdom. The millennial kingdom is but one segment of God's prophetic plan. It will follow a time of great tragedy and horror. It will be the transition era between this present world and the eternal state.

In Luke 1:32,33, an angel came to Mary to announce to her the coming birth of the Messiah. In the majesty and intimacy of this annunciation, the coming kingdom was proclaimed.

> He will be great, and will be called the Son of the Most High; and the Lord God will give Him the throne of His father David; and He will reign over the house of Jacob forever; and His kingdom will have no end.

Yet, when offered by Jesus, the kingdom was rejected. It will however, be established in the future, fulfilling prophetic scriptures proclaimed over many centuries by many prophets. The magnificence of the millennium far exceeds anything we can imagine.

Scripture gives us descriptive glimpses but does not answer all our questions. We know many things with certainty, though we do not know them completely. His kingdom will come and His will shall be done on earth as it is in heaven. The words of the hymnist will be fully realized:

> *The sands of time are sinking,*
> *The dawn of heaven breaks;*
> *The summer morn I've sighed for,*
> *The fair sweet morn awakes.*
> *Dark, dark has been the midnight,*
> *But dayspring is at hand,*
> *And glory, glory dwelleth in*
> *Immanuel's land!*

Notes

Part 1—Signs of the Times

1. John F. Walvoord, *Prophecy: 14 Essential Keys to Understanding the Final Drama* (Nashville: Thomas Nelson Publishers, 1993), p. 1.
2. Ibid.
3. John F. Walvoord, *Armageddon, Oil and the Middle East Crisis*, rev. (Grand Rapids: Zondervan Publishing House, 1990), p. 217.
4. Ed Hindson, *Final Signs: Amazing Prophecies of the End Times* (Eugene, OR: Harvest House Publishers, 1996), pp. 36-37.
5. Ibid.
6. John F. Walvoord, *The Return of the Lord* (Grand Rapids: Zondervan Publishing House, 1955), p. 16.
7. Nathaniel West, *The Thousand Year Reign of Christ: The Classical Work on the Millennium* (Grand Rapids: Kregel Publication, 1993), p. 384.
8. Daniel T. Taylor and H.L. Hastings, *The Reign of Christ on Earth or The Voice of the Church in All Ages* (Boston: H.L. Hastings, 1893), pp. 25-46.
9. Bishop Russell, *Discourse on the Millennium*, cited in Taylor and Hastings, *Reign of Christ*, p. 25.
10. Ibid., p. 26.
11. Larry V. Crutchfield, "Israel and the Church in the Ante-Nicene Fathers," *Bibliotheca Sacra*, vol. 144, no. 575; July-September 1987, pp. 272-76.
12. *The Epistle of Barnabas*, para. 15.1-9. There are many translations of this work, and all will use paragraph or section divisions as cited.
13. Paula Fredriksen, "Tyconius and Augustine on the Apocalypse" in Richard K. Emmerson and Bernard McGinn, eds., *The Apocalypse in the Middle Ages* (Ithaca, NY: Cornell University Press, 1992), pp. 36-37.
14. Richard Erdoes, *A.D. 1000: Living on the Brink of Apocalypse* (San Francisco: Harper & Row Publishers, 1988), p. 1.
15. Ibid., p. 3.
16. Ron Rhodes "Millennial Madness," *Christian Research Journal*, Fall 1990, p. 39.
17. Erdoes, *A.D. 1000*, p. 203.
18. Walvoord, *Armageddon*, pp. 227-28.
19. Result of a poll taken December 2-4, 1994, and reported in *U.S. News & World Report*, December 19, 1994, pp. 62, 64.
20. For an explanation of these two events see Part 2.
21. Ernest R. Sandeen, *The Roots of Fundamentalism* (Grand Rapids: Baker Book House, 1980), pp. 62-63.
22. Ibid., p. 63.
23. Ibid., p. 64.
24. Gary North, "The Sabbath Millennium," *Biblical Economics Today*, vol. VIII, no. 2; February/March 1985), p. 4.
25. Walvoord, *Armageddon*, pp. 21-22.
26. J. Dwight Pentecost, *Things to Come: A Study in Biblical Eschatology* (Grand Rapids: Zondervan Publishing House, 1958), p. 149.
27. G.H. Pember, *The Great Prophecies of the Centuries Concerning the Church* (Miami Springs, FL: Conley & Schoettle Publishing Company, 1984 [1909]), pp. 494-95.
28. Arnold G. Fruchtenbaum, *The Footsteps of the Messiah: A Study of the Sequence of Prophetic Events* (Tustin, CA: Ariel Ministries, 1982), p. 38.
29. Pember, *Great Prophecies*, p. 496.
30. Ibid., p. 497.
31. Fruchtenbaum, *Footsteps*, p. 36.
32. Pember, *Great Prophecies*, p. 496.
33. Ibid., p. 497.
34. Ibid., pp. 497-99.
35. Pentecost, *Things to Come*, p. 155.
36. Taken from ibid., p. 155.
37. Lewis Sperry Chafer, *Systematic Theology*, 8 vols. (Dallas: Dallas Seminary Press, 1948), vol. IV, p. 375.
38. Walvoord, *Armageddon*, p. 219.
39. Ibid., pp. 219-21.
40. Ibid., pp. 222-23.
41. Ibid., pp. 223-25.
42. Ibid., p. 227.
43. Fruchtenbaum, *Footsteps*, p. 65.
44. John F. Walvoord, *Israel in Prophecy* (Grand Rapids: Zondervan Publishing House, 1962), p. 26.
45. Thomas Ice and Timothy Demy, *The Truth About Jerusalem in Bible Prophecy* (Eugene, OR: Harvest House Publishers, 1996).
46. Walvoord, *Armageddon*, pp. 105-06.

47. For more information on recent efforts to rebuild the Jewish Temple see Thomas Ice and Randall Price, *Ready to Rebuild: The Imminent Plan to Rebuild the Last Days' Temple* (Eugene, OR: Harvest House Publishers, 1992); and Thomas Ice and Timothy Demy, *The Truth About The Last Days' Temple* (Eugene, OR: Harvest House Publishers, 1996). This 48-page booklet is part of the Pocket Prophecy series.
48. J. Dwight Pentecost, *Prophecy for Today: The Middle East Crisis and the Future of the World* (Grand Rapids: Zondervan Publishing House, 1961), p. 226.
49. Hal Lindsey, *Planet Earth—2000 A.D. Will Mankind Survive?* (Palos Verdes, CA: Western Front, 1994), p. 221.
50. Chuck Missler, *The Magog Invasion* (Palos Verdes, CA: Western Front, 1995), p. 121.
51. Mark Hitchcock, *After the Empire: Biblical Prophecy in Light of the Fall of the Soviet Union* (Wheaton, IL: Tyndale House Publishers, 1994), p. 156.

52. Hindson, *Final Signs*, p. 151.
53. Charles C. Ryrie, *The Best Is Yet to Come* (Chicago: Moody Press, 1981), pp. 124-25.
54. Thomas Ice and Timothy Demy, *The Coming Cashless Society* (Eugene, OR: Harvest House Publishers, 1996), pp. 85-87.
55. Charles H. Dyer, *The Rise of Babylon: Sign of the End Times* (Wheaton, IL: Tyndale House Publishers, 1991), pp. 208-09.
56. Joseph Chambers, *A Palace for the Antichrist: Saddam Hussein's Drive to Rebuild Babylon and Its Place in Bible Prophecy* (Green Forest, AR: New Leaf Press, 1996), p. 66.
57. Ibid., p. 19.
58. Hal Lindsey, *The Late Great Planet Earth* (Grand Rapids: Zondervan Publishing House, 1970), p. 54.
59. *The Ryrie Study Bible*, NASB (Chicago: Moody Press, 1978), p. 1332.
60. Walvoord, *Armageddon*, p. 120.

Part 2—The Rapture

1. Jeffery L. Sheler, "The Christmas Covenant," *U.S. News & World Report*, December 19, 1994, pp. 62, 64.
2. *Dictionary of New Testament Theology*, s.v. "Snatch," by C. Brown, 3:602.
3. Kenneth Gentry, Jr., *He Shall Have Dominion: A Postmillennial Eschatology* (Tyler, TX: Institute for Christian Economics, 1992), pp. 146, 148.
4. *Webster's New Twentieth-Century Dictionary*, unabridged, 2d ed., s.v. "literal."
5. Paul Lee Tan, *The Interpretation of Prophecy* (Winona Lake, IN: Assurance Publishers, 1974), p. 29.
6. Roy B. Zuck, *Basic Bible Interpretation: A Practical Guide to Discovering Biblical Truth* (Wheaton, IL: Victor Books, 1991), p. 100.
7. Ibid., pp. 100-01.
8. Tan, *Interpretation of Prophecy*, p. 103.
9. Zuck, *Basic Bible Interpretation*, p. 77.
10. David L. Cooper, *The World's Greatest Library: Graphically Illustrated* (Los Angeles: Biblical Research Society, 1970), p. 11.
11. Elliott E. Johnson, *Expository Hermeneutics: An Introduction* (Grand Rapids: Zondervan Publishing House, 1990), p. 9.
12. Charles C. Ryrie, *Basic Theology: A Popular Systematic Guide to Understanding Biblical Truth* (Wheaton, IL: Victor Books, 1986), p. 450.
13. Arnold Fruchtenbaum, "Israel and the Church" in Wesley Willis, John Master, and Charles Ryrie, eds., *Issues in Dispensationalism* (Chicago: Moody Press, 1994), p. 129.
14. Ibid., p. 113.
15. Ibid., pp. 113-15.
16. Ibid., p. 116.
17. Ibid.
18. Ibid.
19. Ibid., p. 117.
20. Ibid.
21. Ibid.
22. Ibid., pp. 117-18.
23. Ibid., p. 118.
24. Ibid.
25. Ibid., p. 124.
26. Ibid., p. 126.
27. Ibid., p. 118.
28. John S. Feinberg, "Arguing for the Rapture: Who Must Prove What and How" in Thomas Ice and Timothy Demy, eds., *When the Trumpet Sounds* (Eugene, OR: Harvest House Publishers, 1995), p. 194.
29. Edward E. Hindson, "The Rapture and the Return: Two Aspects of Christ's Coming" in Thomas Ice and Timothy Demy, eds.,

When the Trumpet Sounds (Eugene, OR: Harvest House Publishers, 1995), p. 158.
30. The quotation and the first six contrasts in the graphic are taken from John F. Walvoord, *The Return of the Lord* (Grand Rapids: Zondervan Publishing House, 1955), pp. 87,88.
31. Hindson, "The Rapture and the Return," p. 157.
32. Many of the points in this section are taken from John F. Walvoord, *Rapture Question: Revised and Enlarged Edition* (Grand Rapids: Zondervan Publishing House, 1979), pp. 274-75.
33. Charles C. Ryrie, *Revelation* (Chicago: Moody Press, 1968), pp. 35, 36.
34. Walvoord, *The Rapture Question*, p. 274.
35. Renald Showers, *Maranatha: Our Lord, Come! A Definitive Study of the Rapture of the Church* (Bellmawr, NJ: The Friends of Israel Gospel Ministry, Inc., 1995), p. 243.
36. Ibid., pp. 127-28.
37. Walvoord, *Rapture Question*, p. 273.
38. These arguments are adopted from Walvoord, *The Rapture Question*, pp. 270-71.

39. Robert Gromacki, "Where is 'The Church' in Revelation 4–19?" in Thomas Ice and Timothy Demy, eds., *When the Trumpet Sounds* (Eugene, OR: Harvest House Publishers, 1995), p. 355.
40. These arguments are adopted from Walvoord, *Rapture Question*, pp. 271-73.
41. Robert L. Thomas, *Revelation 1–7: An Exegetical Commentary* (Chicago: Moody Press, 1992), p. 289.
42. Robert L. Thomas, "2 Thessalonians," in *The Expositor's Bible Commentary*, vol. 11, Frank E. Gaebelein, ed. (Grand Rapids: Zondervan Publishing House, 1978), pp. 324-25.
43. Hindson, "The Rapture and the Return," p. 161.
44. Showers, *Maranatha*, pp. 255-56.
45. Tim LaHaye, *No Fear of the Storm* (Portland, OR: Multnomah Press, 1992), p. 18.
46. Ibid., p. 18.
47. Timothy P. Weber, *Living in the Shadow of the Second Coming: American Premillennialism, 1875–1982* (Grand Rapids: Zondervan Publishing House, 1983), p. 81.

Part 3—The Tribulation and the Antichrist

1. For a more thorough treatment of these passages, see J. Randall Price, "Old Testament Tribulation Terms," in *When the Trumpet Sounds*, Thomas Ice and Timothy Demy, eds. (Eugene, OR: Harvest House Publishers, 1995), pp. 57-84.
2. One of the most readable and extensive discussions on the chronology of the 70 weeks is found in Harold W. Hoehner, *Chronological Aspects of the Life of Christ* (Grand Rapids: Zondervan Publishing House, 1977), pp. 115-39. A more popular presentation is Herb Vander Lugt, *The Daniel Papers* (Grand Rapids: Radio Bible Class, 1994).
3. Hoehner, *Chronological Aspects*, p. 139.
4. Charles H. Dyer, "Jeremiah" in *The Bible Knowledge Commentary: Old Testament*, John F. Walvoord and Roy B. Zuck, eds. (Wheaton, IL: Victor Books, 1984), p. 1168.
5. Stanley D. Toussaint, "The Contingency of the Coming of the Kingdom" in *Integrity of Heart, Skillfulness of Hands: Biblical and Leadership Studies in Honor of Donald K. Campbell*, Charles H. Dyer and Roy B. Zuck, eds. (Grand Rapids: Baker Book House, 1994), p. 224.

6. Price, "Old Testament Tribulation Terms," p. 71.
7. Ibid., p. 72.
8. "2 Thessalonians," *The Expositor's Bible Commentary*, 12 vols., Robert L. Thomas, Frank Gaebelein, gen. eds. (Grand Rapids: Zondervan Publishing House, 1978), 11:224-25.
9. Charles C. Ryrie, *The Holy Spirit* (Chicago: Moody Press, 1965), p. 108. For a more thorough treatment of these passages, see Price, "Old Testament Tribulation Terms," pp. 57-84.
10. John F. Walvoord, *The Holy Spirit* (Findlay, OH: Dunham Publishing Co., 1958), p. 229.
11. Ibid., p. 231.
12. Ibid., p. 230.
13. Arthur W. Pink, *The Antichrist* (Swengel, PA: Bible Truth Depot, 1923), p. 62.
14. For an extensive treatment of the rebuilding of the temple see Thomas Ice and Randall Price, *Ready to Rebuild: The Imminent Plan to Rebuild the Last Days' Temple* (Eugene, OR: Harvest House Publishers, 1992).
15. J. Dwight Pentecost, *Things to Come: A Study in Biblical Eschatology* (Grand

Rapids: Zondervan Publishing House, 1958), p. 337.
16. Ibid., pp. 336-37.
17. These three reasons were gleaned from Arnold Fruchtenbaum, "The Nationality of the Anti-Christ" (Englewood, NJ: American Board of Missions to the Jews, n.d.).
18. Ibid., p. 8.
19. Ibid., pp. 11-22.
20. Ibid., pp. 24, 26.
21. John F. Walvoord, *Major Bible Prophecies: 37 Crucial Prophecies That Affect You Today* (Grand Rapids: Zondervan Publishing House, 1991), pp. 314-15.
22. Charles H. Dyer, *World News and Bible Prophecy* (Wheaton, IL: Tyndale House Publishers, 1993), p. 204.
23. Walvoord, *Major Bible Prophecies*, p. 315.
24. Ibid., p. 319.
25. Many people believe that the progress being made toward a cashless society is preparation to facilitate the work of the Antichrist. However, such technology is not itself the mark of the beast—even though it may be used by him. See our *The Coming Cashless Society* (Harvest House Publishers, 1996) for a more in-depth discussion.
26. Walvoord, *Major Bible Prophecies*, p. 344.
27. John F. Walvoord, *Prophecy: 14 Essential Keys to Understanding the Final Drama* (Nashville: Thomas Nelson Publishers, 1993), p. 125.
28. John F. Walvoord, *The Prophecy Knowledge Handbook* (Wheaton, IL: SP Publications, 1990), p. 587, emphasis added.
29. Robert L. Thomas, *Revelation: An Exegetical Commentary*, 2 vols. (Chicago: Moody Press, 1992, 1995), 2:183-84.
30. Dyer, *World News*, p. 217.
31. Walvoord, *Major Bible Prophecies*, pp. 319, 320.
32. Ibid., p. 341.
33. Arnold G. Fruchtenbaum, *The Footsteps of the Messiah: A Study of the Sequence of Prophetic Events* (Tustin, CA: Ariel Ministries, 1982), pp. 122-26.
34. Ibid., pp. 123-24.
35. Ibid., p. 125.
36. We are following events as outlined in Fruchtenbaum, *Footsteps*, pp. 135-91.
37. For more extensive interaction with preterism see H. Wayne House and Thomas Ice, *Dominion Theology: Blessing or Curse? An Analysis of Christian Reconstructionism* (Portland, OR: Multnomah Press, 1988), pp. 249-334.
38. Charles C. Ryrie, *Basic Theology* (Wheaton, IL: Victor Books, 1986), p. 465.
39. John F. Walvoord, *Daniel: The Key to Prophetic Revelation* (Chicago: Moody Press, 1971), pp. 219-20.
40. Ibid., p. 235.
41. John F. Walvoord, *The Church in Prophecy* (Grand Rapids: Zondervan Publishing House, 1964), pp. 129-30.
42. John F. Walvoord, *The Millennial Kingdom* (Findlay, OH: Dunham Publishing Co., 1958), pp. 257-58.
43. Ryrie, *Basic Theology*, p. 468.

Part 4—Armageddon and the Middle East

1. Charles H. Dyer, *World News and Bible Prophecy* (Wheaton, IL: Tyndale House Publishers, 1991), pp. 237-38.
2. Arnold G. Fruchtenbaum, *The Footsteps of the Messiah: A Study of the Sequence of Prophetic Events* (Tustin, CA: Ariel Ministries, 1982), p. 254.
3. Ibid., p. 218.
4. Not all premillennial and pretribulational interpreters place Armageddon at the end of the tribulation. See J. Dwight Pentecost, *Things to Come: A Study in Biblical Eschatology* (Grand Rapids: Zondervan Publishing House, 1958), pp. 346-55.
5. Fruchtenbaum, *Footsteps*, pp. 216-53.
6. Ibid., p. 216.
7. Ibid., p. 217.
8. Ibid., p. 223.
9. Ibid., pp. 201-04.
10. Ibid., p. 233.
11. Ibid., p. 239.
12. Ibid., p. 248.
13. Ibid., p. 217.
14. Ibid., p. 155.
15. Paul Feinberg, "The Mideast March to Megiddo," in William T. James, ed., *Foreshocks of Antichrist* (Eugene, OR: Harvest House Publishers, 1997), pp. 270-71.
16. Ibid., p. 262.
17. Ibid., pp. 263-64.
18. For more information on the rapture, see Part 2.
19. See Part 5, Question 6 for a brief explanation of this interval. See Fruchtenbaum, *Footsteps*, pp. 256-63, for a full discussion of this time period.
20. For a fuller discussion see Part 5, "The Millennium."

21. David Larsen, *Jews, Gentiles, and the Church: A New Perspective on History and Prophecy* (Grand Rapids: Discovery House, 1995), p. 316.
22. Ibid., p. 317.
23. See Fruchtenbaum, *Footsteps*, pp. 77-83; and Harold W. Hoehner, "The Progression of Events in Ezekiel 38–39" in Charles H. Dyer and Roy B. Zuck, *Integrity of Heart, Skillfulness of Hands* (Grand Rapids: Baker Books, 1994), pp. 82-92.
24. Fruchtenbaum, *Footsteps*, pp. 78-79.
25. Harold W. Hoehner, "The Progression of Events in Ezekiel 38–39," in Charles H. Dyer and Roy B. Zuck, *Integrity of Heart, Skillfulness of Hands* (Grand Rapids: Baker Books, 1994).

26. Fruchtenbaum holds that the invasion "must take place at least 3½ years or more before the tribulation starts" (*Footsteps*, p. 81), so that the 7 years would be completed by the middle of the tribulation, though not all who hold this view require such a large time period.
27. Fruchtenbaum, *Footsteps*, p. 82.
28. Charles C. Ryrie, *Basic Theology* (Wheaton, IL: Victory Books, 1986), p. 476.
29. John F. Walvoord, *Armageddon, Oil and the Middle East Crisis* (Grand Rapids: Zondervan Publishing House, 1990), p. 227.
30. Ibid., p. 219. See Part 1 for more information.
31. Walvoord, *Armageddon*, p. 120.

Part 5—The Millennium

1. John F. Walvoord, *Prophecy: 14 Essential Keys to Understanding the Final Drama* (Nashville: Thomas Nelson Publishers, 1993), p. 139.
2. David L. Larsen, *Jews, Gentiles, and the Church: A New Perspective on History and Prophecy* (Grand Rapids: Discovery House, 1995), pp. 310-11.
3. J. Dwight Pentecost, *Things to Come: A Study in Biblical Eschatology* (Grand Rapids: Zondervan Publishing House, 1958), pp. 563-79.
4. Jack S. Deere, "Premillennialism in Revelation 20:4-6," *Bibliotheca Sacra*, 135 (July–March 1978): 58-73.
5. Roy B. Zuck, *Basic Bible Interpretation* (Wheaton, IL: SP Publications, Inc., 1991), pp. 244-45.
6. Harold W. Hoehner, "Evidence from Revelation," in *A Case for Premillennialism: A New Consensus*, eds. Donald K. Campbell and Jeffrey L. Townsend (Chicago: Moody Press, 1992), pp. 249-50.
7. Nathaniel West, *The Thousand Year Reign of Christ: The Classic Work on the Millennium* (Grand Rapids: Kregel Publications, 1993), p. 327.
8. This argument was made by S. Lewis Johnson, unpublished classnotes from Revelation 228, Dallas Theological Seminary, Fall 1976.
9. Kenneth L. Gentry, *He Shall Have Dominion: A Postmillennial Eschatology* (Tyler, TX: Institute for Christian Economics, 1992), p. 335.
10. West, *Thousand Year Reign*, p. 384.
11. Daniel T. Taylor and H.L. Hastings, *The Reign of Christ on Earth or the Voice of the Church in All Ages* (Boston: H.L. Hastings, 1893), pp. 25-46.
12. Henry Alford, *Alford's Greek Testament*, 4 vols. (Grand Rapids: Guardian Press, 1976), vol. IV, part II, pp. 732-33.
13. For an excellent survey of the biblical covenants see Paul N. Benware, *Understanding End Times Prophecy: A Comprehensive Approach* (Chicago: Moody Press, 1995), pp. 31-74.
14. John F. Walvoord, *The Millennial Kingdom* (Findlay, OH: Dunham Publishing Company, 1959), pp. 298-99.
15. Philip Schaff, *History of the Christian Church*, 8 vols. (Grand Rapids: Eerdmans, 1910), II:614.
16. Ibid., pp. 618-19.
17. For a clear overview of the history of biblical interpretation, see Zuck, *Basic Bible Interpretation*, pp. 27-58.
18. Charles C. Ryrie, *Basic Theology* (Wheaton, IL: SP Publications, Inc., 1986), p. 511.
19. Larsen, *Jews, Gentiles, and the Church*, p. 316.
20. Ibid., p. 317.
21. Arnold G. Fruchtenbaum, *Footsteps of the Messiah: A Study of the Sequence of Prophetic Events* (Tustin, CA: Ariel Ministries, 1982), pp. 256-63.
22. John F. Walvoord, *Major Bible Prophecies: 37 Crucial Prophecies That Affect You Today* (Grand Rapids: Zondervan Publishing House, 1991), p. 404.
23. Ibid., p. 405.
24. Fruchtenbaum, *Footsteps*, pp. 121-26.
25. Walvoord, *Major Bible Prophecies*, p. 390.
26. Fruchtenbaum, *Footsteps*, p. 366.

27. Ryrie, *Basic Theology,* p. 449.
28. Walvoord, *Millennial Kingdom,* p. 23.
29. Benware, *Understanding End Times,* p. 284.
30. Walvoord, *Millennial Kingdom,* p. 318.
31. Ibid., p. 319.
32. Walvoord, *Millennial Kingdom,* p. 307.
33. Pentecost, *Things to Come,* pp. 482-87.
34. Benware, *Understanding End Times,* p. 282.
35. See in this same series by the authors, *The Truth About the Last Days' Temple,* pp. 25-26, 39-43.
36. Walvoord, *Millennial Kingdom,* pp. 310-11.
37. Jerry M. Hullinger, "The Problem of Animal Sacrifices in Ezekiel 40–48," *Bibliotheca Sacra* 152 (July–September 1995), p. 280.
38. Ibid. p. 281.
39. Ibid., p. 289.
40. Arnold G. Fruchtenbaum, *Israelology: The Missing Link in Systematic Theology* (Tustin, CA: Ariel Ministries, 1993), p. 810.
41. Pentecost, *Things to Come,* pp. 503-04.
42. Walvoord, *Major Bible Prophecies,* p. 391.
43. Ibid., p. 390.
44. Fruchtenbaum, *Footsteps,* pp. 287-312.
45. Ibid., pp. 312-17.
46. Larsen, *Jews, Gentiles, and the Church,* p. 310.
47. John F. Walvoord, *The Nations in Prophecy* (Grand Rapids: Zondervan Publishing House, 1967), pp. 170-71.
48. Paul Lee Tan, *The Interpretation of Prophecy* (Dallas: Bible Communications, Inc., 1974), p. 352.

Recommended Reading

Part 1—Signs of the Times*

Alnor, William M. *Soothsayers of the Second Advent*. Old Tappan, NJ: Fleming H. Revell Co., 1989.

Benware, Paul N. *Understanding End Times Prophecy: A Comprehensive Approach*. Chicago: Moody Press, 1995.

Boyer, Paul. *When Time Shall Be No More: Prophecy Belief in Modern Culture*. Cambridge, MA: The Belknap Press of Harvard University Press, 1992.

Chambers, Joseph. *A Palace for the Antichrist: Saddam Hussein's Drive to Rebuild Babylon and Its Place in Bible Prophecy*. Green Forest, AR: New Leaf Press, 1996.

Chandler, Russell. *Doomsday: The End of the World. A View Through Time*. Ann Arbor, MI: Servant Publications, 1993.

Dyer, Charles H. *The Rise of Babylon: Sign of the End Times*. Wheaton, IL: Tyndale House Pub., 1991.

———. *World News and Bible Prophecy*. Wheaton, IL: Tyndale House Pub., 1993.

Erdoes, Richard. *A.D. 1000: Living on the Brink of Apocalypse*. San Francisco: Harper & Row Pub., 1988.

Fruchtenbaum, Arnold G. *The Footsteps of the Messiah: A Study of the Sequence of Prophetic Events*. Tustin, CA: Ariel Ministries, 1982.

Hindson, Ed. *Final Signs: Amazing Prophecies of the End Times*. Eugene, OR: Harvest House Pub., 1996.

Hitchcock, Mark. *After the Empire: Bible Prophecy in Light of the Fall of the Soviet Union*. Wheaton, IL: Tyndale House Pub., 1994.

Hodges, Zane C. *Power to Make War: The Career of the Assyrian Who Will Rule the World*. Dallas: Redención Viva, 1995.

Hoehner, Harold W. *Chronological Aspects of the Life of Christ*. Grand Rapids: Zondervan Pub. House, 1977.

Hunt, Dave. *Cup of Trembling: Jerusalem and Bible Prophecy*. Eugene, OR: Harvest House Pub., 1995.

———. *How Close Are We? Compelling Evidence for the Soon Return of Christ*. Eugene, OR: Harvest House, 1993.

Ice, Thomas, and Timothy Demy. *The Coming Cashless Society*. Eugene, OR: Harvest House Pub., 1996.

———. *The Truth About 2000 A.D. & Predicting Christ's Return*. Eugene, OR: Harvest House Pub., 1996.

———. *The Truth About Jerusalem in Bible Prophecy*. Eugene, OR: Harvest House Pub., 1996.

———. *The Truth About The Last Days' Temple*. Eugene, OR: Harvest House Pub., 1996.

———. *When the Trumpet Sounds: Today's Foremost Authorities Speak Out on End-Time Controversies*. Eugene, OR: Harvest House Pub., 1995.

Ice, Thomas and Randall Price, *Ready to Rebuild: The Imminent Plan to Rebuild the Last Days' Temple*. Eugene, OR: Harvest House Pub., 1992.

LaHaye, Tim. *The Beginning of the End*. Wheaton, IL: Tyndale House Pub., 1991.

LaLonde, Peter and Paul LaLonde. *The Mark of the Beast*. Eugene, OR: Harvest House Pub., 1994.

Larsen, David L. *Jews, Gentiles, and the Church: A New Perspective on History and Prophecy*. Grand Rapids: Discovery House, 1995.

Lindsey, Hal. *The Final Battle*. Palos Verdes, CA: Western Front, 1995.

———. *The Late Great Planet Earth*. Grand Rapids: Zondervan Pub. House, 1970.

———. *Planet Earth—2000 A.D. Will Mankind Survive?* Palos Verdes, CA: Western Front, 1994.

Missler, Chuck. *The Magog Invasion*. Palos Verdes, CA: Western Front, 1995.

Oropeza, B.J. *99 Reasons Why No One Knows When Christ Will Return*. Downers Grove, IL: InterVarsity Press, 1994.

Pate, C. Marvin and Calvin B. Haines, Jr., *Doomsday Delusions: What's Wrong with Predictions About the End of the World*. Downers Grove, IL: InterVarsity Press, 1995.

Pentecost, J. Dwight. *Prophecy for Today: The Middle East Crisis and the Future of the World*. Grand Rapids: Zondervan Pub. House, 1961.

---

* We do not agree with some of the viewpoints expressed in the books in Part 1.

274   Recommended Reading

────. *Things to Come: A Study in Biblical Eschatology*. Grand Rapids: Zondervan Pub. House, 1958.

Ryrie, Charles. *The Best Is Yet to Come*. Chicago: Moody Press, 1981.

Walvoord, John F. *Armageddon, Oil and the Middle East Crisis*. Grand Rapids: Zondervan Pub. House, 1990.

────. *Israel in Prophecy*. Grand Rapids: Zondervan Pub. House, 1962.

────. *Major Bible Prophecies: 37 Crucial Prophecies That Affect You Today*. Grand Rapids: Zondervan Pub. House, 1991.

────. *Prophecy: 14 Essential Keys to Understanding the Final Drama*. Nashville: Thomas Nelson Pub., 1993.

────. *The Prophecy Knowledge Handbook*. Wheaton, IL: Victor Books, 1990.

────. *The Return of the Lord*. Grand Rapids: Zondervan Pub. House, 1955.

Zuck, Roy B. *Basic Bible Interpretation*. Wheaton, IL: SP Publications, Inc., 1991.

Part 2—The Rapture

Beechick, Allen. *The Pre-Tribulation Rapture*. Denver: Accent Books, 1980.

Blackstone, William E. *Jesus Is Coming*. New York: Revell, 1898, 1908, 1932.

Boyer, James L. *Prophecy: Things to Come*. Winona Lake, IN: BMH Books, 1973.

Brookes, James H. *Maranatha*. New York: Fleming H. Revell Co., 1889.

────. *Till He Come*. New York: Fleming H. Revell Co., 1895.

Darby, J.N. *Will the Saints Be in the Tribulation?* New York: Loizeaux Brothers, n.d.

Duty, Guy. *Escape from the Coming Tribulation*. Minneapolis: Bethany Fellowship, 1975.

English, E. Schuyler. *Re-Thinking the Rapture*. Neptune, NJ: Loizeaux Brothers, 1954.

Feinberg, Paul D. "The Case for the Pretribulation Rapture Position" in Richard R. Reiter, Paul D. Feinberg, Gleason L. Archer, Douglas J. Moo, *The Rapture: Pre-, Mid-, or Post-Tribulational?* Grand Rapids: Zondervan Pub. House, 1984.

Fruchtenbaum, Arnold G. *The Footsteps of the Messiah: A Study of the Sequence of Prophetic Events*. Tustin, CA: Ariel Ministries, 1982.

Harrison, William K. *Hope Triumphant: The Rapture of the Church*. Chicago: Moody Press, 1966.

Hoyt, Herman A. *The End Times*. Chicago: Moody Press, 1969.

Ice, Thomas and Timothy Demy, eds., *When the Trumpet Sounds: Today's Foremost Authorities Speak Out on End-Time Controversies*. Eugene, OR: Harvest House Pub., 1995.

Ironside, H.A. *Not Wrath, But Rapture*. New York: Loizeaux Brothers, 1946.

LaHaye, Timothy. *No Fear of the Storm: Why Christians Will Escape All the Tribulation*. Portland, OR: Multnomah Press, 1992.

Lindsey, Hal. *The Rapture: Truth or Consequences*. New York: Bantam Books, 1983.

Mayhue, Richard L. *Snatched Before the Storm? A Case for Pretribulationism*. Winona Lake, IN: BMH Books, 1980.

Pache, René. *The Return of Jesus Christ*. Chicago: Moody Press, 1955, 1975.

Pentecost, J. Dwight. *Things to Come: A Study in Biblical Eschatology*. Grand Rapids: Zondervan Pub. House, 1958.

Ryrie, Charles C. *What You Should Know About the Rapture*. Chicago: Moody Press, 1981.

Scofield, C.I. *Will the Church Pass Through the Great Tribulation?* Philadelphia: Philadelphia School of the Bible, 1917.

Showers, Renald. *Maranatha: Our Lord, Come!* Bellmawr, NJ: The Friends of Israel Gospel Ministry, 1995.

Stanton, Gerald B. *Kept from the Hour: Biblical Evidence for the Pretribulational Return of Christ*, 4th ed. Miami Springs, FL: Schoettle Pub. Co., 1956, 1991.

Strombeck, J.F. *First the Rapture*. Eugene, OR: Harvest House Pub., [1950], 1982.

Thiessen, Henry C. *Will the Church Pass Through the Tribulation?* New York: Loizeaux Brothers, 1941.

Walvoord, John F. *The Blessed Hope and the Tribulation*. Grand Rapids: Zondervan Pub. House, 1976.

────. *The Rapture Question*. Grand Rapids: Zondervan Pub. House, [1957], 1979.

────. *The Return of the Lord*. Grand Rapids: Zondervan Pub. House, 1955.

────. *Major Bible Prophecies: 37 Crucial Prophecies That Affect You Today*. Grand Rapids: Zondervan Pub. House, 1991.

────. *Prophecy: 14 Essential Keys to Understanding the Final Drama*. Nashville: Thomas Nelson Pub., 1993.

Wood, Leon. *Is The Rapture Next?* Grand Rapids: Zondervan Pub. House, 1956.

Part 3—The Tribulation and the Antichrist

Dyer, Charles H. *World News and Bible Prophecy*. Wheaton, IL: Tyndale House Pub., 1993.

Fruchtenbaum, Arnold. "The Nationality of the Anti-Christ." Englewood Cliffs, NJ: American Board of Missions to the Jews, n.d

———. *The Footsteps of the Messiah: A Study of the Sequence of Prophetic Events*. Tustin, CA: Ariel Ministries, 1982.

Hoehner, Harold W. *Chronological Aspects of the Life of Christ*. Grand Rapids: Zondervan Pub. House, 1977.

Hunt, Dave. *A Cup of Trembling: Jerusalem and Bible Prophecy*. Eugene, OR: Harvest House Pub., 1995.

Ice, Thomas and Robert Dean. *Overrun by Demons: The Church's New Preoccupation with the Demonic*. Eugene, OR: Harvest House Pub., 1990.

Ice, Thomas and Timothy Demy, eds. *When the Trumpet Sounds: Today's Foremost Authorities Speak Out on End-Time Controversies*. Eugene, OR: Harvest House Pub., 1995.

Ice, Thomas and Randall Price. *Ready to Rebuild: The Imminent Plan to Rebuild the Last Days Temple*. Eugene, OR: Harvest House Pub., 1992.

Jeffrey, Grant R. *Prince of Darkness: Antichrist and the New World Order*. Toronto: Frontier Research Publications, 1994.

Lindsey, Hal. *The Late Great Planet Earth*. Grand Rapids: Zondervan Pub. House, 1970.

McGinn, Bernard. *Antichrist: Two Thousand Years of the Human Fascination with Evil*. San Francisco: Harper Collins, 1994.

Pentecost, J. Dwight. *Things to Come: A Study in Biblical Eschatology*. Grand Rapids: Zondervan Pub. House, 1958.

Pink, Arthur W. *The Antichrist*. Swengel, PA: Bible Truth Depot, 1923.

Price, Randall. *In Search of Temple Treasures: The Lost Ark and the Last Days*. Eugene, OR: Harvest House Pub., 1994.

Showers, Renald. *Maranatha: Our Lord Come!* Bellmawr, NJ: The Friends of Israel Gospel Ministry, 1995.

Thomas, Robert L. *Revelation: An Exegetical Commentary*. 2 vols. Chicago: Moody Press, 1992, 1995.

Walvoord, John F. *Daniel: The Key to Prophetic Revelation*. Chicago: Moody Press, 1971.

———. *Israel in Prophecy*. Grand Rapids: Zondervan Pub. House, 1962.

———. *Major Bible Prophecies: 37 Crucial Prophecies That Affect You Today*. Grand Rapids: Zondervan Pub. House, 1991.

———. *The Nations in Prophecy*. Grand Rapids: Zondervan Pub. House, 1967.

———. *Prophecy: 14 Essential Keys to Understanding the Final Drama*. Nashville: Thomas Nelson Pub., 1993.

———. *The Prophecy Knowledge Handbook*. Wheaton, IL: SP Publications, 1990.

———. *The Revelation of Jesus Christ*. Chicago: Moody Press, 1963.

Part 4—Armageddon and the Middle East

Chambers, Joseph. *A Palace for the Antichrist: Saddam Hussein's Drive to Rebuild Babylon and Its Place in Bible Prophecy*. Green Forest, AR: New Leaf Press, 1996.

Dyer, Charles H. *The Rise of Babylon: Sign of the End Times*. Wheaton, IL: Tyndale House Pub., 1991.

———. *World News and Bible Prophecy*. Wheaton, IL: Tyndale House Pub., 1993.

———. "The Identity of Babylon in Revelation 17–18, parts 1 and 2." *Bibliotheca Sacra* (vol. 145; nos. 575, 576), pp. 305-16, 433-49.

Feinberg, Charles L. *The Prophecy of Ezekiel: The Glory of the Lord*. Chicago: Moody Press, 1969.

Feinberg, Paul. "The Mideast March to Megiddo," in William T. James, ed., *Fore-*

shocks of Antichrist. Eugene, OR: Harvest House Pub., 1997, pp. 255-73.

Fruchtenbaum, Arnold. *The Footsteps of the Messiah: A Study of the Sequence of Prophetic Events*. Tustin, CA: Ariel Ministries, 1982.

Hoehner, Harold W. "The Progression of Events in Ezekiel 38–39" in *Integrity of Heart, Skillfulness of Hands: Biblical and Leadership Studies in Honor of Donald K. Campbell*, Charles H. Dyer and Roy B. Zuck eds. Grand Rapids: Baker Books, 1994, pp. 82-91.

Ice, Thomas and Timothy Demy. *The Truth About 2000 A.D. and Predicting Christ's Return*. Eugene, OR: Harvest House Pub., 1996.

276   Recommended Reading

———. *The Truth About Jerusalem in Bible Prophecy.* Eugene, OR: Harvest House Pub., 1996.

James, Edgar. *Arabs, Oil, and Armageddon.* Chicago: Moody Press, 1991.

James, William T. *Storming Toward Armageddon: Essays in Apocalypse.* Green Forest, AR: New Leaf Press, 1992.

Jeffrey, Grant R. *Armageddon: Appointment with Destiny.* Toronto: Frontier Research Publications, 1988.

Lindsey, Hal. *The Final Battle.* Palos Verdes, CA: Western Front, Ltd., 1995.

Lindsey, Hal, with C.C. Carlson. *The Late Great Planet Earth.* Grand Rapids: Zondervan Pub. House, 1970.

Pentecost, J. Dwight. *Things to Come: A Study in Biblical Eschatology.* Grand Rapids: Zondervan Pub. House, 1958.

Rosen, Moishe. *Beyond the Gulf War: Overture to Armageddon?* San Bernardino, CA: Here's Life Pub., 1991.

Ryrie, Charles C. *Basic Theology.* Wheaton, IL: SP Publications, 1987.

Thomas, Robert L. *Revelation: An Exegetical Commentary.* 2 vols. Chicago: Moody Press, 1995.

Walvoord, John F. *Armageddon, Oil and the Middle East Crisis.* Rev. ed. Grand Rapids: Zondervan Pub. House, 1990.

———. *Daniel: The Key to Prophetic Revelation.* Chicago: Moody Press, 1971.

———. *Israel in Prophecy.* Grand Rapids: Zondervan Pub. House, 1962.

———. *Major Bible Prophecies: 37 Crucial Prophecies That Affect You Today.* Grand Rapids: Zondervan Pub. House, 1991.

———. *The Nations in Prophecy.* Grand Rapids: Zondervan Pub. House, 1967.

———. *Prophecy: 14 Essential Keys to Understanding the Final Drama.* Nashville: Thomas Nelson Pub., 1993.

———. *The Prophecy Knowledge Handbook.* Wheaton, IL: SP Publications, 1990.

———. *The Revelation of Jesus Christ.* Chicago: Moody Press, 1963.

Yamauchi, Edwin. *Foes from the Northern Frontier.* Grand Rapids: Baker Books, 1982.

———. "Russian Attacks?" *Biblical Archeologist,* Spring 1983: 96-97.

———. "The Scythians: Invading Hordes from the Russian Steppes" *Biblical Archeologist,* Spring 1983: 90-95, 98-99.

Part 5—The Millennium

Benware, Paul N. *Understanding End Times Prophecy: A Comprehensive Approach.* Chicago: Moody Press, 1995.

Bultema, Harry. *Maranatha! A Study of Unfulfilled Prophecy.* Grand Rapids: Kregel Publications, 1985.

Campbell, Donald K. and Jeffrey L. Townsend. *A Case for Premillennialism.* Chicago: Moody Press, 1992.

Deere, Jack S. "Premillennialism in Revelation 20:4-6," *Bibliotheca Sacra* 135 (January–March 1978): 58-73.

Feinberg, Charles L. *The Prophecy of Ezekiel: The Glory of the Lord.* Chicago: Moody Press, 1969.

———. *Millennialism: The Two Major Views,* 4th ed. Chicago: Moody Press, 1980.

Fruchtenbaum, Arnold G. *Footsteps of the Messiah: A Study of the Sequence of Prophetic Events.* Tustin, CA: Ariel Ministries, 1982.

———. *Israelology: The Missing Link in Systematic Theology.* Tustin, CA: Ariel Ministries, 1993.

Larsen, David L. *Jews, Gentiles, and the Church: A New Perspective on History and Prophecy.* Grand Rapids: Discovery House, 1995.

Martin, Alfred and John A. Martin. *Isaiah: The Glory of the Messiah.* Chicago: Moody Press, 1983.

McClain, Alva J. *The Greatness of the Kingdom: An Inductive Study of the Kingdom of God.* Winona Lake, IN: BMH Books, 1959.

Pentecost, J. Dwight. *Things to Come: A Study in Biblical Eschatology.* Grand Rapids: Zondervan Pub. House, 1958.

———. *Thy Kingdom Come.* Wheaton, IL: SP Publications, Inc., 1990.

Peters, George N.H. *The Theocratic Kingdom,* 3 vols. Grand Rapids: Kregel Publications, 1984.

Ryrie, Charles C. *The Basis of the Premillennial Faith.* Neptune, NJ: Loizeaux Brothers, 1953.

Tan, Paul Lee. *The Interpretation of Prophecy.* Dallas: Bible Communications, Inc., 1974.

Townsend, Jeffrey L. "Is the Present Age the Millennium?" in *Vital Prophetic Issues: Examining Promises and Problems in Eschatology,* pp. 68-82. Roy B. Zuck, ed. Grand Rapids: Kregel Publications, 1995.

Walvoord, John F. *Major Bible Prophecies: 37 Crucial Prophecies That Affect You Today.* Grand Rapids: Zondervan Pub. House, 1991.

———. *The Millennial Kingdom.* Findlay, OH: Dunham Pub. Co., 1959.

———. *The Nations in Prophecy.* Grand Rapids: Zondervan Pub. House, 1967.

———. *Prophecy: 14 Essential Keys to Understanding the Final Drama.* Nashville: Thomas Nelson Pub., 1993.

West, Nathaniel. *The Thousand Year Reign of Christ: The Classic Work on the Millennium.* Grand Rapids: Kregel Publications, 1993.

Zuck, Roy B. *Basic Bible Interpretation.* Wheaton, IL: SP Publications, Inc., 1991.

Index

Numbers

144,000 160, 177
200 million 197
75-day transition 211

A

A.D. 1000 23
A.D. 2000 21-22, 38
A.D. 70 41, 44
abomination of desolation 139, 144, 166
allegorical interpretation 242
amillennialism 33, 35, 90, 237, 242
Antichrist 56, 68, 70, 139-140, 144, 146,
    153, 156, 174, 234
apostasy 34, 50-51
Armageddon 183-185, 200, 203, 206, 209,
    215
  battle of 66
Augustine 230

B

Babylon 71, 188-189, 204
birth pangs 134
bowl judgments 168
Bozrah 193

C

China 197
church 93-94, 264
church age 9, 11, 44
conversion of Israel 169
current events 215

D

Daniel's 70 weeks 123, 130
date-setting 24, 29, 37, 40
Davidic covenant 249
Day of Atonement 31
Day of Pentecost 32
day of the Lord 131
destruction of Jerusalem 29
Diocletian 29
dispensationalism 33
dispensationalists 30

E

earthquakes 34, 74
Edgar Whisenant 35
end times 9
Ephesus 47
Epistle of Barnabas 20
establishment of Israel 53
eternal state 239
Europe 70
European Common Market 150
European Economic Community 150
evangelism 116

F

false prophet 234
famines 74
Feast
  Day of Atonement 31
  of First Fruits 31
  of Passover 31
  of Pentecost 32
  of Tabernacles 31
  of Trumpets 31
  of Unleavened Bread 31
  of Weeks 31
feast cycle 31-32
figures of speech 87
first fruits 31
futurism 29, 91-92
futurists 27, 30

G

generation 43, 73
Gentiles 175, 250, 259, 263
Gog 69, 202
great tribulation 128
great white throne judgment 235

H

Hal Lindsey 73
heaven 228
historicism 27, 34
historicist 27, 91
Holy Spirit 111, 136-137, 253

I

idealism 29
idealist 27, 91
imminence 42, 107
imminency 105
Israel 44, 59, 61, 63, 65, 93-94, 159, 174,
    231, 262

J

J.N. Darby 30
Jerusalem 65, 192, 203, 217, 249
Jesus Christ 209
Jonathan Edwards 37
judgment of Gentiles 259
judgment of Israel 259
judgment of Satan 235

K

kingdom of God 133, 225

L

lake of fire 234
Laodicea 46-47
last days 9
literal interpretation 84-85, 87-88

M

Magog 69, 202
man of lawlessness 111
maranatha 107
mark of the beast 71, 165
Meshech 68
Middle East 215, 217
midtribulationism 81
millennial kingdom 228, 246
millennial rest 17
millennial temple 255
millennium 20, 33, 35, 223, 229, 231, 237,
   259, 265
Mount of Olives 196, 210
mystery 102

N

natural disasters 34, 125
new covenant 252
New Jerusalem 240
newspaper exegesis 14
Nostradamus 38

P

partial rapture 81
Passover 31
Pentecost 32
Pergamum 47
Petra 193
Philadelphia 47
postmillennialism 33, 36-37, 90, 237, 243-
   244
Posttribulationism 82
premillennialism 33, 80, 89-90, 241
preterism 27, 170
preterist 27, 91
pretribulationism 80, 112
prewrath rapture 82

R

rapture 9, 11, 32, 43, 51-52, 55, 77-78,
   80, 97-98, 100, 102, 105, 111, 114
regathering of Israel 63

remnant 168
restoration of Israel 263
Rosh Hashanah 31
Rosh, prince of 68
Russia 69

S

sacrifices 256-257
Sardis 47
Satan 162, 225, 233-235
seal judgments 74, 160
second coming 9, 98, 100, 195, 239
septa-millennial 34
   theory 17-20, 31
   view 21
seven churches 45, 47
signs 10, 12, 14
signs of the times 55
Smyrna 47
speculations 12-13
stage-setting 10

T

tabernacles 31
temple 67, 142-143
ten-nation confederacy 160
Thyatira 47
timing of prophecy 32
tribulation 9, 55-56, 75, 108, 110, 119,
   121, 123, 125, 128-129, 158, 160,
   169, 174, 238
trumpet judgments 160
trumpets 31
Tubal 68
two witnesses 160

U

unleavened bread 31

W

wars 74
William Miller 34
world missions 117

Other Good Harvest House Reading

Fast Facts on Bible Prophecy

Thomas Ice and Timothy Demy. Ice and Demy, creators of the Pocket Prophecy series, have compiled their works into this A-to-Z end-times resource. Includes more than 175 in-depth Bible prophecy definitions, background on different interpretations of prophecy, outlines on the timing of prophetic events, and much more.

The Coming Cashless Society

Thomas Ice and Timothy Demy. Could a cashless society be a final stepping stone to the mark of the beast? An intriguing look at what the Bible says about a cashless society and answers on how Christians should evaluate the new technology explosion.

Ready to Rebuild

Thomas Ice and Randall Price. A fast-moving overview of contemporary events which indicate that a significant move to rebuild the Temple is gaining momentum in Israel. Important pictures and charts.

When the Trumpet Sounds

Thomas Ice and Timothy Demy, eds. Twenty-one respected prophecy experts join forces in this definitive, compelling look at prophecy from a premillennial perspective. This powerful, readable summary covers major prophetic issues.